The Book of the Tongass

The Book of the Tongass

EDITED BY

Carolyn Servid

AND

Donald Snow

MILKWEED EDITIONS

Published 1999 by Milkweed Editions
Printed in the United States of America
Cover design by Rob Dewey
Front cover photo by Gerry Ellis/ENP Images
Back cover photo by Richard Nelson
Interior design by Wendy Holdman
Interior illustrations by Nancy Behnken, Richard Carstensen,
Page Else, Katherine M. Hocker
The text of this book is set in Legacy.
99 00 01 02 03   5 4 3 2 1
First Edition

Milkweed Editions, a nonprofit publisher, gratefully acknowledges support from our World As
Home funders: Lila Wallace-Reader's Digest Fund; Creation and Presentation Programs of the
National Endowment for the Arts; Reader's Legacy underwriter Elly Sturgis. Other support has
been provided by the Elmer L. and Eleanor J. Andersen Foundation; James Ford Bell Foundation;
Bush Foundation; Dayton's, Mervyn's, and Target Stores by the Dayton Hudson Foundation;
Doherty, Rumble and Butler Foundation; General Mills Foundation; Honeywell Foundation;
Hubbard Foundation; McKnight Foundation; Minnesota State Arts Board through an
appropriation by the Minnesota State Legislature; Creation and Presentation Programs of the
National Endowment for the Arts; Norwest Foundation on behalf of Norwest Bank Minnesota;
Lawrence and Elizabeth Ann O'Shaughnessy Charitable Income Trust in honor of Lawrence M.
O'Shaughnessy; Oswald Family Foundation; Ritz Foundation on behalf of Mr. and Mrs. E. J.
Phelps Jr.; John and Beverly Rollwagen Fund of the Minneapolis Foundation; St. Paul Companies,
Inc.; Star Tribune Foundation; U.S. Bancorp Piper Jaffray Foundation on behalf of U.S. Bancorp
Piper Jaffray; and generous individuals.

Library of Congress Cataloging-in-Publication Data

The book of the Tongass / edited by Carolyn Servid and Donald Snow. —
1st ed.
p.   cm.
ISBN 1-57131-226-9 (pbk. : alk. paper)
1. Tongass National Forest (Alaska)—History.   2. Tongass National
Forest (Alaska)—Environmental conditions.   3. Tongass National
Forest (Alaska)—Economic conditions.   4. Natural history—Alaska—
Tongass National Forest.   I. Servid, Carolyn.   II. Snow, Donald.
F912.T64B66   1999
33.75'09798'2—dc21   98-49802
                                                                CIP

The Book of the Tongass

Acknowledgments

This book is the result of a complex collaboration among organizations and individuals. It was, from the beginning, a project requiring teamwork, commitment, good faith, a modest budget, and a little luck.

The organizational sponsors who helped develop the manuscript include The Island Institute of Sitka, Alaska, and Gallatin Writers, Inc., of Bozeman, Montana.

For more than fifteen years, The Island Institute's programs have encouraged people to explore how they can best live together in communities and best inhabit the places where they live. Through its core program, the annual Sitka Symposium, the Institute has brought together writers, scholars, students, and citizens from around the country to consider these broad questions within the context of specific themes. Using the lovely setting of Sitka and Baranof Island as a host environment, the Institute's weeklong summer symposia have enabled participants to explore complex private and public issues on political, ethical, social, and environmental fronts with some of the nation's leading writers and thinkers.

Island Institute staff, knowing the turf of Southeast Alaska well, were responsible for recruiting the writers of this book. Moreover, the Institute sponsored and hosted the one and only gathering of those writers, in September 1997. We are grateful to the Henry P. Kendall Foundation for its support of that gathering. And we thank the board, volunteers, and staff of the Institute for the time, effort, dollars, and commitment they have contributed over the years.

Gallatin Writers, Inc., is a newer organization, one committed to the importance of the written word in matters pertaining to environmental integrity. Not strictly literary in its approach, not strictly focusing on policy and economics, Gallatin is an organization composed of writers, scientists, and activists who possess a passion for the American West and a concern for the future of the public lands states of the West. The Gallatin group shares a commitment to discourse, debate, and the open exchange of ideas among honest people of goodwill. Gallatin Writers pursues a nonprescriptive, ecumenical approach to environmental policy, believing that good writing, sound information, and challenging perspectives on the West can only enhance the quality of public decision making.

John A. Baden, chairman of Gallatin Writers, deserves special recognition for his role in bringing this book to print. He found the financial support and provided the fiscal management that helped create the original manuscript. But more than that, his entrepreneurial leadership continues to nurture projects such as this one—books that perhaps would not find their way to readers but for the innovative agency of small, nonprofit groups such as Gallatin.

We especially thank Jeff Olson of the Ford Foundation for his vision in helping to support Gallatin Writers. We also acknowledge Dick Larry, an annual Montana visitor who has encouraged and supported Gallatin's efforts from the beginning.

Emilie Buchwald, publisher of Milkweed Editions, knew a good idea when she heard it, and we are grateful for her willingness to take a chance on a book about an American place as remote as

Southeast Alaska. Her comments and deft editorial pen greatly improved this manuscript.

Finally, we acknowledge and thank the writers, scholars, and storytellers whose work appears in this volume. The ones who wrote original, commissioned manuscripts toiled under a tight deadline, for small pay, yet gave their best. Special thanks go to Nora Marks Dauenhauer and Dick Dauenhauer, linguists and scholars, who gathered and recorded the two ancient stories included in these pages. The Tlingit elders who allowed their people's stories to be set down in print have done an enormous service to those from cultures that now suffer from the absence of such a tradition. We are humbled and made grateful by their efforts.

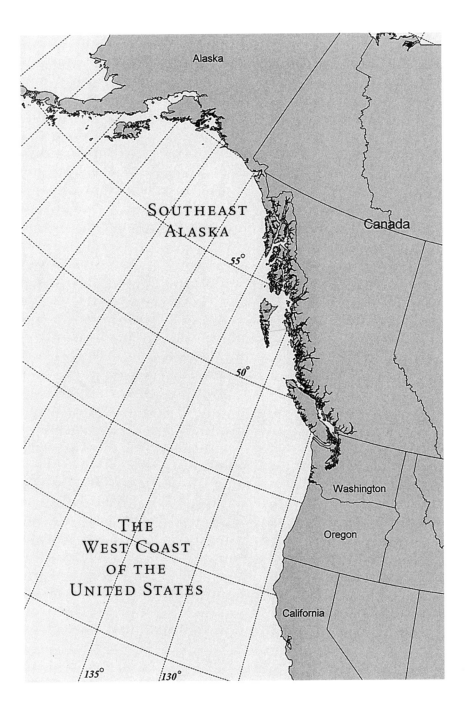

Alaska

SOUTHEAST
ALASKA

Canada

55°

50°

THE
WEST COAST
OF THE
UNITED STATES

Washington

Oregon

California

135°   130°

Page Else, Sitka Conservation Society

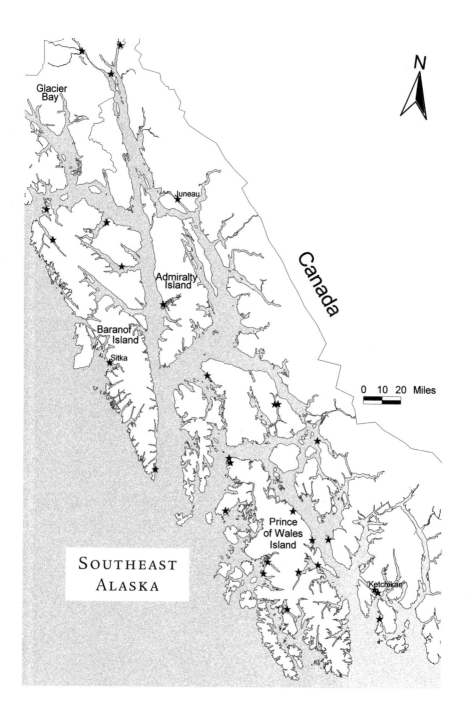

Glacier
Bay

Juneau

Canada

Admiralty
Island

Baranof
Island

Sitka

Prince
of Wales
Island

SOUTHEAST
ALASKA

Ketchikan

N

0 10 20 Miles

Page Else, Sitka Conservation Society

The Book of the Tongass

raven, *Katherine M. Hocker*

Introduction

DONALD SNOW

When you encounter any portion of Southeast Alaska for the first time—as I did in June 1996—you are struck immediately by the richness of the place. There is an almost comic exaggeration of size, scale, and numbers.

I remember vividly the airplane landing in Sitka on that leaden day in June. The long flight direct from Seattle sliced through two miles of clouds above Baranof Island, the big island where Sitka is located. I remember the first lightening of gray as the jet nosed down, then the gauzy white-gray as we began to break through the belly of the cloud-beast, then the amazing colors and shapes of the barrier islands beneath. I thought at first they were animals, those dozens of tiny islands dimly visible with their aprons of white churning sea water. I thought they were whales, perhaps, or sea lions spun over on their backs to watch the big aluminum bird.

When my eyes and my mind came together on the logic of what I was seeing for the first time, I focused on what everyone must focus on in the land of the Tongass National Forest: the trees. Each small island was black with trees. They grew to the rough edges of each island, where the water boiled and crashed against a narrow rim of rocks. It was as if the trees had erupted from the sea itself—as if the sea were filled with trees, and here and there they burst out in tall pockets we call islands. Not an inch of *land* was visible, but trees were everywhere.

I had never seen such trees. And the world shall never see them again.

Size, scale, and numbers. When you walk the streets of Sitka in June, bald eagles wheel everywhere overhead. Looking up Katlian Street past the fish-processing plants along the shore north of town, you see eagles on piers, eagles on the buildings, eagles perched on the radio towers of the fishing boats known as long-liners. The ravens are even more plentiful and remarkable. They must be the largest ravens in the world, and they are surely the most vocal. Everywhere in Sitka during daylight hours, you are surrounded by the mechanical-toy *whonking* of ravens, by the wood-spoon-on-kettle *donging* of ravens, by the whispers, croaks, and polyglot jokes of ravens. You keep turning around, thinking someone down the street has called your name. But there is no one there. A ventriloquist raven sits on a pole overhead, pretending he isn't looking at you.

The mountain peaks of Southeast are astounding in their size, clarity, and color, as I found out the second morning I was there. Normally, their craggy heads jut up into the bellies of the clouds, and all you can see are the black, solid, forested slopes of their arms and lower shoulders. But when the clouds finally tear and fly away, you see impossible emeralds and whites; you see rocks so vivid with life and moisture they seem to turn orange, then back to shining blacks and silvers as the sun passes. You see a sky that makes you ache with blue—a blue you learn in a day not to take for granted here. You think you see bears everywhere, at distances impossible even for bears.

There are said to be a thousand of them on Baranof Island alone. The island runs about a hundred miles north and south, and thirty miles across at its widest point. In my scale of normal living, that's about the amount of country I would circumscribe by highway if I drove from Missoula to Helena, Montana, and back again in one day, going first over McDonald Pass, then home by way of Flescher Pass near the former residence of the Unabomber. If I think of a thousand grizzly bears in that amount of land, I think of a different planet.

Then you learn in casual, understated conversation that Baranof is not the richest of the bear islands; that there are much heavier concentrations of eagles elsewhere in Southeast; that the peaks behind Sitka that have astounded you are but the smallest taste of what you find elsewhere in the region. There are canyon-deep glaciers spilling into the sea. There are true fjords. There are islands carved from the limestone known as karst, and beyond them, a veritable jigsaw puzzle of geology. There is a living presence of the Pleistocene.

There are bars and taverns like the Pioneer and the Fo'c'sle. There are people who each day see things that you have never in your life imagined.

Richness. Five species of salmon, each one perfectly adapted to the freshwater-saltwater-freshwater cycle of its life. Each species breaks down further into bands of fish that find their way back to the streams of their birth. They sort out and divide, sort and divide again at sea, and return home at once, on cue, listening, or smelling, or navigating by some nexus of time and space that we cannot even dimly imagine. They do it perfectly, have done it perfectly for tens of thousands of years. Their numbers once defeated our powers of calculation, and in Southeast the runs are still healthy compared to, say, the wild runs of the Columbia.

And with them, in the bays and inlets and open seas that weave in and out of the Southeast archipelago, are the halibut, the black cod or sablefish, the rockfish and shellfish and herring of one of the richest marine environments on earth. Browsing through the superb artifact collections at Sitka's Sheldon Jackson Museum, you are apt to be amazed at the cunning with which the native people of Southeast pursued the fruits of the sea. They trapped salmon in woven weirs along creeks and rivers, speared and netted and snagged them. They devised masterful halibut hooks of wood, bone, and tooth—hooks with shanks as big as your wrist, to capture fish larger than adolescent humans. They lived with a year-round bounty of fish and shellfish, seal meat and oil, the lovely Sitka black-tailed deer, and other meat-giving species.

On the totem poles they left in every village, you find the faces of the animals who represent the interpenetration of forest, bog, stream, sky, and sea. Raven casts his sidelong glance as you stare back at his static profile. Bear looks lens-to-lens at you, omnivore facing omnivore. Frog stares broadly with eyes that seem to reach over the top of her head. And Salmon, the special, silver person—she who enriches the forest upon her death, whose young ones are but a swimming eye when they depart, only to return as adults in sexual frenzy—she reappears in the carver's hands from the wood her body helped make. Transfixed by these poles, you realize right away the collective ecological wisdom of the people who made them. You understand how well they knew, how deeply they felt, the sacred sustenance of their lives.

And yet, amid the richness and splendor of Southeast, the size, scale, and numbers also give pause. As several chapters in this book will show, board feet in these parts are often expressed in billions, which implies a massive richness—but board feet also means the killing of trees, hundreds of thousands of acres of some of the greatest trees on earth in the greatest temperate rain forest on earth. Think of the stately Sitka spruce and you think of Chopin and sounding boards in the world's finest pianos, but in the same thought, you also must make room for the cellophane that wraps packages of cigarettes. Think of the soft-needled western hemlock and the strength it offers to hold a house together, but at the same time, consider rayon. As the decades since World War II have proved, we cannot reflect on the Tongass National Forest without taking into account the fifty-year sweetheart deals between the U.S. Forest Service and multinational wood-pulp corporations. We cannot avoid the fact that these trees of the "ageless forest," trees that may be four hundred years old but took millennia to create, have sold for a few dollars a stump.

Like it or not, we cannot face the past, present, or future of Southeast Alaska and the Tongass without taking account of timber. If there seems to be an overload of timber talk in the pages of this anthology, it's only because timber and the Tongass are woven together in one story. And it is often a story fraught with ironies.

In addition to the timber that has been removed from federal public lands in Southeast—lands that comprise 95 percent of the region—most of the Southeast Alaska Native corporations have chosen to clear-cut the land selections they made under the Alaska Native Claims Settlement Act of 1971. This cutting has generated its own controversies within Native communities, and has made many people ponder the effects of introducing the concepts of short-term cash flow and asset liquidation to people who lived in one place for millennia without damaging the natural basis of their own sustenance. Of the 1 million acres that have been clear-cut in the Tongass, over half have been cut by Native corporations, which are not held to the environmental standards applied to logging on federal lands. They are also not bound by restrictions against shipping raw, round logs overseas.

It was the timber war on the Tongass National Forest, perhaps more than any other factor, that has brought this anthology into being. Logging turned the Tongass into a national issue, but the place itself, by around 1990, had already attracted an international constituency. This book is not a polemical attack on logging, or mining, or milling, or any other aspect of resource extraction. Those attacks have already been mounted, and the tide of the battle has turned. It is time now to make a new assessment of Southeast Alaska and, we hope, a new contribution to discussions of sustainability.

It is the aim of this anthology to help provide a realistic new context in which people can think about the Tongass and the future of Southeast Alaska.

The year 1997 was a signal year for the Tongass National Forest. The huge Ketchikan pulp mill closed in March. With the earlier closure of Southeast's other large pulp mill in Sitka, the fifty-year contracts that monopolized the Southeast Alaska timber industry are out of the picture. The Forest Service's new Tongass Land Management Plan lays out a revised blueprint for timber harvest, recreation, and habitat conservation for the coming decade. And while trees will still be taken down, it is no longer clear who the timber industry players will be.

The question now on everyone's mind is "What's next?" What will happen in Southeast Alaska as the timber cut continues to decline? Will communities less picturesque, less favored by location than Sitka also continue to thrive, as Sitka did when its mill closed in 1993? Will chambers of commerce in every Southeast town now redouble their commitments to the enterprise Edward Abbey called "industrial tourism"? Will Alaskans attempt to substitute one assault on the Tongass for another, in the hope that the great old-growth forests can somehow attract new tourism revenues to replace the income lost from the hundreds of high-paying jobs in the mills?

And what about the rest of the country and its growing awareness of the treasures in the Tongass National Forest? How will the national interest be taken into account? As long as the big logs rolled off the forest and the ships steamed on to the Orient with their loads of dissolving pulp, it was easy to make a case for development of the Tongass. Economists needed only to count the volumes and dollars, the income levels and expenditures. But now, the economy of Southeast Alaska has become more diffuse, more nebulous. The counters are less able to account for an "amenity economy" based on the valuation of environmental quality, if indeed that is where the Southeast economy is headed. How do we begin to reconcile local needs for dignified livelihood with national demands to keep old-growth forests intact?

Local people, Alaska's people, and people who live elsewhere but value Southeast Alaska need wise counsel as they debate and puzzle over the future of the Tongass National Forest. They need to be reminded—perhaps some need to be convinced—that the most important questions about Southeast Alaska in this time of painful transition are not questions of dollars and measurements, but rather questions about values and ideals. The key questions are about stewardship—of the land and waters, and the communities that depend utterly upon them.

Those are the questions that interest the authors of this anthology, all of them writers with deep, long experience in Southeast. When Carolyn Servid and I asked them to help assemble this book, we made clear that we wanted to fulfill three purposes:

First, to celebrate and honor the legacy of the forest itself. Perhaps we cannot ever comprehend a forest as powerful, rich, and diverse as the Tongass, but in humble ways we can express our feelings for it.

Second, to recognize the ongoing value of humanity and human communities in and around the Tongass. People have lived in these forests—mostly at the ecotones of forest and sea—for thousands of years. The forests and waters have taken care of the people, have sheltered and nourished them and have been at the core of their material and spiritual lives. The people have given back (though not always well) and need to be encouraged to give back more, and in better ways—better for both forests and people.

And third, to ponder the future of Southeast Alaska and the

Tongass National Forest, not so much by offering prescriptions for a future, but by suggesting a set of shared values that may radiate from the personal to the societal and back again. A strong theme here is the theme of *subsistence,* for subsistence implies reciprocal nourishment and humility. If people can be encouraged to think of their lives in more elemental terms, and less in terms of mortgages, payments, and the pressures that come of monetary abstractions, they may be freer to imagine a future based on reciprocity with nature.

This anthology ends with Carolyn Servid's musing on the importance of reciprocity between human communities and the forest, on what might be thought of as a kind of collaboration between the people who are grappling with the difficult issues of the Tongass and the land itself. Her emphasis on the idea of collaboration is fitting here, for this book itself is the product of a healthy collaboration.

My 1996 visit to Sitka came at the invitation of the Island Institute. Carolyn and her husband and colleague Dorik Mechau had asked me to be part of the Institute's excellent Sitka Symposium, an annual gathering of writers, scholars, students, and citizens who explore themes of human values and their intersection with nature. I went gladly, stayed a week, and went home having gained far more than I gave.

A few months after returning home, I scurried off again to a gathering of the writers who had contributed to the small anthology published by Milkweed Editions, *Testimony: Writers Speak On Behalf of Utah Wilderness.* We met at the Sundance Resort in Provo Canyon, Utah, and there I encountered Emilie Buchwald, publisher and editor at Milkweed Editions. When Emilie explained her plans for a series of place-centered books on the theme of Literature for a Land Ethic, I found myself thinking about the Tongass and all I had learned in the company of Carolyn, Dorik, Richard Nelson, and others from the Sitka Symposium. I suggested to Emilie that she consider a *Testimony*-type book about the Tongass National Forest, and she responded that she had already been in contact with a person named Carolyn Servid!

The idea next rebounded to Gallatin Writers, Inc., in Bozeman, Montana, where, for the past six years, I have been working with Dr. John Baden and his staff to craft a series of seminars that bring together emerging Western writers with ecologists, economists, and other scientists to discuss innovative approaches to natural re-source and environmental issues in the American West. It was John Baden who came up with the funding to support the creation of this manuscript. As is typical of John, we sealed the deal with a handshake and a promise. He urged the best we could do, then let things take their natural course.

So, the collaboration . . . is among the people at the Island Institute, who gathered together the writers and major themes of the book; at Gallatin Writers, Inc., who provided the "seedbed" and the initial funding; and at Milkweed Editions, who put its capital and expertise behind the production, marketing, and dis-tribution of this volume. But the true inspiration came from the forests of the Tongass. May this collection be a human offering in return.

Long before the U.S. Forest Service laid out the boundaries of the Tongass National Forest, the indigenous people of the region—Tlingit, Haida, and Tsimshian—claimed it as their home. The issues faced by those indigenous people since Western settlement are thorny and complex. To give the reader an overview of those complexities, we have included an essay written by an attorney for the Sitka Tribe of Alaska and reviewed by members of the tribe. We hope his description of Native customary and traditional relation-ships to the land, together with a historical account of significant legal landmarks that affected those traditional relationships, will offer an understanding of the dilemmas facing the original human inhabitants of this region.

To complement this factual perspective on Native issues, we've included two Tlingit stories as well—tales, used with permission, that will at least offer a small sense of how some of Southeast's indigenous people encountered what we today call the Tongass. These stories are notable for their stark departure from linearity, from the modern frame of mind as it applies to nature and the abstract thing we nominate as "resources." Yet the stories persevere, and hold up beautifully, and are beautiful, and perhaps are more necessary today than ever before.

A word of explanation will help readers who may be uncertain about how to read these written forms of stories that come from an oral tradition. The two Tlingit stories included here were told in Tlingit and recorded on tape. They were written down in Tlingit, the way they were told, and then translated into English, keeping the Tlingit oral style in mind. While much about the context is lost—the storyteller's voice and gestures and performance—the English translation and the format try to capture how the stories sound. Though their short lines make them look like poems, they are not. Rather, the lines reflect the rhythm and pace of the story's telling. Breaks in the lines indicate a pause in the delivery. Longer pauses are marked with punctuation—a period or comma or semicolon. If you read the stories aloud, paying attention to those pauses, you will begin to get a sense of the cadence of the stories as they were told, of the rhythm of the storyteller's voice.

The last voice I heard, the last time I was in Sitka, came as an utterance that seemed to be both above and ahead of me at the same time. I was admiring a wolf pelt on a rack in the street in front of Sitka's lone furrier—admiring, amazed, and saddened at once, as is often my complex of feelings when I visit the remarkable village of Sitka-by-the-Sea. The voice croaked low enough that I could not hear clearly, but as in certain dreams when we awake and cannot remember the details of the dream, yet feel its essence, I felt the essence of the words.

"Go home" was the sense I had of the voice. It was not a reprimand or a rebuke, not a voice telling me to get out, but more of an urging. Perhaps "come home" was more the sense of it, but as in dreams, I was not sure. "Come home."

When will we come home?

The shadow of black wings passed as I turned to head back to the airport.

DONALD SNOW is executive director of Northern Lights Institute as well as director of the Environmental Writing Institute at the University of Montana. Through the university's environmental studies program, he teaches graduate courses in environmental writing and natural resource policy. He lives in Missoula, Montana.

Townsend's warbler, *Katherine M. Hocker*

Up the Inside Passage—
Bridge to the Past

JACKIE CANTERBURY AND CHERI BROOKS

On maps showing northwestern North America, Southeast Alaska dangles from British Columbia like green fringe. A cluster of emerald islands and a lean strip of coast compose Alaska's slender panhandle. The climate and vegetation here are nothing like the rest of the state, which is broad, cold, inhospitable, and dry. Southeast Alaska, in contrast, is wet and mild and sustains one of the largest, lushest rain forests in the world: the Tongass National Forest.

At seventeen million acres, the Tongass is the country's grandest national forest, larger than the state of West Virginia by acres, but scattered across more than a thousand islands—the Alexander Archipelago—and stretched along the narrow Pacific coastline. East of the coastal mountains lies the frigid northern expanse of British Columbia; west of the mountains, tranquil waters reflect a palate of green. Giant Sitka spruce trees grow in river valleys and line the narrow fjords that were created as the glaciers retreated and the seas rose and filled the carved channels that dissect the coast into nine thousand meandering miles of intricate shoreline. Tree-covered slopes catch moisture from the sea and turn it into mist. Western hemlock mixes with Sitka spruce, deep green blending with blue-green, fringed by yellow cedar in a shaggy patchwork.

The Alexander Archipelago, a jigsaw of islands, fashions a buffer against storms that batter the outer Pacific coast. The shelter of the islands forms the Inside Passage—a maritime highway to

Alaska that begins in Seattle. "The scenery gains everything from being translated through the medium of a soft, pearly atmosphere, where the light is as gray and evenly diffused as in Old England itself," wrote one traveler up the Passage during the 1880s. "The calm of the brooding air, the shimmer of the opaline sea around one, and the ranges of green and russet hills, misty purple mountains, and snowy summits on the faint horizon, give a dream-like coloring to all one's thoughts."

Walking in the Tongass can feel like treading across a lumpy sponge. Sooner or later you will step onto a rotten lump, camouflaged by sphagnum moss, or stumble into a hole, formed when fungi slowly swallowed a decomposing log. Huckleberry and blueberry bushes can be waist high. Bright green ferns and lichens hang from the branches of the large conifers that stretch more than a hundred feet into the sky and overlap in the canopy. You can lie on the ground, look up, and never see the sky.

The Tongass is the last stronghold of creatures that are scarce or nonexistent in the lower forty-eight states: wolves, brown bears, wolverines, marten, river otters, marbled murrelets, goshawks, and bald eagles, of which Southeast Alaska has the highest density in North America. The central feature of the landscape, though, is water. Water runs down mountains in rushes and rivulets and downpours directly from sorrowful skies. Streams and rivers form a complex system that intersects and interacts with the forest. Five kinds of salmon—red, silver, king, humpbacked, and chum (called "dog salmon")—spawn in Tongass waterways. Southeast Alaska is one of the last places where salmon still shimmer like stepping stones in the channels. The fish are so plentiful that brown bears (known as grizzlies elsewhere) congregate every summer around certain streams, such as Anan Creek, where you can see as many as twenty bears at once gorging themselves on salmon.

Though Alaska's Panhandle stretches for five hundred miles

along the Northwest coast—from Misty Fjords to Glacier Bay—and includes the capital city of Juneau, only seventy-four thousand people live there. More than three times that number live in Anchorage, and Alaska's attention mostly faces north toward the oil resources that have made the state rich. The slow-paced lifestyle of "Southeast" harks back to a time when people felt more a part of their surroundings. While Alaskans love the land, this relationship does not have a detached glow like a scene outside a picture window. Many make their living from the forest and sea, and depend on the fish and deer and wood they harvest. The majority of rural Southeast Alaskans rely to some degree on subsistence hunting and fishing to feed their families.

Despite its remoteness, the Panhandle, in many ways, is more akin to the Pacific Northwest than to Arctic Alaska. Its larger towns have adopted some of the earnest, arty, highbrow culture of Seattle, Portland, and Vancouver. Coffee bars, vegetarian restaurants, and bookstores have multiplied in Sitka, Ketchikan, and Juneau during the past decade. Bright, idealistic people migrate to Alaska, some hoping to fulfill a long-held American dream about the last frontier, to live closer to the land. Southeast is also home to a transient culture of loggers and fishermen who work seasonally and only seldom put down roots. Some say it is the realm of misfits, malcontents, and outlaws. But those with the strongest foothold in the region are the Tlingit, Haida, and Tsimshian peoples, whose cultures developed in the long-ago time when great ice fields covered the Pacific Northwest.

Ketchikan is Alaska's southernmost substantial city. Lying on Revillagigedo Island, which Captain George Vancouver named after a Spanish count, Ketchikan begins with mazes of gray dock and ascends from shore on wooden boardwalks and steps that climb steep, forested hillsides. Ketchikan has only forty miles of city streets, but boat traffic often backs up along the Tongass Narrows when cruise ships glide in during the warm season. Knickknack shops selling T-shirts, canned salmon, and baleen carvings sandwich loggers' bars and canneries along the waterfront.

Misty Fjords National Monument includes the east side of Revilla (as it's usually shortened) and part of the adjacent mainland. Misty is a remarkable sanctuary of waterfalls, tall timber, and sheer granite rock, home to both Alaska brown bears and mountain goats. West of Revilla, separated from Ketchikan by Clarence Strait, lies Prince of Wales, the third-largest island in the United States and the source of Alaska's biggest trees. Prince of Wales is accessible only by plane or boat, but more than thirty-five hundred miles of logging road crisscross this 135-mile-long island. The big trees and rich soils lured the timber industry to Alaska and made the island a hub of Northwest logging. Prince of Wales is also a stronghold for the Alexander Archipelago wolf. Wolves reside on most of the Tongass's southern islands but not on the large northern ones—Admiralty, Baranof, and Chichagof—which are home to brown bears.

The town of Wrangell lies north on the mainland at the mouth of the Stikine River. The mighty Stikine breaks through the coastal range that divides Canada from the United States, and its valley forms a highway between two distinct climates. The country east of the coastal mountains has much greater extremes in temperature—hotter summers and colder winters—and Wrangell is exposed to some of this interior climate. While Ketchikan sometimes get 160 inches of rain per year, Wrangell only gets about 80.

Russian traders settled Wrangell in 1834 and built a stockade, Fort Dionysius, to prevent the Hudson's Bay Company from trading upriver on the Stikine. When the Russians leased Southeast Alaska to the Hudson's Bay Company in 1840, Fort Dionysius became Fort Stikine, a British fur-trading post. When Alaska became a United States territory in 1867, the settlement became Fort Wrangell. Gold seekers surged through Wrangell en route to inland mining sites via the Stikine during the gold rushes of 1874–76 and 1897–1900. *The Wrangell Sentinel* printed its first issue in 1909; now it is the oldest continuous publication in Alaska.

The town of Petersburg lies on Mitkof Island, which is only seventeen miles long. Petersburg is a wealthy fishing town of about three thousand, and it is said to have many fishing millionaires. A Norwegian named Peter Buschmann started a cannery in the small town in 1898 because the area reminded him of Norway and promised a steady supply of ice from the nearby LeConte Glacier. Commercial fishing for halibut, salmon, and shrimp remains the town's mainstay. Southeast Alaska's history was full of canneries, but most did not survive. Petersburg's did. The town is called Little Norway and still reflects the charm of its Norwegian roots.

Baranof Island, 105 miles long, lies between Chatham Strait and the Gulf of Alaska. It is named for Aleksandr Baranof, a skillful businessman and longtime head of the Russian-American Company. "Sitka-by-the-Sea," as Alaskans call this quaint fishing town, sits on Baranof's west side. Its Russian heritage lingers in the Orthodox Church that overlooks the center of town. Sitka's beauty has lured retirees from the lower forty-eight, who have built large houses along the waterfront. Once dominated by the economies of fur trading, timber pulping, and salmon and halibut fishing, Sitka has now become a fashionable tourist center, though it retains its Alaskan character.

The Tlingit called Admiralty Island *Kootznahoo*—Fortress of the Bears. One of the highest concentrations of brown bears in the world—one per square mile by some estimates—lives on Admiralty Island, which is preserved as a national monument. Salmon-filled streams and abundant deer and marine animals provide the bears with a diverse and bountiful food supply. Admiralty's brown bears sometimes stand taller than nine feet and weigh more than a thousand pounds, making them among the largest land animals in North America.

Juneau, Alaska's capital, has thirty thousand residents, including a host of white-collar workers who wear the latest Patagonia clothing, sip espresso, and discuss state politics. While towns like Ketchikan are transitory—people come and go with the season— Juneau is more stable and modern. City streets once were lined with gold, but today McDonald's sits only a block away from the famous Gold Nugget Saloon.

Long before the Alaskan gold rush, before the arrival of Europeans, trees supported Southeast Alaska's first inhabitants. About ten thousand years ago groups of humans who crossed the Bering land bridge settled along the northwest coast, taking advantage of its abundant natural resources. Wood provided the raw materials for their homes, furniture, canoes, clothing, ceremonial objects, totems, and tools such as halibut hooks. Tlingits lived throughout Southeast Alaska. Their rivals, the Haidas, lived farther south in the Queen Charlotte Islands and on the southern tip of Prince of Wales Island. Tsimshian people were rooted even farther south; but in 1887 a large group, led by Anglican missionary William Duncan, moved to Annette Island across the channel from Ketchikan.

Vitus Bering, a Danish navigator working in the service of the Russian czar, led the first European expedition to Alaska. In 1728 he proved that a narrow strip of the Pacific separated North America from Asia by sailing through the narrow strait that now bears his name. Not for another decade, during his second voyage east from Siberia, did Bering sight Mount Saint Elias on the Alaskan mainland. Bering's colleague on his second expedition, Aleksei Chirikov, who sailed farther south, sighted what is believed to be Prince of Wales Island on July 15, 1741, the day before Bering saw Mount Saint Elias. Chirikov sent two longboats to explore the coastline, but both disappeared without a trace.

The voyage of Bering and Chirikov actually revealed little about *alayeksa*—the Great Land—as the Aleut people called it. Crew members suffered from scurvy and bad weather. Bering allowed his ship's scientist, George Wilhelm Steller, barely a day to explore the scientific wonders of Kayak Island along the Aleutian chain. This caused Steller to bemoan an expedition in which "ten years of preparation had led to but ten hours of exploration."

The Russians had long suspected that they could reach North America by sailing east from the coast of the Kamchatka Peninsula in Siberia, but it was centuries before their eastern frontier expanded that far. In Russia, furs were currency and sable was king. Cossacks and *promyshlenniki* (fur traders) led the eastern expansion, following the sable. After depleting this fur-bearing mammal, the *promyshlenniki* pushed the Russian frontier farther, to Alaska. The sea otter provided Russia with a timely response to the Canadian beaver, which had cut significantly into its European fur market. Sea otter pelts were traded primarily in China, allowing Russia to import exotic Asian commodities such as tea, silk, and porcelain.

The czar granted a charter for the establishment of the Russian-American Company in 1799, the same year that Baranof founded the city of Mikhailovsk (present-day Sitka), named for the Archangel Michael. Tlingits, who always resisted the Russians, destroyed the town in 1802, but Baranof came back in 1804 with a larger force and drove the Natives from the island. The rebuilt settlement of New Archangel became the capital of Russian America.

At the close of the eighteenth century, English, French, and Spanish explorers journeyed to Alaska, challenging Russian dominance to varying degrees. The most accomplished navigator was Captain James Cook, who initiated the age of scientific navigation and charted much of the Pacific. Cook went to the North Pacific in 1778, in part to determine the existence of the fabled Northwest Passage. The English had long hoped to find a sea passage through North America that would provide them with a direct route to Asia. Many sixteenth- and seventeenth-century maps illustrate passageways through the continent, via Hudson Bay or the Mississippi River, but exploration gradually revealed such routes to be wholly imaginary.

Cook was the first captain to sail the full extent of Alaska's coastline and map its main features. He sailed into what is now called Cook Inlet, which he thought might be a navigable river providing a route to the Atlantic. But the voyage of Vancouver in 1794 disproved this claim. Vancouver finally put to rest the myth of the Northwest Passage and mapped the contours of the last uncharted temperate region of the world, including the Southeast Alaska coastline.

Cook's voyage alerted the Hudson's Bay Company to the abundance of fur-bearing mammals off Alaska's shores. Later, "Boston traders" endeavored westward and even armed the Native people against the Russians. In 1825 the governments of Russia, the United States, and England signed an agreement protecting their mutual interests, and the Hudson's Bay Company eventually was able to lease portions of Russian America and to trade directly with the Natives.

But by the mid–1800s, hunting had depleted Alaska's fur resources substantially. The colony became a burden to Russia's imperial government. The market for fur was declining, and it was only a matter of time before the United States would take Alaska, as it had already stretched into Oregon Territory. In 1867 the United States bought Alaska from the Russians for $7.2 million. Many in the States considered it a foolish investment until someone discovered gold in the Yukon in the late 1870s. After that, America's frontier soon stretched northwest, toward Alaska. The gold rush brought mining camps, salmon canneries, and settlers to Southeast. Alaska's abundant natural resources fostered Manifest Destiny on a grand scale, as prospectors rushed to drill, mine, hunt, lumber, and fish the last frontier and sell its scenery.

For a long while, though, Southeast remained tranquil, and

people continued to live a simple life among the towering trees and salmon streams. George T. Emmons, a naval officer and collector of Indian art, explored the Alexander Archipelago in the early 1900s and described the region to his friend Teddy Roosevelt as "one immense forest of conifers." Emmons recognized the value of the timber on many of the islands, especially Prince of Wales, and convinced President Roosevelt to set aside several of the larger islands as a forest reserve. Roosevelt signed a bill creating the Alexander Archipelago Forest Reserve in 1902. In 1908 the government added to the reserve the Baranof Island group and the adjacent mainland area near Juneau and renamed it the Tongass National Forest after the southernmost regional group of Tlingits.

Until the 1960s, small businesses, fishermen, and independent logging and milling operators provided the foundation of the Southeast Alaskan economy. The rich natural environment enhanced the quality of life for a scattered population, isolated from the lower forty-eight states. There were few roads. Small-scale logging took place along beach margins. Loggers cut trees with handsaws, then slid them downslope to the water where they were bundled, rafted, and towed to small sawmills. After the Forest Service took over management of the Tongass, however, it set about trying to sell rights to the timber in order to stimulate development in Southeast Alaska.

During the Second World War the agency administered a spruce-log program to supply clear-grained Sitka spruce to the Canadian deHavviland aircraft company for use in the noses and wings of British mosquito bombers. After the war, when the country faced a shortage of newsprint, the Forest Service worked to bring the pulp industry to the Tongass. Down south, a postwar housing boom was helping to transform the Forest Service from a forest-protection agency into a forest-production army. The Tongass Timber Act of 1947 allowed the Forest Service to open up the Tongass to large-scale timber production, despite the claims of

Tlingit and Haida peoples that the forests were part of their traditional hunting and fishing grounds.

Once the way was cleared for industrial forestry, the Forest Service took pains to attract timber companies to the Alaskan wilds. During the 1950s the agency brokered two contracts; subsequently, the Ketchikan Pulp Company built a mill in Ketchikan, and the Alaska Lumber and Pulp Company built a mill in Sitka. In return for building and operating the mills, the companies were guaranteed access to thirteen billion board feet of Tongass timber over fifty years. The pulp mills in Sitka and Ketchikan turned Tongass old-growth trees into dissolving pulp, the raw material for rayon, cellophane, and other products. As the lumber export market expanded during the 1960s and 1970s, the Tongass timber-sale program also expanded, and the contract holders began exporting lumber and logs to the Far East.

The pulp mills provided high-paying, year-round jobs but also changed the economies of Ketchikan and Sitka. More than a hundred independent logging and milling companies were "forced to bankruptcy, acquired, or otherwise driven from the logging business" because of the long-term contracts, according to a 1981 court decision. The new timber economy changed the Panhandle's slow-paced lifestyle. The population grew, money began flowing into Southeast, politicians began letting the timber companies call the shots, and a great bureaucratic fortress was built in the Forest Service's Alaska region.

Clear-cut logging has devoured more than a million acres of rain forest in Southeast Alaska (on both private and public lands), but logging has especially affected some of the thickest and densest stands, which provide crucial habitat for wildlife. Sitka black-tailed deer, for instance, depend upon large trees for food and shelter during the winter snowfalls. Wolves, in turn, depend upon the availability of deer. Dense groves of large trees are actually rather rare in the Tongass. Most "forest lands" are really bogs, muskegs, alpine meadows, or stands of stunted or branchy timber. Only a fraction of the Tongass contains "high-volume" stands; because such stands contain the most valuable trees, they are cut first by loggers.

A land-claims settlement with Native Alaskans multiplied the environmental effects of the two fifty-year contracts. Though Native Alaskans accused the federal government and (after 1958) the state of Alaska of encroaching upon their ancestral lands, the government postponed any negotiation of such claims until after 1968. That was the year that Atlantic Richfield Company and Humble Oil and Refining Company struck oil in Prudhoe Bay. It was necessary to build a pipeline from Prudhoe Bay to the ice-free port of Valdez, and oil companies required transportation corridors and rights-of-way through lands claimed by Native peoples. In effect, oil development could not proceed without their blessing.

The architects of the 1971 Alaska Native Claims Settlement Act tried to revise prior United States–Indian policies—rejecting a reservation-based concept in favor of one that would provide Natives with a productive role in a growing state economy. The act granted $962.5 million and forty-four million acres to Alaskan Natives, who, in exchange, surrendered their claims to their ancestral lands. The settlement made Natives the largest private landowners in Alaska; collectively, they acquired about 12 percent of the state. Native corporations formed to manage these new assets. In 1971 the annual convention of the Alaskan Federation of Natives stated, "In the white man's society, we need white man's tools."

As part of the settlement agreement, some Native corporations selected more than half a million acres of timberlands, formerly in the Tongass. To earn profits for stockholders, most of these lands were quickly clear-cut. Klukwan, for instance, a village corporation from the vicinity of Haines, selected land on Long Island in the southern part of the Tongass. Trees grew tall and wide on Long

Island's limestone substrate—some of the biggest trees in Alaska—yet few were able to glimpse them. Klukwan logged all of its lands, leaving behind a panorama of clear-cuts stretching ten thousand acres. Klukwan was savvy in its investments; in 1990 each of its 253 shareholders received a dividend of $36,000. In 1996 the corporation paid out $65,000 per shareholder. But Long Island stands bare.

Native corporations, for the most part, have liquidated their Southeast Alaskan holdings. Ketchikan Pulp Company and Alaska Pulp Corporation—after decades of milling Tongass old growth into pulp, often purchasing four-hundred-year-old trees for the price of a cheeseburger—shut their doors during the mid-1990s. In late 1997 Ketchikan Pulp Company auctioned off bulldozers, forklifts, chain saws, and digesters to the highest bidder. Both companies blamed market forces, timber shortfalls, environmentalist protests, and government regulations for closing the mills before the fifty-year contracts were complete. But the truth was, they already had taken many of the most valuable trees.

Corporate timber interests have clear-cut some of best places in Southeast Alaska—for instance, much of Prince of Wales Island, Long Island, Dall Island, and the area surrounding the village of Hoonah—but many wonderful and wild forests remain. Some places, such as Misty Fjords, Admiralty Island, and Glacier Bay, have been set aside permanently by Congress for future generations to enjoy. Other extraordinary areas—Honker Divide, Cleveland Peninsula, East Kuiu Island, and Poison Cove—will stand or fall depending on future Forest Service decisions.

Timber harvesting in the Tongass has declined considerably in recent years, but biologists say that logging levels must decrease even more if Southeast is to preserve its rare biological diversity. For the Tongass is a fragmented forest of islands. Even the mainland effectively is segmented by mountains and river valleys. The landscape is steep and rugged, especially toward the north, where mountains rise to four thousand feet on some large islands and to more than ten thousand feet on the mainland. Ocean passageways create formidable barriers for animals. For large species with large home ranges, such as bears and wolves, the Tongass's island geography challenges their need to move around. For small animals like mice, this geography provides an evolutionary opportunity, creating pockets of species particular to an island or group of islands.

Tongass wildlife has adapted to the rain forest and to Southeast Alaska's singular landscape. The small Sitka black-tailed deer is found only along a narrow arc of coastal forest. Brown bears need approximately forty square miles of home-range territory, something they find in the vast Tongass forest but in few other places. Bald eagles are common along the Southeast coastline where fish are plentiful; they tend to raise their young in large spruce trees that have limbs strong enough to support their enormous nests. The rufous hummingbird migrates to Southeast Alaska from Mexico, a two-thousand-mile journey. Males arrive before the huckleberry and blueberry bushes flower but feed on the sugary sap that spills from old-growth trees.

The Tongass has a great deal to offer, but it is not limitless. The tranquil islands, the abundant wildlife, and the rich natural resources all remind us of a time—we might not remember it individually but we feel it collectively—when our entire continent was still wild. We have spread across North America into nearly every nook and cranny of nature, transforming it into a uniform and ubiquitous landscape of strip malls, highways, tract homes, trailer parks, fields and pastures, tree farms, and carefully ordered parks.

Reckless fools might underestimate the power of the wild, which can be a deadly mistake for a careless individual. The greater error, perhaps, is to underestimate the fragility of nature, a blunder that tears down the web of life. Southeast Alaska is gentler than many wild places. Its rugged tree-lined mountaintops are tamed by warm rains that invite rich biological diversity. The Tongass is the last primeval rain forest in North America. Though it seems unchanging and timeless—for we have no clock to measure the biological and evolutionary time that shaped it—we must deal with the forest in the here and now, within a political space and inside an economic framework. We can only hope the Tongass has time on its side.

JACKIE CANTERBURY is a biologist who has lived and worked in the Tongass National Forest for about twenty years. She has worked for the Forest Service studying birds in old-growth forest ecosystems and as an activist for the nonprofit organization Forest Service Employees for Environmental Ethics. She got involved in conservation issues many years ago when she moved to Ketchikan, the hub of logging activity on the Tongass. Jackie has a husband, Jack, and a golden retriever, Huxley. They all live in Ketchikan.

CHERI BROOKS is a writer and editor based in Oregon where she seeks out the last vestiges of that state's ancient forests with her daughter and two dogs. She has written magazine articles and research papers about the history and politics of Southeast Alaska, which she feels provides a window into America's past—and, perhaps, a key to its future.

leader of Sitka spruce sapling, *Richard Carstensen*

Heart of the Forest

RICHARD CARSTENSEN

Alaska's largest tree may still be out there hiding, and part of me wants to find it. Over the past three years I've become enchanted by big trees. Searching through the great stands of the northern temperate rain forest, measuring, venerating, I've grown increasingly convinced that the champion living Sitka spruce is on no forester's map.

But the elusiveness of such a tree is worth more to me than discovering it. I hope we never learn enough about the Tongass to assure ourselves we've fingered that particular forest grail. Perhaps tree hunters, like fly fishers, need to temper desire with restraint: catch and release. At times our catch is so wild and sensitive that we hold a judicious flame to the data card. One forest encounter lingers longest in my memory. It deepened my sense of what is most sacred—and least touchable—about my chosen home.

Reaching the place took days. My friends and I ferried south from homes in Juneau to Prince of Wales Island. We eased my laden Honda Civic over rutted gravel roads, launched our three kayaks, and paddled deep into the South Prince of Wales Wilderness. Dangling into the storm nursery called Dixon Entrance at Alaska's southernmost extremity, this is one of the least visited wilderness areas in the state. In fifteen days' kayaking we passed one recreational party. Near the turnaround point in our 150-mile paddle, I noticed on my aerial photos a small patch of very large trees at the head of a long narrow bay. Adding to the enticement, the geology map showed a thin strip of carbonate bedrock running precisely beneath that stand of big trees. It was the only rock of its type in hundreds of square miles.

Carbonates are water-soluble rocks such as limestone and marble. On northern Prince of Wales Island, abundant carbonate bedrock supports a landscape of fluted spires and bewitching sinkholes called karst—and on its sweet, acid-buffered soils, the violated remains of the state's once-greatest forest. The South Prince of Wales Wilderness has almost no such riches or liabilities. Unproductive, mostly granitic bedrock and exposure to the climatic tantrums of Dixon Entrance give this wilderness a deserved reputation for steep, wave-mauled beaches; impenetrable salal thickets; and lovely, industrially worthless bonsai forests.

Unable to resist the hint of a pearl disguised among trade beads, we made a four-mile detour into the beckoning bay. Next morning in steady drizzle we parked our kayaks on a riverbank and scrambled over a cream-colored limey outcrop into the first completely intact big karst forest I'd ever seen. Broad mudflats in the estuary had protected this stand even from the intrepid hand loggers, whose hulking rotted stumps dispirit nearly all of our most productive coastal stands.

We spent the day measuring trees in the most outstanding one-acre patch of this forest. Two immense Sitka spruces were seven and eight feet in diameter at breast height, and one stretched upward to a dizzying two hundred feet. The surrounding acre contained 126,000 board feet, an extraordinary volume of wood. It confirmed my suspicions that the greatest of the karst bedrock forests—now leveled or highgraded—were fully the equal of our mightiest river-bottom stands on well-drained sands and gravels.

The day of measuring, estimating, reducing a forest to numbers was quite enough for me. Most naturalists are long on art and short on science. With a few hours of daylight remaining, I went for a walk before dinner. The aerial photos suggested another narrow band of big Sitka spruces back up a nearby stream, at a bend in the channel. The stream would require fording, so I packed wading sandals.

Dusk is when the big furry things come out. In tangled stink currant and devils club I bashfully called "Yo mama, comin' through," but it seemed indecorous to ruffle a silence so unused to human voices. I spoke only a few times, then forgot, as unseen gatekeepers admitted me to a forest no person could ever earn.

However accurate our measure or penetrating our ring count, a first meeting with big trees should be subjective. I've stood impressed but irreligious before labeled five-foot oak boles on mowed lawns, or muttered my respects to redwoods from trodden park trails, too self-conscious in the crowds to *feel* their age or immensity. But here, alone, a mile up an unnamed creek, a week's paddle from the nearest far-flung town, I drifted, dumbed crown gazer. For two hundred yards, each streamside giant seemed larger than the last, culminating in five behemoths, elephantine root buttresses staking deep into river gravel, highest foliage mounting into mist.

In deference to the Alaska Register of Big Trees, I'll guess that a couple could have dethroned the current champion spruce at Exchange Cove, northern Prince of Wales. At the moment, that wasn't of interest.

I like those trees unjudged.

BIOREGION BOUNDARIES

Those streamside trees announced an astonishing fertility for a latitude so far north that it intersects Hudson Bay and the Labrador Sea. Straight west from Prince of Wales Island across the Pacific Ocean lies Russia's Shantar Archipelago, where sea ice persists for eight months of the year and the beach is backed by grassy tundra. The big trees of Southeast Alaska are the pampered heirs of a marine endowment, with front-row seats on the warm northeastward-drifting Alaska Current. To best appreciate this gift of climate, it helps to come here not by sea or air, but over land.

You can enter Southeast Alaska by land only through a few roaded passes. You could of course climb over an ice field on foot, or float down one of the handful of major rivers that cut low through otherwise continuous, braided mountain ranges. By any of these routes you would witness a profound ecological transition.

Approaching Southeast Alaska from the east through equivalent latitudes of boreal British Columbia (about fifty-five to sixty degrees north), the dry land bears a spartan mosaic of slender white and black spruces and modest trembling aspens. None are large and few are old, since fire reigns here. Atlin, British Columbia, gets about twelve inches of annual precipitation. Added to the often-torched and near-desert conditions are trying extremes of temperature, from ninety-five degrees Fahrenheit in summer to minus fifty in winter. Across all of Canada, these are the facts of life for northern plants and animals. The exception is the Pacific coast.

Vegetation maps of British Columbia usually use some suggestive shade of green to show the lush, maritime hemlock and spruce forest. Confined mostly to the wet side of the Boundary Ranges, this rich green color leaks inland along the Skeena, Stikine, Taku, and Alsek River valleys. I have to smile at these maps, because an Alaskan rain-country naturalist would paint those same valleys as conduits of cold and desiccation—probably some icy shade of blue or gray—bringing exotic boreal elements like caribou and subalpine fir to the portals of our balmy bioregion. In Juneau, where precipitation is about seven times greater than Atlin's, this continental influence has a name that turns up our collars and our thermostats: the Taku Wind.

I concede, however, that after a week of acclimating to the wimpy moisture-starved fire forests of the interior, then driving back toward the generous coastal humidity, I can appreciate what the dry-country Canadian perceives as green, inland-penetrating fingers. Lushness is relative, after all. When the short-branched, skinny spires of white spruce fill out, begin to interlace canopies, when an actual understory appears, through which hikers no longer amble but bushwhack, I know I'm coming home. Soon I'll see big trees.

SUBSTRATES

Moisture availability doesn't limit tree growth on the Tongass. In fact, moisture ubiquity is often the problem. Tree roots must stand free of the water table, and except on the best-drained sites, our water table lies at or close beneath the surface. The simplest test for water table depth is to sit down on the ground. Southeast Alaskans tend not to do that without rain pants or a lot of site reconnaissance.

Let's say you need to sit upon a substrate of unknown origin. Particle size is an important consideration. Particles range in size from boulders (head diameter or bigger) down through cobbles, gravel, and sand, and finally into the invisibly small categories called silt and clay. An undiscriminating substrate maker like a glacier or a bulldozer or a landslide may leave a chaotic mixture of all of these particle sizes. The water-holding capacity of that *unsorted* mixture will depend on how much clay, silt, and fine sand it contains. Most of the commercial-sized forest of the Tongass, of eight thousand board feet per acre or more, occupies a blanket of unsorted glacial debris called *till*, smeared with variable thickness over an undulating train wreck of unpredictable bedrock types. The till forests and the stands growing from thin soils over bedrock are usually moderately drained, hemlock-dominated, and of intermediate size.

If on the other hand your mystery substrate is *sorted*, or made of particles all about the same size, then it was almost certainly laid down underwater. (In drier bioregions like the Sonoran Desert, sorted and layered deposits may also be created by wind, but on the Tongass there's precious little unvegetated surface for wind to play with.) A caked layer of impermeable silt suggests quiet water; maybe it was an old lake bed, or a raised tidal flat, or a lens of fill in a river's overflow channel. This silt bed is now ill suited for picnics, houses, or big forests. It's probably marked by some variety of wetland.

Only when we come to coarser, sorted, *alluvial* deposits left by more quickly flowing waters do we enter the realm of very large trees. One example is the nearly level floodplain of a larger stream or river. For millennia, accumulating sands and gravels provide drain field and nutrients to huge forests with devils club and foam-flower understories and a larger spruce component (the commercially preferred species) than on till-covered valley walls.

Another optimum type of forest substrate is called an *alluvial fan*. Streams descending steep bedrock slopes suddenly slow down on lowland terraces, dumping their loads. By migrating from side to side for centuries over these deposits, streams build fan-shaped landforms with the largest particles at the apex and the smallest at the base. Fan forests rival floodplain forests in magnificence. The Forest Service habitat database for the Tongass presently contains enough information to give a rough estimate of what percentage of our fan and floodplain surface has been clear-cut. This has not been done.

On steeper forested slopes rocks sometimes lie eloquently *on top of* the moss, giving meaning to the phrase "angle of repose." This is a *colluvial fan,* formed by rockfall rather than by streams. Some of these former slide paths are colonized by forest and gradually stabilized, with only occasional rocks wedged loose by frost from cliffs above, or kicked free of the fragile ferny duff by passing animals. Especially near the bases of these fans one sometimes finds huge trees, beneficiaries of steady nutrient replenishment and excellent drainage. Logging of steep colluvial fans, so dependent on tree roots for anchorage, is like tearing the scab off a wound; it brings renewed landslides and irreparable soil loss with the first hard rains.

The common denominator among all of these substrates that support big trees is good drainage. All examples, so far, have been unconsolidated *surficial deposits*. Big trees may also grow directly on bedrock when it too offers good drainage. The obvious example is karst. A forest on soluble limestone or marble may be subtly or unmistakably distinctive. At its most striking, weird rain-polished fins and pallid knobs jut up through the mosses and maidenhair ferns. Greened-over sinkholes, as deep as they are wide, gape between tree trunks. It's a challenge to mentally strip away the plants and thin soils in order to visualize the bedrock foundation of a karst forest. But to appreciate the internal drainage, and the near impossibility of surface flow or ponding, a walk down to the beach is enlightening. Here in the tide zone the naked bedrock looks like Swiss cheese, sculpted into pits and arches, and everywhere pocked with sharp-edged craters like sun-cups on summer snowfields.

As on alluvium, almost all of the productive lowland karst forest has been clear-cut. Whenever I notice a surviving old-growth forest on karst, I paddle ashore to check it out. But until I found the miraculously spared stand on South Prince of Wales Wilderness, I'd only been able to guess at the karst forest's original structure and understory composition. For several decades after the turn of the century, hand loggers with axes and crosscut saws patrolled every beach in the Alexander Archipelago. Their prowess was legendary. The "pumpkins"—clean, fat spruces often lacking branches for the first hundred feet above the ground—fell during this period. The invention of barge-mounted cable winches called steam donkeys allowed hand loggers to drag even the largest logs from great distances down to salt water.

Today these "highgraded" forests are typically dominated not by spruces but by less commercially valuable western hemlock trees left standing by the hand loggers. Branches and foliage of these hemlocks spread out dramatically after the demise of the pumpkin spruces, and saplings grow up swiftly to plug the gaps, creating a thick, relatively shorter and more uniform canopy. To a deer, such shady forests have disappointing understories; critical winter forage plants like five-leaved bramble and bunchberry are sparsely distributed.

The karst stand we measured on South Prince of Wales Wilderness was my first direct insight into what these forests once offered. Two huge spruces towered far above the other trees, which were mostly hemlocks from 100 to 150 feet tall. The resulting multilayered canopy admitted plentiful light to understory plants, which here included a complex mosaic of red huckleberry, salmonberry, sword fern, sapling hemlocks, and false lily of the valley. Each of these, in its own season, is food for deer. Clearly, it would be jumping to conclusions to suggest that all of today's highgraded karst forests once looked like this, but the rarity of this untouched stand underscores the carelessness of failing to follow the "first precaution of intelligent tinkering," in the words of Aldo Leopold: "to keep every cog and wheel."

Substrate, by influencing drainage and nutrient availability, controls potential tree size. Another control is wind, which knocks down entire forests every few centuries on some vulnerable mountainsides. On the most repeatedly storm-blasted sites such as high ridge crests, wind can "train" trees into resistant shapes with prop roots, short tapered trunks, and low centers of gravity. Studies on Prince of Wales Island indicated that wind damage to forests is most extensive on the southeast- to southwest-facing hill slopes, and least extensive on north-facing aspects. This can easily be seen on high-elevation aerial photos of very wind-exposed places like southernmost Prince of Wales. Gale force southeasterlies racing in from the unfettered sweep of Dixon Entrance result in scrubby forests (either perennially *trained* or young blowdown regeneration) on windward slopes. Only on fairly steep northwest-facing colluvial slopes and sheltered stream bottoms is there taller forest, which appears as coarser texture on the photos. |

WHAT'S LEFT?

In 1993 the Wilderness Society won a lawsuit against the Forest Service by exposing the statistical weakness of dividing the forest into four commercial volume classes based primarily on photo interpretation. Until foresters rectify the faulty timber inventory maps, oft-quoted answers to the most basic questions—How much big forest once existed? How much has been taken?—are on hold. Redefining "big forest" is the first problem. The agency is presently trying to move "beyond volume" in its assessment of the forest, recognizing that given stands might have equivalent board footage but very different species composition, canopy cover, stand structure, wildlife value, and susceptibility to erosion after logging.

The courts need the numbers, but our hearts already know; the river bottom lands, the alluvial and colluvial fans, and the great karst forest have been systematically ravaged. Even into recent decades, and especially on Native lands, spruces larger than the current state champion have been discovered by loggers, and dropped unceremoniously. Stumped landscapes and thousands of shocking aerial photos eventually are numbing. I paddle on, or flip past the ugliest pictures, searching for survivors.

How much of the original big-tree forest—say, fifty thousand or more board feet per acre—has been clear-cut? Answering that contentious question again could take years of effort by the Forest Service's astute researchers and statisticians, directing large teams of cruisers and wielding the latest in remote sensing and computerized geographic information systems. Meanwhile, clear-cutting continues, and new experiments with helicopters have revived the old hand logger's practice of plucking out the pumpkins. Now, however, prime trees need no longer be within quick skidding distance of the beach or logging roads. Big trees, ironically, may become victims of attempts at a more benign forestry.

Stands of more than fifty thousand board feet per acre are majestic and increasingly uncommon. But how big were the greatest stands of the Tongass? What percentage of the forest once held stands containing more than one hundred thousand board feet per acre? And what remains? The megastands are no longer found in patches much larger than a single acre.

SCIENTIFIC RECREATION

The fifty thousand-plus board feet per acre question will be a tough nut to crack, even on the ponderous Forest Service anvil. But the one hundred thousand-plus board feet per acre question is more tractable, something a dedicated amateur could peck at with affordable tools and a love of bushwhacking. What's more, really big trees have that *Guinness Book* appeal and are proven tourist attractions, from California's redwoods to Vancouver Island's Sitka spruces. In Juneau, a few years ago, a businessman named Sam Skaggs became intrigued by the big tree question. He had an interest in ecotourism and was a board member of Interrain Pacific, a nonprofit organization dedicated to enhancing public access to geographic information systems within the coastal rain forest bioregion. Could an ecotourism venture—a search for Alaska's last megaforests—also provide data needed by land managers and the concerned public?

Sam took these ideas to Matt Kirchhoff, a wildlife habitat researcher with the Alaska Department of Fish and Game. In response, Matt developed a scoring system for a one-acre patch of big forest. He borrowed in part from national and state procedures for the measurement of champion trees. The height and girth of the largest single tree in the stand contribute half of the total stand score. But as an ecologist, Matt wanted to ensure that tree hunters wouldn't miss the forest for the trees, so he expanded the point system to include the total volume of wood contained within the chosen acre. Measurements are taken with foresters' tools such as Relaskops, diameter tapes, clinometers, and laser range finders. We thus determine tree heights and diameters and the board footage of the selected acre. That acre is not intended to represent the wider surroundings. It characterizes the absolute cream of the watershed. Our data allow us to describe, in addition to the stand score, the forest's canopy structure, species composition, understory mosaic, and habitat values for deer and bear. And we are slowly groping for ways to express on paper that slipperiest and least quantifiable of forest values—the impact of a towering and enduring community on the human heart.

Sam Skaggs founded Alaska Research Voyages, Inc., and one of its first undertakings was the ecological trophy hunt called Landmark Trees. Participants would assist with fieldwork by day and return at night to royal accommodations on the fifty-four-foot sailboat *Arcturus*. When Sam asked if I would lead the first Landmark Trees expedition to Sea Otter Sound on northern Prince of Wales Island, it didn't take me long to decide. If I had recognized how utterly that month of tree hunting would restructure my relationship to the Tongass, I suppose I would have considered the offer for a more seemly period, then agreed even more enthusiastically.

The first Landmark Trees trip impressed me as the essence of respectful ecotourism. It promoted holistic investigation rather than been-there-done-that checklisting. It confronted the country's unsightly wounds as well as its feel-good attractions. We sought ever higher stand scores, playfully competing to toot the bioregion's horn rather than our own. Participants knew their fieldwork and trip fees were paying back the land they visited. We met the imperiled heart of the archipelago.

The Tongass is about exchange and transformation across the

Great Edge: geologic collision, subduction, mountain building; boiling up of rain clouds over steep wooded hillsides; "grease trail" traders bartering smelt oil for lynx fur; translation of wealth from sea to land to sea to land. Fishy sea lion belches swept by sea breeze from their haul-out rocks into the forest leave a pastel green scuz on the windward side of tree trunks. Lichen squamules maybe. The Pacific's very breath inoculates us.

And the bustling land-sea marketplace, the heart of the Tongass, is the anadromous stream: collector of the foamy detritus of a watershed, incubator and cemetery of salmon, stalking ground of North America's best-fed carnivore. Fish streams and big trees have an ancient pact. Roots of living trees stabilize stream banks, and big dead logs in the water maintain deep coho nursery pools. To return the favor, streamsides offer near-perfect growing conditions for Sitka spruces, partly for reasons of improved drainage on alluvium, as I've mentioned. But the plot gets thicker as terrestrial ecologists collaborate with fisheries biologists and laboratory wizards who can now determine how much of the carbon in streamside vegetation comes from the sea. Trees are made of salmon. Salmon are made of insect-processed trees. After a fall outing on this theme, a fourth grade student points to a departing eagle and yells, "Look, flying fish!" and the naturalist grins in bliss. This kind of epiphany should be coaxed from more tourists by more tour guides.

Landmark Trees as ecotourism has scarcely wet its feet. I expect Alaska will soon see an overflow effect from growing interest in the bigger-yet-tamer trees to the south of us. The champion trees of Washington State, for example, are dearly loved. Countless hands have touched them, and eyes are lifted daily to their distant crowns. They stand as much as fifty feet taller and five feet thicker than Alaska's largest. Most are tightly hemmed by second growth, like shackled kings. The Tongass big tree experience, at its best, deemphasizes the lone giant and honors the still-wild forest. Alluvium, devils club, salmon, bear, eagle, and towering spruce trees comprise the core community of the rain-forest bioregion. The health of all surrounding communities, from subalpine meadow to subtidal eelgrass bed, is supported by the "commerce" of the stream and river bottomlands. In Washington and Oregon, primeval riparian communities live only in memory.

Southeast Alaskans need tourism not only as employment, but also as protection from our own rapacity. The world's attention, refocused by a coalition of biologists, conservationists, and eco-tour operators, could stop the sack of the Tongass. But we've done poorly at bringing forest destruction before the scrutiny of visitors, who after all are on vacation, often in flight from their own sad surroundings. The Clear-Cut Successional Interpretive Tour will probably never be a hot seller, but there are subtler and more uplifting ways to speak for the country.

One way is to offer new and more fundamental icons for the northern rain forest. In this anthology, we've chosen to spotlight the spruce, salmon, and deer: the plant, fish, and mammal most revered and directly used by the human residents of Southeast Alaska. Today's tourist has another set of icons, chosen for their charisma and their rarity elsewhere: tidewater glaciers, brown bears, and whales. An operator offering all three is sitting smugly on the grand slam of Alaskan coastal tourism. A visitor returning home with memories of calving ice, a breaching humpback, and a brownie in the ryegrass has "done" the Tongass, at least by present standards.

Encounters with glaciers, brownies, and whales are profoundly moving even for Alaskans who live with them. And there are some conservation benefits from a tour industry structured around the Big Three. Whale biologist Roger Paine believes that every visitor excitedly clutching the deck rail of a whale-watching ship is a potential vote for marine mammal conservation, far outweighing that activity's harassment to the animals. Bear watching is conducted on a much less industrial scale, and we can't significantly increase the contacts between brown bears and tourists without developing new, supervised observation posts like Pack Creek on Admiralty Island, a proposition sure to face criticism.

The unfortunate thing about the glaciers-bears-and-whales fixation is that visitors coveting direct sightings of the Big Three can be distracted from their glorious context. Wilderness guides deal daily with this pesky expectation. Skilled guides are adept at defusing it, opening guests' senses to the liquid trills of thrushes, to silvery flashes of sand lance schools, to sweet tongueburst of licorice fern runners, and to the hair-tickling pungency of skunk cabbage freshly scooped and shredded by something manifestly bigger footed than a deer.

What if every guide made a point of seeking out the most spectacular forest on the journey, be it an afternoon's walk or a week's paddle? What if, by way of introduction, the guide said this: "Frankly, your odds of actually seeing a brown bear on this trip are about one in four. The gift of bears, really, isn't seeing them; it's just that wonderful, mammalian whole-body knowledge that they're *nearby,* sniffing, listening to you. But there's something unforgettable on this trip that I *can* show you, if you're game. It's much bigger than a bear, and it can't run. We found it a couple weeks ago, way back off the beach. I'm gonna take you on a fifteen-minute bushwhack into the beating heart of the rain forest."

CONSERVATION CRUISERS

While Sam Skaggs and I waited for ecotourists to discover Landmark Trees, the project took directions that neither of us envisioned during its first summer aboard *Arcturus*. Examining our data from Prince of Wales Island later that winter, already imagining an eventual *Atlas of Tongass Landmark Trees,* I chafed under the snail's pace at which we were scouting a land area more than twice the size of the rain forest of western Washington and Oregon. We needed help from resident Alaskans.

With Sam's encouragement, I proposed free Landmark Tree workshops in summer 1997 for members of the Sitka Conservation Society, and for Narrows Conservation Coalition, in Petersburg. The Sitka workshop would be followed by a Landmark Tree expedition in the Peril Strait region, aboard Lynn Schooler's charter boat, the *Wilderness Swift*. Since Lynn and I volunteered our time, Southeast Alaska Conservation Council (SEACC) and Alaska Conservation Foundation covered our travel and operating expenses.

June 30, 1997, Askulk Pass. Our pilot, Lynn Schooler, ran five eager tree hunters in his light inflatable skiff from our tent camp to the wide bay-head estuary. He planned to spend the day filming brown bears, and would listen for our radio call that evening. Our team consisted of Marc Wheeler and Angie Schmitz from the Juneau SEACC office, naturalist Kathy Hocker, longtime conservationist Dana Owen, and me. Over the past few days they'd become adept timber cruisers, at ease with volume tables and stereo photo interpretation. All were old hands at brush travel, undaunted by thorns and blowdown. That would help. Landmark trees rarely just stood there next to the trail. Besides, there wasn't any trail.

On the beach we rendezvoused with our new Sitka friends Barth and Mary Alice Hamburg, who'd come in their own skiff, the *Seaweed*. A landscape architect with the Forest Service, Barth was spending his weekend helping with our Landmark Trees assessments. He'd heard from forester colleagues of an exceptional stand several miles back into Askulk Pass, a long valley connecting two bays. The pass fell within a recent, congressionally designated roadless area. On this expedition we were sampling the full range of land-use designations, from protected to potentially loggable.

Single file, we waded through chest-high grass and fireweed toward the forest, mostly following the mashed-down swaths of grazing bears. Sign was heavy—scats and uprooted skunk cabbage—and we appreciated the relative safety in our numbers. Just inside the trees, a hare-sized animal bounded away, and I belatedly recognized it as a month-old fawn. It was lucky to be alive in this brownie metropolis.

The guys who cruised this valley years ago told Barth they found superlative but widely spaced spruces in the open-canopied floodplain forest just a short distance upstream from the tidal flats. They urged us not to stop there, however, but to continue deeper inland into Askulk Pass, almost to the headwaters of the stream draining out to the bay on the far side. There they'd found equally large but more closely spaced trees, forming a much higher volume forest on a gently sloping alluvial fan. The fan originated in a gully on one valley wall and spread smoothly across the entire valley floor.

The foresters' advice was hard to heed. The lower floodplain forest had trees much larger than any we'd so far seen in the Sitka area. The spectacular terrain of Baranof, Kruzof, and southwestern Chichagof Islands—the primary use area for the people of Sitka—is more precipitous than that of Prince of Wales Island, where our first Landmark Trees efforts focused. Although a great deal more timber has been cut from Prince of Wales's mellower topography, the more predictably concentrated big valley-bottom forest near Sitka has been more thoroughly eliminated. The Askulk Pass forest was more than we dared hope for. Three times we stopped to measure trees. One was 205 feet tall and 87 inches in diameter at breast height, the largest I'd found on the northern Tongass. We didn't expect anything bigger on the fan forest farther inland. But only half of a Landmark Trees score comes from the dimensions of the largest individual; the rest is based on the gross board feet of the surrounding acre.

The trees within a hundred feet or so of this 205-foot spruce were not exceptional. Because trunks were set far apart, the open forest canopy admitted plentiful light to the understory, where the frequently reworked, gravelly floodplain had an extremely healthy thicket of devils club and salmonberry. Already our knees and forearms tingled from scratches and embedded needle tips. But the promised fan forest did indeed look striking on the aerial photos. We packed up and pressed on.

Two hours later we emerged into a quarter-mile-long sedge fen, created in part by episodic beaver floodings. At the far end of the meadow stood our fan forest, and we could tell even from a distance that the hike had been worth it. A pair of yellowlegs criticized as we sloshed past their camouflaged nest into one of the great hidden treasures of the Tongass.

For lack of time we skipped a thorough reconnaissance of the entire fan and set quickly to work measuring. It was obvious that the fan supported the largest contiguous acreage of very high volume forest that I'd ever seen. The center of the acre we selected held an amazing cluster of spruces, born before Columbus. One reached 210 feet tall; two were 200; one was 190; two were 180. In the awesome surroundings, they hardly stood out.

The grandeur mitigated the difficult work. Often our Relaskop handlers couldn't find the rod person only a few feet away through the thorny leaves. But the numbers were finally turned in. Askulk Pass was our second-highest-scoring Landmark Trees stand. And the stand volume, at 141,700 board feet, was the highest we'd ever measured.

We were sweaty and dehydrated. Rare sunny skies made for contrasty lighting, and I took only a few stark mug shots of massive boles and weary hunters. Marc gathered our drained water bottles and headed off to fill them at a nearby stream, but hurried back empty-handed at the sound of a large animal splashing. Drinks could wait. We rapidly recorded the understory flora. Then we dragged our tape in three stages, 680 feet, on a fixed bearing back to the beaver meadow.

Out in the fen we marked a more relocatable "witness tree." We finally got a satellite triangulation reading from our handheld global positioning system unit, which wouldn't operate back under the spruce canopy. I wrote the latitude and longitude into our data form, intrigued but uneasy with this hand-me-down power. Global positioning is a Gulf War invention developed to guide missiles into an enemy's broom closet. Released to potentially subversive civilians like us, its precision is intentionally damped but still remarkable. An earlier era of military hand-me-downs, at the close of World War II, gave us the first systematic aerial photo coverage of Southeast Alaska, still the base for today's topographic maps.

Industrial logging has sponsored equally revealing imagery, but little of it has trickled down to more peaceful applications. If you need high-resolution color aerial photos of Tongass timber production land, you'll find file cabinetsful, usually reflown and updated every decade or so. Photo coverage of unharvestable wilderness areas is patchy and old by contrast. Fortunately, many parts of the national forest were photographed before their recent removal from the timber base. The laminated prints of the Askulk Pass megastand that proved so instrumental to our bushwhack dated back to 1977; they bore grease-pencil marks I preferred not to decipher. If there's any tool in the land manager's kit with the potential to empower conservationists, it's aerial photography. The public paid for those photos, and the great majority of federal employees I know are pleased, even anxious, to show them to us.

On our long hike back to the beach, thrilled with this incredible yet scarcely talked-of valley, we tried to imagine it as a showcase for the giant alluvial forests of the Tongass. Aerial photos and timber-shop rumors indicated equally magnificent stands in the bay on the far side of Askulk Pass. What a traverse for an ecotourist!

Fantasy: Fresh from your home in Cleveland, you get dropped off at Askulk Pass by a Sitka floatplane pilot to spend the evening watching sedge-grazing brown bears. The bears ignore your admiration because you watch them through a spotscope mounted in the tree platform adjoining your sturdy Forest Service rental cabin. Next day, following directions in your Landmark Trees Atlas, you backpack inland on a well-maintained trail, passing the largest conifers you've ever seen. That night you sleep in a reserved hut on a small lake near the watershed divide. Varnished onto the tabletop in this hut are enchantingly detailed aerial photos under a 3-D viewer. This stereoscope makes the biggest trees rise prominently above those of less productive forests. The photo caption informs you that the intact alluvial community is ecologically precious and vanishingly rare, and you resolve to pay closer attention on the next day's hike out to Exit Bay. Somewhere along that walk, your senses honed by discovery of huge clawed footprints in the mud, you freeze in terror as a seven-foot bird launches from a low branch overhead. Recovering, heart racing, you experience the "Flying fish!" epiphany. Alluvium, big trees, brown bears, eagles, devils club, and salmon are forever married in your soul. You're met on the beach by a charter boat from Hoonah, where you go to spread around more tourism dollars. When you get home you recommend the trip to your congressional delegation.

Nice, we thought, except for the part about the bears. Our imaginary ecotourist couldn't sidestep that impact, the well-intended but certain harassment and displacement. And would bear hunters use the huts? How does one safeguard the forest's heart, by baring it or by ripping down the trail signs? We tossed around a few more fantasies and finally settled on the more attainable goal of our beach pickup, dinner, and warm sleeping bags.

But the subject will arise again, as long as wilderness—official or de facto—remains on the Tongass. Ecotourism has slipped its collar and is running amok through many a Southeast city and village and their decreasingly pristine surroundings. The wilderness ethic of many small tour operators, in view of economic alternatives like large-scale logging, is "use it or lose it." Partly self-serving, partly cold realism, it hasn't matured into a coordinated community response to threats or opportunities.

In the economy of the spirit, wildness is our working capital. We can't borrow much harder on it, as a nation or as individuals. In a dream, the furry thing sighs, begins to rise. We wake up shaken, afraid of the wildness we crave, ashamed of the wildness we advertise. I erase from record the alluvial fringe of big spruces along that unnamed creek on South Prince of Wales Wilderness. No blaze or cut stump or boot track marked the game trails that led me there. In a life among wild places, I've never walked farther from my own domestic effrontery, or closer to nature's forgiveness, free as water in the world's last tree temples. Yet even there, in the shadows of a musky grotto under the largest, wildest spruce, lay a brittle piece of faded pink survey flagging. May what it claimed be forgotten.

RICHARD CARSTENSEN is a naturalist from Juneau, Alaska, with a special interest in the biogeography of the Alexander Archipelago. Most of his work is done through the Discovery Foundation, a nonprofit organization that teaches natural history to the youth and educators of Southeast Alaska. He is coauthor and illustrator of The Nature of Southeast Alaska: A Guide to Plants, Animals, and Habitats *(Alaska Northwest Books, 1992) and the Alaskan contributor to* Enduring Forests *(The Mountaineers, 1996). With help from resident and visiting volunteers, Richard is continuing the Landmark Tree program under a fellowship from Interrain Pacific.*

sphagnum moss, *Richard Carstensen*

The Tongass Rain Forest—
An Elusive Sense of Place and Time

PAUL ALABACK

The Tongass forms the heart of the world's largest temperate rain forest. The perhumid or continually wet rain forest covers the rugged archipelago and fjordland coast from Vancouver Island north to Prince William Sound in Alaska—a stretch of more than a thousand miles. Not only is it the biggest cold rain forest in the world, it also includes some of the most intact and ecologically valuable wilderness areas left on the planet. In wilderness reserves like Admiralty Island or Kitlope or Misty Fjords, aside from a narrow strip of forest along bays where boats can easily be moored, humans have seldom ventured and have taken little. Sitka black-tailed deer thrive in the old growth, where enough light pierces the canopy to grow choice foods for a large, herbivorous mammal. Salmon still fill the rivers and streams, and brown bears—known locally as "brownies"—roam on trails that date back over millennia. This is a place where our impact has been so localized and so recent that we still have a good chance of creating an existence that allows for the coexistence of the myriad life-forms of this forest. Our challenge is to see if we can really understand this place, its biota, and its sense of time enough to find our place within it.

It's hard to deny that the Tongass is a wet place, and it is water, perhaps more than any other variable, that drives the Tongass's ecosystems. A deep green permeates the forest, from the dense carpet of feather mosses on the floor to the intertwined thickets of blueberry bushes. Huge mounds of mosses and liverworts wedge in at the base of large branches in the upper canopy and the dense carpet of needles on top, from one hundred to as much as two hundred feet above the ground. From the spongy forest floor to the lichens festooning the upper branches of patriarch trees, the Tongass impresses even the most hardened rain forest veteran. A constant ooze of water wells up when you walk over the ground. Is it any wonder that general rules of thumb for forests often break down in this strange, wet microcosm?

But *wet* is a relative term. Tropical forests can be incredibly wet as well. There, humidity leads to runaway molds and flourishing relatives of the pineapple family. In the West and North, brown (or white) landscapes predominate in winter; forty inches of rain, as in Seattle, seems like an amazing deluge. But in Southeast Alaska, raindrops in standard weather gauges add up to two to ten times what is recorded in Seattle and occur year round; little of the moisture evaporates. Just try hanging out clothes on a typical day in coastal Alaska. Without some source of heat, they are more likely to mold than to dry. So not only is it as wet as a tropical rain forest, but the moisture sticks around even more than it would in the tropics because of the continually cool temperatures. Thus, coastal Alaska has one of the highest rates of runoff—the difference between rainfall and evaporation—in the world.

In the Tongass, the massive amounts of moisture lead to both the rapid leaching of nutrients and speedy soil development. Soils that form in thousands of years in New England do so in only a few centuries here. Even for plants, this is too much moisture. The fastest growth of trees occurs where steep slopes or porous soils can let some of the water drain away so that oxygen can get to the roots.

From a human perspective, the constant moisture is quite a pain to deal with. Flying low to the ground through dense fog that is wrapped around an intricate labyrinth of glacially scoured spirelike mountains in Southeast Alaska can be an especially harrowing but common experience for residents of Southeast Alaska. Planning when to work on the roof, even in summer, can tax the most meticulous Day-Timer. Many forest trails go through extensive areas of unique soils that turn to deep slimy mud when they're wet and disturbed by trampling, unless they are covered with boards. One needs a certain attitude to enjoy the pleasures of jogging, playing baseball, or shooting baskets outdoors. There is no such thing as cancellation due to rain. Nothing would ever get done. Everyone owns rubber boots and rain gear, even for town life.

To understand the Tongass and the myriad issues that face it—especially in terms of how people have changed and are changing their relationship to this ecosystem—you really need to think about how the bizarre climate affects plants and all the animals that depend on them. Most forest regions in the West have terrible problems with poor forest regrowth after logging or natural wildfires. If tree seedlings are not planted within a few years, these lands will be overtaken by drought-tolerant weeds, shrubs, or other plants for years or even decades. Not so in coastal Alaska. Hemlock seedlings come up in nearly uncountable numbers just two years after logging. Most of the lower forty-eight is beset by ever-increasing invasions of exotic species, threatening to change ecosystems in fundamental, irreversible ways. Not so in the Tongass. There is a growing consensus that in most forested regions in the United States, people have fundamentally altered the ecology and functioning of forests, even in the most remote wilderness areas. Not in the Tongass. The differences have a lot to do with rain.

Perhaps the best way to try to get an idea of how the Tongass works is to look at the most fundamental ecological process in forests: change. Walking through an old-growth forest lends the easy impression that this is the forest immortal. Massive patriarch trees, some four to six feet in diameter and older than seven hundred years, suggest that this forest has been here forever and has always been the same. But in fact what makes the Tongass so complex, so diverse and difficult to understand, is that it is actually a product of centuries, if not millennia, of natural disturbances. Its response to these disturbances is what makes it unique. Disturbance is the scalpel that gives the forest its shape and character.

Most forests in North America are profoundly affected by fire. The spectacular fires that scoured thousands of acres in Yellowstone in 1988 are but one example. Even in the Northeast and in the Midwest, fires historically played a key role in opening up the forest, recycling nutrients, favoring oaks and pines over maples and other hardwoods, providing more nutritious forage for deer. In most places there is a warm, dry season and lightning storms that eventually lead to natural fire. But not so in coastal Alaska. Fire is extremely rare. Flooding, glaciers, and volcanoes are the most spectacular events that beset the region now and then, but it is wind in combination with the omnipresent moisture that shapes the forest here.

In October, when New England is in full, vibrant color and much of the country enjoys a crisp "Indian summer," coastal Alaska typically experiences its most intense downpours and winds. One October in Ketchikan, it rained as much as in Seattle over an entire year. This is the time when the forest trees are most susceptible to being toppled by winds. But the scalpel can be coarse and hard to predict. It is quite rare that all trees in any given area fall at once. One study suggested that the most common event is for two to four trees to go down at a time. Apparently when one of these rain forest giants tumbles, it usually takes a few others with it.

So why is it that trees of the Tongass are falling down so often in such small pockets? It would seem that if the wind were strong enough to knock over one tree, it would knock down the entire forest, like a hurricane or a typhoon. The answer seems to lie in several factors working together. First, these are wet soils—so wet that in many places the soils never dry out. Plants have a pretty tough time extracting nutrients from saturated soils. All the action occurs in the thick organic layer on top, so even the largest roots of two-hundred-foot-tall trees usually lie within a foot or so of the soil's surface. The combination of heavy rains and windstorms is quite effective in knocking over tall, shallow-rooted trees. But this still does not explain the small patches of blowdown.

Many of the old rain forest trees are hollow, or partially hollow, from slow-growing rot and decay that works up from the roots. When the massive winds of the Tongass topple a few old giants, standing trees have bark ripped off in swipes from falling trees or branches. In these wounds, tiny spores lodge and grow, spreading more rot to invade new trees. It doesn't take much wind to blow over a hollow-bottomed giant. In some instances, trees may fall from their own weight, even on calm days. So this seems to explain why some trees go down more readily than others. In fact, most trees break at midstem, not by having their root mass ripped out and tipped over.

Another important factor again links back to water. Since drainage is key in governing how fast and how high trees grow, variation in soils is crucial to the character of the forest. Southeast Alaska has some of the most complicated and varied geology of any region on the continent. Sandstones, mudstones, limestones, metamorphics like schist, volcanics, granites—they are all there. The varied geology, in combination with a long glacial history, has led to an incredibly complex routing of water across the land. Wet pockets and dry pockets occur sporadically. While we are most impressed with the magnificent, tall trees that often grow in small patches on the Tongass, the landscape is mostly a peat bog.

Many flat areas accumulate so much water that they can sustain only short, stunted trees or peat. These are some of the most unusual ecosystems of coastal Alaska. More than twenty species of sphagnum moss occur here, making the Tongass one of the most species-rich bog environments in the world. Scientists have debated whether these peat bogs are killing the adjacent forest or whether the bogs are turning into forest. Evidence suggests that change is occurring in both directions. Dig into a peat bog and you can often find perfectly preserved remains of forest trees. Dig down into a forest floor and you may find ancient layers of buried peat.

The great trees of the Tongass occur along streams, bathed in nutrient-rich sediment, or on steep mountain slopes or rich benches that mark old shorelines or landslides. They also flourish in the less acidic limestone soils. Only 4 percent of the land area of the Tongass is even capable of growing the giant trees. What appears to the raven above as an impenetrable green thicket is actually a mosaic of tiny peat bog depressions, great nutrient-rich microsites surrounded by a plethora of other types and conditions. The boundary between holes in the forest formed by peat bogs and adjacent tall trees is usually gradual, reflecting continuous changes in nutrients and drainage. Over mountains, a full range of tree heights can be seen, reflecting old disturbances, the routing of water, and changes in geology. Variations in soils, causing abrupt differences in plant communities, often occur over a range of feet rather than acres. Thus, it is easy to see why logging, which has occurred over less than 5 percent of the land area, has still had a profound effect on the Tongass, because it has nearly always been confined to these relatively rare, specialized habitats.

The rugged terrain is the key to explaining why some places are more likely to blow down than others. The steeply carved islands of Southeast Alaska's many fjords often funnel and redirect winds. In Hawk Inlet on Admiralty Island, when gales blow from the southeast across the huge Chatham Strait, the wind blows mostly to the north in the bay. Most trees are braced against these northerly winds. But gusts blowing through channels and rugged mountains often lead to high-velocity blasts of upper air pockets that occasionally touch land and knock over a patch of forest. It works just like the riptides that form as water plows its way through these same channels during midtides. One recent study showed that on a particularly windy island, forests growing on exposed, southeast-facing ridges tend to blow over in large patches and thus rarely attain the great tree ages that you see on other parts of the Tongass. The west coast of Prince of Wales Island and parts of Admiralty Island are famous for catastrophic windstorms every few centuries. Much of the clear-cut logging on Prince of Wales in the 1970s and 1980s was concentrated in these unique forests. The most spectacular problems with postlogging windthrow, not too surprisingly, also occurred in this area. Edges created by logging certainly did not create the sculpting for aero-dynamics that occurs naturally along the ancient bog forest margins.

Once a forest hole has been created by a wind gust, all the moisture-loving but light-starved plants have a rare opportunity. In one study, I found elderberry seedlings germinating within a matter of weeks following a wind disturbance, their long-buried seeds finally seeing the light of day. Surrounding trees that were left standing increased their growth within a few months. For these plants, there is no time to lose. A disturbance creates an optimal microenvironment with lots of light, moisture, and nutrients. But it won't last. Soon the hole will fill in with the branches of surrounding trees. So nature favors plants that can rapidly fill in the hole in the forest, and there are many candidates. For many plants, this is also the only time that sex results in offspring that might have a chance to make a new generation in the forest. Most of the time they all die, either quickly after germinating or more slowly, withering in the dark forest. Since seeds have so little chance, the parent plant must sprout vegetatively to keep things going, sometimes for hundreds of years.

Over the millennia, the forest has continued its fight against the elements in this way. Because of its remarkable ability to snap back quickly and survive storms, it has become the ageless forest. Individual trees die, but the forest remains. While the old-growth Douglas fir stands of the Pacific Northwest can be well described by naming the dominant behemoths—whose ages correspond with the great fires—such naming and individuation have little meaning in the Tongass. This forest is the product of generation upon generation of trees growing up in a partially open, complex mosaic. Thus, it is the age of the forest, not of any individual tree, that is key. The Scandinavians call this phenomenon forest continuity. My studies suggest that for a forest to start from scratch—say, from a clear-cut or another catastrophic disturbance—it will take at least three or four centuries to develop the complexity typical of the ageless forests you see today. Dominant trees in these old-growth forests can be anywhere from one hundred and fifty to seven hundred years old.

The actual location of openings or thickets may change slightly, but most animals can always count on the forest, the landscape, being pretty much the same. Is it thus any surprise that many animals of the Tongass are adapted to the dense forest, whereas in most other places, animals are adapted to large openings and clearings? Walk through this forest slowly. Look at all the clues. Even the understory herbs like dwarf dogwoods creeping across the forest floor may be centuries old but owe their origin to a specific disturbance. Often you can see countless generations of patriarchs: centuries-old behemoths above, recently fallen trunks below them, and hollow, rotting logs beside them. In soft, spongy mounds on the ground, you can readily kick your foot into a thousand strands of stringy red fibers. Dig into this soil and you can see signs of wood from trees even more ancient. Their remains give the soil a reddish or brownish color and a slight feel of peat or microsponge—clues that go back a thousand years.

The Tongass fails to satisfy people's fascination with order, pattern, and perfection. Every time wind blasts through a patch of forest, taking down a few trees, it causes change. Not only are new generations and old survivors allowed a chance to alter their lives and roles, but the existence of the new hole changes the forest mosaic. One study near Juneau found that these holes tend to expand. When a rough edge has been created in the forest, the forces of nature are going to smooth it out, much as a sharply angled stone on the beach will be smoothed by water. Most likely, a few more trees will soon be taken from that spot. This is not a random process. It depends on the time of year, the direction of the wind, the height above the canopy of any given tree, how massive the branches and needles that can catch the wind are, how the wind moves over obstacles in the forest. All of these factors will determine the next tree to fall. After the largest patriarch goes down, the die begins to roll for some of the smaller trees. Complexity breeds complexity. It is not a question of how long the forest will take to return to what it was, for every disturbance is unique. It may never return to what it was. From the perspective of a vole or a carab beetle, the forest is always changing; but for the raven flying above, it's pretty much the same.

There is a huge scientific debate raging in the Tongass over what kinds of windstorms may have begotten the forest we see today. In some places, huge gales occasionally sweep the forested mountain slopes, leaving twenty-acre piles of felled trees. A study of one island on the Tongass suggested that these intense storms may have affected a sizable percentage of the area—providing a perfect excuse for those who favor massive clear-cuts to say their logging is simply an emulation of nature. But the forest tells a much more complex story. It is not a large patchwork like a nice orderly tapestry we might want to weave, but a mosaic, every piece a different shape, each overlapping some others, and all with a different story of disturbance. If only we could more easily adapt the view of one of these patriarchs, it would be so much easier to see what is important, what is the scalpel and what is the ax, where and how often each force plays a role, and to what ultimate effect.

It would seem that if this climate is so unusual—and all we have thought about so far seems to derive from this idea—then to get a global perspective on this forest we need to start looking for all the other places in the world with a similarly strange climate. After more than ten years of searching, all I can say is that the more we look, the more difficult the task becomes. The kind of climate possessed by the Tongass is truly rare. There are only a few spots on the globe with temperate rain forests, cool summers, and over sixty inches of rain annually. Most are small pockets standing on the shores of an ocean and at the base of large mountains. Winds blow from the sea, bathing these few forests in moisture and buffering them from the cold air that brutalizes continental interiors during the winter.

The world's second-largest temperate rain forest lies along eight hundred miles of the rugged fjordland coast of southern Chile and Argentina. It also is a wet place, with lush, beautiful forests. But because of events going back hundreds of millions of years, this forest has a completely different cast of characters for a similar ecological drama. The trees are broadleaf evergreens, a life-form rarely found in North America. The live oaks of Georgia and Florida, the Pacific madrone, and the golden chinquapin of northern California are among the few examples. But unlike these specimens that grow only in very mild climates, the Chilean and Argentinean broadleaf evergreens—mostly southern beeches or *coigües*—grow next to glaciers, near mountaintops, and in deep snow. Their leaves are very small, a fact suggesting that there must be some special advantage to tough, small evergreen leaves in a coastal rain forest. These southern forests possess amazingly dense thickets, with layer upon layer of vegetation. The upper forest is generally less dense, but the lower forest is much thicker, often with a nearly impenetrable solid-stemmed bamboo called *quila*. This is the bamboo that is so ideally suited for carving into the flutes and panpipes made famous in Andean music.

No great bears or sea eagles grace these forests. No salmon historically invaded their streams. A strange array of small mammals, diminutive deer, and birds that are more often heard than seen make it clear that you are not in North America. But the winds and rains do come. In fact, the forty-degree latitudes in Chile are called the "roaring forties" because of their nearly continuous gales blowing all the way across the southern Pacific from Antarctica or New Zealand. Just as much rain drenches these forests, but winters are much milder. Plants such as the bizarre *pangue* with leaves six feet across and huge spines on the undersides grow here. So do bromeliads. *Pangue* and bromeliads both grow in the tropical rain forests of Costa Rica and down in the sub-Antarctic Chilean forests. Brilliant flashes of scarlet come from fuchsia—the same plant that graces gardens in the Northern Hemisphere—that grow in profusion in windthrow pockets and other openings throughout Patagonian rain forests.

It is the same in most of the other rain forests in the Southern Hemisphere. They all evolved as isolated pockets with many unique species. New Zealand, Tasmania, and higher elevations in southeast Australia, New Guinea, and other places harbor these resplendent forests. A few more pockets of native forest formerly eked out an existence along the stormy, rainy coasts of Ireland, Scotland, and Norway.

The Patagonian rain forests possess some of the world's oldest trees (many over three thousand years old). More plant species generally occur in these southern forests as well. Many of the large game species such as the *huemul* deer are seldom seen—they are victims of overhunting, poaching, or both. Just in the last decade, foreign investment has led to rapid forest clearing. Human-caused fires have ravaged many places despite the high rainfall. Exotic tree plantations have replaced much of the northern extent of these forests.

In terms of an intact ecosystem with all the major plant and animal species roughly as abundant as they were when the first European explorers arrived, the Tongass and adjacent British Columbia stand alone.

It's little wonder that temperate rain forests have been among the last to have been exploited for timbering. The two most extensive temperate rain forests in the world occur along incredibly remote and rugged coastlines that defy any kind of convenient transportation system. Deep fjords make bridge construction prohibitive or impossible. Steep slopes make roads expensive and unstable. Flying in these wet coastal regions is some of the most hazardous air travel in the world. Boats fare little better, unless you can wait for good weather and tides. Distances are vast as well. In the case of the Tongass, the haul from Juneau to the nearest major U.S. port is seven hundred miles. And then there is the matter of the rain. Construction techniques suited for solid ground have little place in soggy, peaty forests.

Following the exploitation of the easily accessible forests of the Pacific Northwest through the 1940s, Alaska and British Columbia were the obvious next places for the timber industry after World War II. Like the forests around Seattle and Vancouver, the Tongass is wet, and it possesses many of the same tree and shrub species, so it seemed logical that the northern rain forest should adapt well to logging and development strategies worked out in the Pacific Northwest. But things haven't quite gone that way. Apparently our sense of place was flawed.

Some of the fastest-growing trees in the temperate zone are found in the Pacific Northwest. Mild winters, abundant moisture, and sunny summers provide nirvana for both forest trees and city dwellers. But once in a while these forests can experience serious drought, or a series of successive droughts, which, combined with lightning storms or human-caused ignitions, can lead to the most spectacular and destructive fires on the continent. Indeed, some of the veteran Douglas firs from northern California to southern Canada appear to have come in after massive fires about five hundred years ago. What blazes they must have been!

When clear-cuts were first tried in coastal Alaska, loggers declared them far more successful than in southern locales. Within just two years, in 1954, a mile-square clear-cut on Prince of Wales Island was covered with tree seedlings all the way across. It appeared that the forest would just bounce right back. Likewise, studies of fisheries suggested no massive die-off attributable to logging. Industry ads declared logging to be the savior of the forest. They claimed that openings created by clear-cutting were leading to increased tree growth, better habitat for wildlife such as deer, and improved growth rates of salmon fry. The largest timber sale in Forest Service history called for logging 95 percent of the commercial-sized trees on more than a million acres of what is now Admiralty Island National Monument and adjacent lands. Yet when it was first proposed in the 1960s the clear-cutting was declared to have "no negative environmental impacts." From an impatient human perspective of time, in terms of five to twenty years, everything seemed fine.

But further investigations proved these sunny declarations illusory. In this case it was our flawed sense of time. Through decades of study, we have found that the rapid growth of seedlings is only the first chapter in the story. With clear-cutting, all trees are felled in forest stands ranging from forty to hundreds of acres. The logging typically occurs within one or two years. In the Tongass, ground disturbance caused by clear-cutting seems to be minimized since most of the available nutrients are contained in the soggy organic mat on top of the soil. But in contrast to wind and decay disturbances, in which only a few trees at a time typically fall, clear-cuts leave hardly any survivors. All the extra light and warmth now flooding the open forest patches are a godsend for plants whose growth has been suppressed by the presence of the big trees. In the Tongass, unlike in other western forests where logging occurs, the rapid opening of large acreages sets in motion an entirely peculiar set of conditions.

I have walked through countless clear-cuts of all ages on every major island of Southeast Alaska. For more than twenty years, my colleagues, students, and I have measured thousands of stem diameters, shrub heights, tree seedlings, and mosses and lichens in these disturbed settings. A remarkable pattern has emerged from our studies. Thirty or forty years after clear-cutting in the Tongass, a dense forest has begun to develop. After the thorough disturbance generally comes a clean, dense, even-aged stand of trees. Open pockets and old trees are rare. Just as in the tropics where biologists speak of primary and secondary forests, we call these second-growth, or secondary, forests. The most famous secondary forests are the exotic radiata pine plantations of southeastern Australia. So many trees and leaves are crammed together, scarcely 1 percent of open sunlight can make it to the forest floor, leaving little solar radiation for shrubs, herbs, and other plants that grow low to the ground—not much food for a plant eater like a deer.

What is unique about the secondary forests of the Tongass is that they persist for such a long time. In Oregon and Washington, studies have suggested that dense, second-growth forests last for only a few decades before opening up and developing lush, rich understory layers. In the Tongass, by contrast, it appears that a century or more is required for the forest to open up sufficiently to spur a lush ground-layer growth, but it is still without the richness of the original forest. Simply thinning the forest to open it up artificially seems to benefit only a few species of plants, for nature is much more complex than the tasks of artificial thinning suggest. When we change the disturbance intensity or frequency, or the type of disturbance, we change the forest. With an ageless forest, we are talking about centuries of change set in motion by clear-cutting.

Our challenge is to see how we can cheaply and effectively sculpt the forest so that it has more of its original mosaic of patches laid upon one another—not a simple task in the ageless forests of the Tongass. We have to stretch our comprehension to resemble that of an old tree or even an island. As Aldo Leopold said, we have to "think like a mountain." Countless storms, changes in climate, changes in biotic composition have occurred—many of them within the lifetime of a forest patriarch. Many clues probably lurk in the history of these places—clues that may lead us on a path of enlightenment: both what this forest really is and how we may better work within its fabric on its own terms.

Legends from the Hoonah people tell of what Glacier Bay was like before the advance of ice hundreds of years ago. As the ice melts now after retreating from its "little ice age" optimum, lakes and other features are reappearing. The natural order does come back. The Tsimshian people also remember the time before the great cedar migrated up the coast after the last large ice advance a mere three thousand years ago. With the arrival of the cedar came a flourishing of culture, so useful was the tree for making canoes, string, and weatherproof housing. Now a climate shift over the past twenty years giving the Tongass unprecedented mild winters has led to invasions of trees into alpine meadows and the appearance of secondary forests in avalanche tracks. Change is constant. The question is, how well can we learn from what the forest has to teach us? And how, within a more tolerable human time frame, can we figure out ways to sculpt the forest back into a pattern that fits the bigger picture?

The harsh cycle of disturbance caused by clear-cut logging has little analog in the Tongass or any other temperate rain forest. Wildlife studies show, for example, that few animal species benefit from these ephemeral habitats. Deer, the quintessential opportunists from suburban gardens to industrial tree farms, have met their match with coastal Alaska clear-cuts. After the secondary forests close in, twenty to thirty years after cutting, they are habitat for mites, porcupines, some foliage-gleaning birds—but not deer. There is nothing for deer to eat. New experimentation with selective logging techniques shows more promise for something that may better meld with the animals and plants of the archipelago. Still, our greatest challenge will be to help guide the extensive secondary forests back toward richer, more diverse forests in a reasonable period of time. Clear-cutting sets in motion a powerful juggernaut of change that has been fiendishly difficult to redirect.

The big stands of the Tongass were once among the most spectacular forests of North America. Consider the Maybeso Valley, where the region's first industrial-scale clear-cut occurred. The Maybeso grew thousands of acres of Sitka spruce trees, four to ten feet in diameter, 180 feet in height, many four hundred years old or more. No forest of such dimensions exists in the Tongass today. The Maybeso Valley was the core of this rain forest. Any modest success we may have in accelerating its melding back into the larger patchwork could be key to building a more sustainable relationship to the land for us and our successors. The Maybeso attests to our power to transform this forest in a blink of time. But do we have the will and the wisdom to bring it back to center stage?

There is little doubt that a diverse, productive rain forest of some kind eventually can regain its hold on this remote rainy coastline, just as it has done following glaciers, mudslides, and hurricane-force winds. But are we willing to wait? And can it happen before climate change and other stresses we may induce interfere with this age-old process once again? Will all the key animals, insects, and other players be able to persist and procreate effectively enough across this vast archipelago to be ready when the ageless rain forest reemerges from the old clear-cuts? There are plenty of uncertainties. But since human impact has thus far been confined to a relatively small part of the Tongass, since our impact has taken place over a short period of time, since exotic plants and animals do not appear to be invading and irreversibly changing this forest, and since we are not able to alter the basic scalpel of change—wind—it seems a good bet that this is one of the more likely places on Earth to survive human impact with minimal casualties.

In this rugged, majestic place, where our abuses of the land have been much simpler than in more subdued terrains, it is likely that the forest may be able to teach us the few vital lessons that we need to be able to adapt to a life that fits this place and time, both for us and for the surrounding forest. First, this forest has adapted to a uniquely wet and cold climate. Subtle changes in soils or climate within as little as dozens of feet create fundamentally distinctive circumstances. People who live in this forest need to consider these subtleties as well. Second, many parts of the Tongass owe their existence to events that occurred a century or more ago. An extended sense of time is elusive in this fast-moving slave-to-the-clock world that we have created. Our consciousness of this forest over the past century has tended to depreciate the importance of knowing the intracacies of place and time as these plants do. It is now up to the current generations of Tongass residents to develop a more profound appreciation and understanding of this place—to learn how better to heal the wounds of the forest and, more importantly, to demonstrate that we can carve out an existence here that enriches and sustains the complexity of this forest, not only on our rushed time scale, but also on that of the giant forest patriarchs, which are the heart of the Tongass.

PAUL ALABACK first became interested in natural history and ecology while growing up in suburban Chicago working with volunteer organizations on restoring prairies along old railroad rights of way. His first interest was in the vast array of bird species and the habitats they depend on. This quickly turned to an interest in plants and forests in particular and their interactions with wildlife. Fascinated by the lush and remote forests of the Pacific Northwest and Alaska, he studied both botany and forest science at the University of Washington in Seattle, then did graduate work at Oregon State University, specializing in the forest ecology of Southeastern Alaska. He has spent the subsequent twenty years studying the ecology of trees, mosses, ferns, herbs, and shrubs of temperate rain forests throughout the Americas. His particular interest is in how climate controls the function and diversity of these forests, and how they respond to both natural and human-induced disturbances. He was the ecologist for the Pacific Northwest Research Station of the U.S. Forest Service for eight years, and in 1993 he joined the faculty at the University of Montana, where he currently teaches and does research on forest ecology and conservation biology with field sites from Alaska to Argentina spanning semidesert grasslands to rain forests.

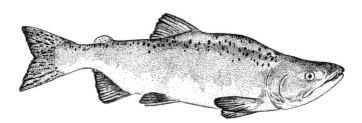

male pink salmon, *Katherine M. Hocker*

Salmon in the Trees

BRAD MATSEN

*One of the great dreams of man must be to find someplace between the
extremes of civilization and nature where it is possible to live without
regret.* BARRY LOPEZ

I'd better tell you right off that I have never seen spawning salmon
actually *in* the spruces, hemlocks, alders, or any of the other trees
in the rain forest of the Alexander Archipelago. I *have* seen them in
the creeks, of course, during the warm months when they arrive
from the sea, vital and silver, only to turn into ragged monsters to
surrender to their descendants. I take a one-two punch of mortal-
ity and renewal every time I stand on a muddy bank and watch
those beautiful fish turn so poignantly into tatters right before
my eyes, with their next generation tentatively on deposit in the
streambed gravel. They disguise themselves and then disappear al-
together, as though they are determined to blend with the moss,
bark, silt, debris, and earth of the place.

It's hard to resist thinking of those fabulous, recently departed
salmon as ornaments dangling from the branches of the trees, clattering around up there like wind chimes. What we started to suspect—that cutting down the rain forest would kill the salmon—has
proved to be true: trees need fish as much as fish need trees. And as
it turns out, wishing that salmon really spawned in the trees of the
miraculous bit of territory we call the Tongass isn't just a matter of

having a hyperbolic imagination. At a potluck in Ketchikan a few years ago, a geologist showed up with hard evidence that salmon eventually do make their way into trunks, branches, leaves, and needles, especially the royal old growths of the outer islands. The menu that evening was predictably delicious: baked halibut, hot dish, salad, and wine, the food of every winter anybody has ever spent in a Southeast Alaska town. The company was similarly comfortable, about a dozen of us who ate, then helped our hosts take some art off the walls for the slide show. Then, for an hour, we sipped decaf and wine while the geologist, an exuberant man named Jim Baichtel, told us about his enchantment with the limestone karst of Prince of Wales Island.

His slides were portraits of lush trees and groves; clear-cut ridges, saddles, and valleys; and people on claustrophobic expeditions into the labyrinth of caverns and tunnels that underlie the familiar surface terrain. In some of the pictures, spelunkers are hanging on ropes in dead-drop shafts more than five hundred feet deep, grinning. In others, dusty cavers bathed in the glow of head-lamps and strobes are wedging themselves through subterranean gaps barely as wide as their hips. They are equipped with special straps on their boots, Jim explained, to allow their comrades to extricate them when they get stuck. Over the rattling of the projector, he also told us stories about the geologic skeleton that shapes the archipelago and serves the trees and the salmon.

Imagine a braid of half a dozen gigantic strands of ancient rock winding along a southwest-to-northeast line like an enormous plait of hair, braided and laid against the continent. These six tendrils are the remnants of distinct terranes, pieces of drifting crust that docked against the old, old rock of the North American plate and fused together over the past couple of hundred million years. The rocks vary wildly in origin, age, and kind, but all of them seem to conform to two generalities: they were once buried deeply, then were uplifted and exposed by glaciation and erosion, and their grain is consistently parallel to the long axis of the archipelago. A great fault, one of the most obvious and beautiful in the world, cleaves the entire assemblage in a fracture more than three hundred miles long, now occupied by the waters of Chatham Strait and Lynn Canal.

To the east on the mainland lies what pioneer geologist John C. Reid called "a truly stupendous body of granite." We know it now as the Coast Range, the uncountable crags that pucker into the sky at the thoroughly unnatural border between Southeast Alaska and British Columbia. To the west, the island rocks are metamorphic and sedimentary melanges that include gneisses, schists, phylites, slates, limestones, and marbles. In most places, the limestone and marble are ten thousand feet thick, and the quarries at Tokeen and Marble Island have barely touched what is estimated to be eight hundred million tons of high-quality marble that would be the envy of any Renaissance sculptor. The four great columns in the facade of the State Capitol in Juneau are Tokeen marble; from 1909 to 1932, more than a dozen quarries dispatched shipments of the rock around the world.

The point of Jim's entertaining explanation of the geology of the region was to lay the groundwork for his argument against cutting what's left of the old-growth trees in the archipelago. The outer islands, he told us, very likely were among the first to emerge from the ice ten thousand or so years ago, and some patches of terrain might even have remained ice-free throughout the cold times. They were refugia for animals including bears, deer, and salmon, and quite possibly for humans who rode out some pretty rough times together or just moved through the remains of the island group on their way to better living to the south. Jim and others also figured that the relationship between karst, trees, salmon, and every other living thing is not well enough understood to permit the removal of a single, terribly consequential element of this version of life's formula: the trees. The biggest, healthiest old-growth trees grow where they grow because the porous limestone beneath a thin covering of soil and organic debris is nothing less than a massive storm drain. The karst filters the sweet, steady rain into caves, caverns, underground channels, and the sea.

The karst, the trees, the caves, the salmon, even the people, Jim said, are parts of an immensely interdependent, complex system about which we still know very little. The returning salmon definitely pack nitrogen and other essential ingredients of forest life in their bodies, and they surrender them year after year after year. The fish rot quickly and find their way into the trees through the guts of bears, humans, birds, and other animals that leave their droppings in the forests. Eagles and ospreys haul rotting salmon around like take-out waiters, depositing their remains in the uplands, where the porous understory and rock deliver the meal to root webs. The rocks, gravel, and soil form a capillary system of sorts to actually conduct the nutrients of the waterway upland into the forest, and into the trees as vapor in that leg of the hydrologic cycle. In the past decade, field science is finally quantifying this transfer of energy from fish to stream to flora. I was reminded that night in Ketchikan of a wry bit of enviro-humor:

How does a Buddhist order a hot dog?

Make me one with everything.

The removal of the trees and fish of the archipelago in ignorance of their true value to the system of life into which they are woven is not without precedent. We humans have limped along with oversimplified notions about taking what we call natural resources from places like the Tongass chiefly because we perceive ourselves to be at the center of the cycle of consumption. We are also impeded in our judgment by the human life span, less than a hundred years, and economic systems that contain no real long-range vision. Only in the last quarter of this century have we begun to understand that this old-growth forest has far more value than the dollars contained in top-grade wood products and the cosmetic charm of the glades and groves for hikers. The forests also purify water, store carbon, and enable salmon, bears, humans, wolves, birds, deer, insects, worms, and countless plants and creatures to exist. In a complex relationship with all other life, the trees stabilize the giant organism we call the earth. Salmon have helped to deliver the news.

Salmon have been food for as long as other critters have been around to eat them, and human myths, ceremonies, and respect have been engendered as much by gratitude for a meal as by appreciation for their enigmatic spirits. Pacific salmon are anadromous—the word means "up-running." They are born in freshwater, migrate to the sea to mature, return to freshwater, and spawn. (The opposite is catadromous, down-running, like most eels that return to the sea to spawn.) All salmon but the steelhead are semelparous: they die after spawning once. Atlantic salmon, of the genus *Salmo*, are anadromous but not semelparous, and steelhead, too, spawn more than once.

A classic example of ordering-a-hot-dog wisdom links fish to rocks to trees. Salmon probably became anadromous to adapt to the cycles of ice and water that have dominated their range since the Pleistocene, when they evolved to their present form in the cold, nutrient-poor freshwater of northern latitudes. From time to time, great glaciers completely hushed the continental rivers and lakes beneath crackling blankets of ice, driving the fish to sea. Salmon are among the quickest studies in the evolutionary drama, able to change so rapidly in just a few generations that geneticists favor them for experiments in mutation and adaptation. Salmon evolved the physiological and biochemical traits necessary to migration, homing, and survival in both fresh and salt water, and further refined themselves into hundreds of races distinctly bound to specific watersheds. Every salmon is a member not only of its broad taxonomic species like king or coho, but also of a natal subgroup from its particular stream or river, marked by distinct traits such as scale color, size, flesh color, and even taste to a predator.

Georg Steller, the legendary German naturalist who sailed to within a few hundred miles of the Tongass with Vitus Bering on his second voyage to North America in 1741–42, was the first to list the species of Pacific salmon. The names he gave them are Russian in origin because Steller and Bering were on the czar's payroll. Fifty years later, Johann Julius Wilbaum, a German ichthyologist, used Steller's notes to formally describe the members of the genus *Oncorhynchus: O. tsawytscha* (chinook), *O. kisutch* (coho), *O. nerka* (sockeye), *O. keta* (chum), *O. gorbuscha* (pink), and *O. masou* (cherry). Later, we described *O. amago* and *O. mykiss* (steelhead). We know them, too, by the seasons of their return, and by the names of the rivers and tributaries to which they are bound as surely as red cells are to the blood flowing in arteries, veins, and capillaries. A king salmon is a king salmon, but a king from the outer watersheds of Prince of Wales Island is subtly but clearly a salmon with an accent different from that of a king from an Admiralty Island drainage on Chatham Strait.

Each species, and in some cases each race or run within a species, carries in its genetic code a schedule for fresh and saltwater migration. All five species of salmon that spawn in North American rivers are represented in the Tongass.

Chinook salmon, adapted to long or steep rivers, build strength and size during as many as five years at sea after a year in freshwater. A seiner off Prince of Wales Island caught a 145-pounder, though surely bigger chinooks have lived and live now.

The coho's anadromous rhythm is similar to that of a chinook, its closest relative, though its sea time is shorter: usually only eighteen months or two years. If salmon were automobiles, cohos would be sports cars, fast, agile, and compact. The biggest ones, late in the season when all the fattening is done, can weigh twenty pounds.

The annual cycles of the sockeye are the most varied of the tribe, from a few weeks to three years in freshwater, and from one to four years in the sea. Their life spans are so varied because they are more dependent on ecological combinations—patterns and sizes of lakes, streams, and rivers—than any other salmon. Some biologists spend their entire careers on the complicated sockeye, trying to predict the timing and size of the runs for commercial packers who want to know how much money to borrow to finance their seasons, and how much to pay the fishermen who always think it's not enough. (The kokanee, a close cousin of the sockeye, has even abandoned its anadromous instincts in favor of life as a smaller fish in landlocked lakes.)

Chums are the blue-collar salmon, dependable, nothing fancy, the most widely distributed of all species, once ranging from Korea around the Pacific Rim to Monterey Bay, California. Second only to chinooks in size, the workerlike chums usually return in two waves, summer and late fall, when they are the last of the salmon to reach their home rivers. They leave their streams within months of spawning and after two to five years at sea return with a territorial precision notable even among salmon.

Pinks, by comparison, are zoom salmon. After just a few months in freshwater and a single winter at sea, they return in great swarms of three- to six-pound fish. Throughout their range from the Sea of Japan to the Sacramento River, "humpies" spawn in alternating big and small years, and we know why. Because of their short life cycles, one year's pink salmon never mix with another year's, so runs in odd- and even-numbered years have become genetically isolated and radically different in size.

(Until 1992, steelhead were included in the *Salmo* tribe, but taxonomists reclassified the species as *O. mykiss*, true Pacific salmon. They are the only members of the *Oncorhynchus* tribe that make whoopee more than once.)

All Pacific salmon share common patterns of emergence,

maturation, and reproduction that bind them to their streams and shape them for survival in the ocean. Chief among the survival mechanisms of the species is sheer abundance, since going the distance from egg to spawner is a numbers game. Ask anyone who's spent a summer on a counting tower. If S is the number of salmon that must return to perpetuate a healthy run, fertilized eggs must number thousands of times S. (My numbers are not scientific fact, but comparisons of magnitude that vary for each species.) Hundreds of times S must survive the delicate emergence into alevin, flashing bits of protein becoming living creatures in full view.

These transparent, eyed beings hunker down in the substrate of their natal streams and feed off their own egg sacs during the still months of winter and early spring when predators are likely to leave them be. Then, still hundreds of times S must survive to become fry, real fish with their egg sacs consumed, their bodies zipped up, their fins and tails developed. As juveniles or smolt, the new fish begin actively eating and being eaten. Herons, gulls, eagles, ospreys, and other birds thin their numbers as the salmon work their way downstream to the sea; seals, sea lions, otters, and bigger fish wait hungrily in the estuaries. On most rivers at the end of the twentieth century, the salmon are also put in dire straits by logging that destroys their spawning habitat, by pollution, dams, and urban sprawl. Once they're in the sea, predators, including fishermen, claim their shares of the salmon runs, further reducing S until, finally, the survivors reach home to spawn. Though their powers of navigation are studied and celebrated, it is probably their genetic programming that allows a few to stray in every run. That way, they can survive the natural destruction of their spawning streams by ice, floods, and fire. They are, sadly, having trouble adjusting to the chain saw.

The earliest treaties, agreements, and conciliations among the people of the Pacific Rim sorted out rights to salmon, first as matters of tradition, then as matters of law, but always because salmon are vital as food. The Tlingit and Haida people of the ancient Tongass watersheds defined their band and family relationships according to ancestral rights to particular streams and salmon runs. Only in the 1950s were those fishing rights—part of the first land settlement between the early people and the recently arrived Americans—officially abrogated by the courts of the United States. By that time, the industrial fleets and packers were in full flower, migrating north each year to take advantage of the last thriving salmon runs on the planet. By midcentury, the salmon had been through total collapse and renewal several times, in part because the fishers and packers did not live in the watersheds they plundered and did not tend them.

For thousands of years in the human relationship with salmon, though, nobody trapped, caught, or ate anything anonymously. The links between water, fish, trees, and people were not scientifically defined, but they were perfectly clear and understood in taboos and traditions. Commerce in distant markets and cash economies broke those instinctive bonds forever and replaced them with the impersonal networks of industrial fishing, canning, and freezing. Now, salmon reach tables around the world, but most carry no ecological return address. Stewardship has proven to be impossible at a distance.

To modern people, dams, timber, and great cities are part of the vision of paradise, engineers are priests, and the forces of nature are mere puzzles with certain solutions. Coastal and watershed destruction to encourage commerce is not an aberration of industrial culture but a definitive characteristic, and no nation can claim restraint on behalf of salmon. Even today, as the somber notes of acute ecosystem crisis are sounding on dozens of North American watersheds, politicians support destructive logging and mining practices in Alaska and British Columbia, assuring us that they will not harm the few healthy salmon runs that are left.

Whether they are motivated by long-range vision or short-term greed, the people of the Pacific tacitly agree to the bargain that is killing off salmon. Millions of other people in Asia and Europe are already paying the true price for similar alterations in their relationships with the habitat of Pacific and Atlantic salmon. The mainland drainages of the Tumen, Amur, Anadyr, Markova, Elbe, Danube, Rhine, Thames, Spey, Hudson, and Connecticut Rivers and the numberless shorter watercourses of the Newfoundland, Kurile, and Japanese archipelagos once were graced by salmon every year. As miner's canaries for the health of watersheds, salmon carry a message of distress by their absence. A salmon watershed without salmon is no longer singing the song of life. Until recently, early and modern people relied on superabundance and their ability to move on if they overfished a salmon run or trashed a stream or other life-support system. Alaska, including the fragile watersheds of the Tongass, is the last place to run to.

Putting up Pacific salmon on an industrial scale began in 1864 on the Sacramento River when the Hume brothers—William, George, Robert, and Joseph—arrived with a tinsmith, Andrew Hapgood. Sixty years before they came west, Nicolas Appert, a vintner, beer maker, and chef had invented the canning process and won Napoleon Bonaparte's twelve-hundred-franc prize for coming up with a way to feed advancing armies. Subsequent refinements in the process eliminated some of the spoilage that plagued canners and armies; tin cans replaced glass jars; and, finally, Pasteur tied bacteria to disease. Not incidentally, he figured out why food rotted and what to do about it. In 1840 the first canned salmon in North America was packed on the Bay of Fundy, not too far north of Maine, the childhood home of the Humes and Hapgood.

At first, the packers cut out their cans with tin snips; soldered them by hand; filled each with the very tasty, very expensive salmon that was worth about a dollar a can in England; crimped and soldered tops; and submitted the miraculous package to heat in a retort. A good tinsmith could make a hundred cans a day, and an entire year's pack was less than one hundred thousand cans. Trapping the salmon in the river was easy and cheap, so in short order, Hapgood and the Humes got rich and expanded from their family shed into real canneries. Markets for salmon that would keep for more than a week seemed endless and the rush was on, every bit the equal of an attack of gold fever.

In a few years, a combination of salmon lust on the Sacramento and hydraulic mining, a particularly virulent method that blasted enormous quantities of mud and gravel into the rivers and streams, had just about wiped out the runs and spawning beds in that watershed. So the salmon canners spread north, first to the Rogue River, then to the Columbia, the Fraser, and the smaller watercourses in between. Competitors challenged Hapgood and the Humes, and eventually, fleets of square-riggers sailed for Alaskan waters. As the years ticked over into the American century, the unbridled canners were packing salmon on every spawning river from California to the Arctic Circle, and canned salmon began its eighty-year run as a staple food. From 1870 to 1950, you could open ten cupboards anywhere in Europe or North America and probably find a can of salmon in seven of them.

Though salmon traps and weirs were the mainstays of hundreds of chugging canneries, eventually men in boats had to venture away from the rivers into the sea to supply the packing lines. What we now celebrate as commercial salmon fishing arrived on the Pacific. Every spring, full-rigged ships sailed north from San Francisco to Southeast Alaska, across the Gulf of Alaska, west along the Aleutians, through Unimak Pass, and into the Bering Sea. The Alaska fleet was the last hurrah for the square-riggers, including *Star of India, Abner Coburn, Benjamin F. Packard,* and *Glory of the Seas.* The shorter voyage and supply lines to Southeast Alaska produced permanent canneries and herring reduction plants in virtually every cove and bay in the Tongass. Not until the 1920s, when many of the once vigorous runs of Bristol Bay and Southeast Alaska became pathetic trickles, did anyone give much thought to restraint. The legacy of this excess fell to the local fishermen, who eventually succeeded in wresting much of the power from the packers at statehood. Alaskans banned traps and eventually placed the rights to the fish in the hands of the fishermen by limiting entry to the grounds. The fleets were under control, but until the ecological renaissance of the 1980s and 1990s, salmon and timber were commodities to be extracted, their worth computed by the pound and board foot. Our understanding of the complex dependencies of the rain forest is still incomplete, and we finally suspect that we are living incompetently, that we have evolved unnatural relationships with our food, shelter, and water. The feedback loop of excess and consequence is closing, though, and we are once again, as were early people, realizing that we cut no tree and catch no fish anonymously.

For a short time, I fished for a living under the apparently simple terms of anonymous extraction. It was a wonderful life. One night in a bar in Sitka, another fisherman pointed out that trolling for salmon in Southeast Alaska is one of the last best things a self-indulgent liberal arts major can do for a living. The Pioneer Bar is to commercial fishing what Sardi's is to the theater in New York: it's a big, warm barroom with black-and-white photographs of fishing boats and fishing people instead of stage celebrities covering every inch of the walls. In a meandering but eloquent monologue, my friend argued that literature and history, along with a fear of real jobs, prepared us for hard, dangerous work on small boats, rewarded by great beauty and just enough money to pay the bills.

But even before my friend delivered his inspired vision on that well-lubricated night, I knew that I would have gone fishing for nothing. The water, the forest, the people, and the salmon of the archipelago were enough to claim me. Trollers often fish alone, catch salmon one at a time on hooks, and depend entirely upon guile, instinct, sham, trickery, and luck for success. The kings and cohos we hunted traveled thousands of miles to complete the circles of their lives in the streams they inherited from the previous generation. They are wondrous creatures that have been around for millions of years; they track the magnetic field of the earth to navigate and return carrying nutrients from the deep sea to their ancestral watersheds. Though I was paid to catch them to feed people all over the world, fishing for salmon was anything but a job.

Trolling in Southeast Alaska was this: I am at anchor in the lee of Point Adolphus, an idyllic promontory on the north end of Chichagof Island, directly across Icy Strait from Glacier Bay. There, the Pacific invades the northern reaches of the archipelago through a gap just a few hundred yards wide and, at speeds of up to eight knots, encounters its first major terrestrial obstacle. When the current peaks, the collision churns the water into a symphony of feeding fish, birds, seals, whales, and porpoises. Fishing, therefore, is often great, especially accompanied by the primitive pleasure of knowing that I am just another creature clinging to the very visible marine food web.

The sensory snapshots of that morning evoke fish, water, and trees. The ocean roars and swells, gathering itself into rips and maelstroms of astonishing power, while swarms of thrashing needlefish, herring, and salmon stipple the surface. Synchronized swarms of northern phalaropes flash alternately brown and white, as though to the tapping toe of an invisible choreographer who occasionally orders them from the sky into undulating rafts on the chrome-black water. Beyond the phalaropes, a few miles across the strait through clearing tendrils of fog, are the peaks of the Fairweather Range and the icy uplands of Glacier Bay. The rivers of ice are remnants of the thick skin of frozen water that as recently as fourteen thousand years ago covered not just the strait where I lie at anchor, but the entire hemisphere north to the pole and south to the latitude of Puget Sound.

As I sip my coffee on deck, the water itself enchants me, there on display in its three astonishing states, liquid, gas, and solid. Water is odorless, colorless, and tasteless, a compound of enormous stability, and a powerful solvent that is repelled by most organic substances but attracted by inorganic materials, including itself. Water expands when it's frozen, rather than contracting like most substances, so the solid is lighter than the liquid, which is, of course, why ice floats. If water suddenly started behaving like almost every other molecule and weighed more frozen than as a liquid, life as we know it would depart. Ice would sink to the bottom of the oceans and the summer sun would not be strong enough to melt it at such great depths. Life in the water would cease, the seas as we know them would disappear, the hydrologic cycle upon which our existence is based would grind to a halt. Our food is not only mostly water, but also utterly dependent on it; a one-pound loaf of bread has used up about two tons of water while the wheat was growing. A salmon needs the water of an ocean, a stream, and a forest to grow.

I remember that morning at Point Adolphus like a poker player remembers a pat hand. The sensual feast kindled in me a new awareness of the bonds between the water, forest, and salmon of the Tongass. By the time Jim Baichtel put salmon in the trees for me at that potluck in Ketchikan, most fishermen in Southeast had caught on, too, and joined ranks with environmental advocates and other outraged citizens to force reform of logging practices. Unfortunately, trees and salmon are still commodities to be consumed, rather than deeply connected parts of the same whole, and separating them in the minds of people who eat and use them remains a disservice to all. The jobs-versus-environment paradigm continues to corrupt our political solutions to abusive logging.

And at the fish market, you can buy farmed salmon from pens instead of streams and the sea, further relieving consumers of the demand for stewardship. Maybe we'd get the picture if each farmed salmon carried the truth in a brutal caveat: "This salmon cannot spawn in trees and may be hazardous to your health."

BRAD MATSEN *is the author of eight books, including* Planet Ocean: A Story of Life, the Sea, and Dancing to the Fossil Record *(Ten Speed Press, 1994) and* Reaching Home: Pacific Salmon, Pacific People *(Alaska Northwest Books, 1994). He has written four major documentary television scripts, most recently "Animals: The Shape of Life" for National Geographic Television, an eight-hour series that will air in 2001. His magazine articles and photographs have appeared in* Audubon, Mother Jones, Oceans, Natural History, Whole Earth Review, Alaska, *and dozens of other magazines and newspapers. He has worked as a charter pilot and commercial fisherman, and has spent most of his life in Alaska and the Pacific Northwest. He now lives in Seattle and New York.*

sea lion and seals, *Nancy Behnken*

First Peoples of the Tongass: Law and the Traditional Subsistence Way of Life

DAVID AVRAHAM VOLUCK

Please forgive me, if what I say offends you
It is truly not my intention

It is customary among the people with whom I work to begin any important discussion with such an apology. This care when speaking harkens back to a place and people whose words carry great weight and meaning.

First, it is important you know that I am a non-Native practitioner of Indian law and do not speak for the Native people of Southeast Alaska. I can only try to describe an important force at work within the Tongass. The Tlingit, Haida, and, more recently, Tsimshian Indians have a relationship with the forest and sea that has formed over the millennia. This relationship continues today and is at the heart of many of the laws governing the Tongass.

At the center of the Native customary and traditional way of life are land and the concept of subsistence. It is important to understand that *subsistence* is a white man's word, and it does not capture the traditional way of life. The word *subsistence* often suggests poverty or bare survival, while the experience for Alaska Natives is a rich, vital, and fulfilling way of life.[1]

For our discussion, however, I will use the term subsistence, since it is part of the vocabulary necessary to follow the contemporary politics and law surrounding the Tongass. Subsistence is also the word used to describe the spirit and harvest of other Native and non-Native residents of Southeast Alaska.

The first section of this essay is focused on the traditional subsistence way of life, with an eye toward providing a backdrop for the rest of the discussion. The next section is devoted to a legal and historical account of the Native relationship with the Tongass; it includes a brief description of traditional property law, contact with European and American governments, and the resulting imposition of Western law on the Native people. The next two sections describe the land claims movement and the effects of the Alaska Native Claims Settlement Act on traditional property ownership and the subsistence way of life, then the revival of subsistence rights in the Tongass with the passage of Title VIII of the Alaska National Interest Lands Conservation Act and the Subsistence Priority for federal lands. Finally, I offer some concluding thoughts on why access to the subsistence way of life is critical, not only to the Native right of self-determination, but also to the long-term well-being of humankind.

It is not for me to write fully about the vastness of the land or the deep traditions of the Native people of the Tongass. It is my hope that the story presented here kindles enough interest for deeper learning.

THE TRADITIONAL SUBSISTENCE LIFE

It is critical to a discussion of subsistence that we strive to understand the "subsistence life" as it is played out on the lands and waters of Southeast Alaska. This task is more daunting than it appears. On a general level, the Western mind is constricted by experience, culture, and, most importantly, language. Because my words will be ineffective in explaining major facets of the Native subsistence experience, it is important to stretch the boundaries of our imagination to better understand the Native community of life.

The traditional subsistence life in Southeast Alaska forms a deep web of connections between the people, the land, the sea, the wildlife, and the spirit. On a physical level, it uses the surrounding world as a source of materials and sustenance. Hunting, fishing, and gathering provide the Native people with a protein- and vitamin-rich source of food. Wild fish and game are about one-third higher in protein than store-bought domesticated red meats, and the oils from fish and sea mammals are healthy and efficient sources of energy and quick body heat for people in cold northern climates. Additionally, these wild foods are free of pesticides and chemical additives found in commercially processed food.[2] Customary and traditional foods are essential to the physical health of Southeast Alaska Natives, and changes away from the traditional diet are believed to contribute to incidence of diabetes, heart disease, obesity, and cancer.

In Southeast Alaska, relying on subsistence foods for a substantial part of one's diet is a matter not only of choice, but also of necessity. A number of factors, including great distance from other food sources and a compromised position in the cash economy, combine to make Native communities physically and economically dependent on traditional subsistence resources.[3]

However, it is not appropriate to reduce the traditional subsistence life solely to the act of deriving food. In addition to providing sustenance, subsistence gathering activities build a network of social relationships within the Native community. There is a division of labor among harvesting, preparing, and distributing wild foods. The spirit of sharing is central to a successful harvest. Natives often share portions of their harvest with extended family and with Elders, widows, people without boats, and others who cannot obtain their own supply. Subsistence harvests provide the classroom for passing on traditional values to young people. This education follows the cycle of seasons and the special foods that come only for a brief period during the year. Young harvesters learn slowly, through seasons of experience, the lore and skills preserved through the generations. They accompany experienced harvesters to learn by personal observation and hands-on activity all they can about local geography, weather, animal behavior, techniques of traveling and hunting, and how to preserve and process the foods they harvest.[4]

A life of traditional subsistence is governed by a commonly accepted set of principles. These laws and customs strictly define the rights, obligations, and privileges of tribal members. Traditional law is passed from generation to generation through repetition of legends, observance of ceremonials, and social corrections by community Elders. Subsistence living is not only a distinct way of life, it is also a life-enriching process. Conservation and perpetuation of subsistence resources is part of the traditional subsistence way of life, and is mandated in traditional law and custom. Traditionally, waste was not permitted; all remains not used for food, dress, tools, or other purposes had to be burned or returned to the water. The animal spirits then could report to their kind of the respectful treatment by the people, and thus the animal populations were plentiful each season.[5] Further, all things, including animals, fish, trees, glaciers, and the sea itself, possessed a powerful spirit and were to be treated with great respect:

> That's when he took it out . . . that flame. He threw it into the ground, threw it into the cliff, threw it into the snow. All the animal, what's flying . . . in the water . . . all the fish in there got the Spirit. Everything he throwed in got the Spirit. The tree beginning to grow. Every year it comes out if you look at it. They are alive.
>
> They gave us the spirit. From the Raven what he throwing in. That's why we talk about it. To respect

everything . . . the tree, the rock, the ground, everything. Everything's got the spirit. They don't believe
us. They don't want us to talk about the Spirit.

> —*The Spirit Came to All Things*
> As told by Austin Hammond Sr.
> Shared by Bob Sam, Tlingit storyteller

Unfortunately, to many non-Natives, subsistence hunting and fishing refers solely to the effort of providing necessary food. This limited view was clearly articulated by the non-Native president of a
sport fishing association, who, upon hearing about an Indian
tribe's legal challenge to a state subsistence law, said, "It's not like
anybody really needs it [subsistence fishing]. We got grocery stores,
you know."[6] Even a cursory description of the traditional subsistence way of life makes it evident that the subsistence life is much
more than putting food on the table. As David Case, a leading authority on Native law in Alaska, has noted, the ability of Alaska
Natives to engage in the subsistence life is a measure of their self-
determination. Without full access to fish and wildlife, without the
ritual and community that revolve around subsistence activities,
the way in which Southeast Alaska Natives live would be defined by
standards outside their own cultural values.[7]

HISTORICAL AND LEGAL RELATION TO THE LAND

The People

The Tlingit and Haida Indians have inhabited the Tongass rain forest from time immemorial. Most of the Tongass was controlled by
the Tlingit Indians; the Haida territory principally comprised
Prince of Wales Island and Canada's Queen Charlotte Island to the
south. The Tlingit and Haida Indians speak different languages
and hold dearly to separate and distinct cultures.[8] For purposes of
understanding their legal relation to the land, however, there are

some important similarities. The Tlingit and Haida Indian Nations are divided into two primary blood groups (sometimes referred to as moieties) under the Eagle and the Raven. The Eagle and Raven moieties are separated further into a great many clans. Traditional laws of marriage hold that people marry from the opposite moiety, and children inherit their mother's moiety, clan, and associated property. The clan is the focus of identity. The foundation of tribal authority and law comes from the clan, though an overarching balance is carefully kept between the ultimate Eagle and Raven moieties.

Tlingit and Haida clans are masterful harvesters of salmon, halibut, shellfish, sea weeds, plants, timber, deer, and marine mammals. The fertility of the land and sea is expressed in ceremonial regalia, carvings, songs, and stories. Elaborate artwork of clan crests traditionally adorns houses, clothing, canoes, and totem poles. These beautiful designs provide a constant reminder of identity, history, and ownership. The abundance of food and resources within Tlingit and Haida territories historically allowed surplus and rich trade. In addition to using the land efficiently for its roots, bark, and medicinal plants, Southeast Alaska Natives are strongly oriented to the ocean. Long trading expeditions would take place by cedar canoes north with the Athabascan Indians, east over the mountains with inland Canadian tribes, and as far south as California.

The Tlingit and Haida still hold to a well-defined system of property ownership that was established well before contact with European colonists. Generally speaking, clans own names, songs, stories, and crest designs. Clan property is owned communally, and all members of the clan are charged with safeguarding the clan property from misappropriation. No member of the clan has the individual right to sell or transfer clan property.[9]

Traditionally, the Native people of Southeast Alaska did not hold territory individually like Anglo-Americans; rather, title to the land and resources was tied to the clan and family group. The various clan leaders held oversight of all bays, islands, fish streams, berry patches, and trade routes. This ownership was recognized and reinforced publicly at large ceremonial potlatch parties. Use was by permission only, and as foreign settlements would learn, trespassers provoked a severe response from the clan.

Contact with the Russians and the Transfer of Alaska

Russian explorers and merchants eventually discovered Southeast Alaska and decided to stay when they found the rich fur of the sea otter. Extensive trade with the Tlingit Indians for the sea otter pelts began in the late eighteenth century. In time, Russian disrespect for the traditional hunting laws and mass exploitation of the resource led to warfare with the Tlingits and resulted in the near extinction of sea otter populations. The severe depletion of the sea otter led to a decline in revenue for the Russian colonists at a time when Russia was experiencing economic difficulties from costly foreign wars. These two factors combined with a military vulnerability to both the Tlingit and the ever-expanding United States to make Russian control of Alaska untenable. Czarist Russia eventually negotiated the so-called sale of Alaska to the United States of America.

The United States government purchased the interests Russia held in Alaska with the signing of the Treaty of Cession in 1867. This supposed sale was a curiosity to the Tlingit Indians, since the Russians held little control beyond their stockade fences and lived on the land by permission of the Tlingit leaders. Under Western law, the vague language of the treaty and the fact that Russia held no physical, military, or political authority over Alaska made it unclear what legal effect the Treaty of Cession had on the rights of the unconquered Native people.

Aboriginal Rights

In the abstract, the United States's first dealings in Southeast Alaska were dictated by the principles of federal Indian law. In order to understand the present situation in the Tongass, it is necessary to study the history of federal Indian law and the concept of aboriginal rights.

Federal Indian law and the United States's recognition of aboriginal rights stem from three early-nineteenth-century Supreme Court opinions written by Chief Justice John Marshall, collectively called the Marshall Trilogy. Justice Marshall found the federal government's authority to regulate Indian affairs in the U.S. Constitution: "The Congress shall have Power . . . to regulate Commerce with foreign Nations, and among the several States, and *with the Indian Tribes*."[10] Out of the Marshall Trilogy come the following principles of Indian law: (1) The federal government, not the state governments, has primary authority over Indian affairs. (2) Indian tribes are recognized as sovereign nations with jurisdiction over their own territory and tribal members. This power of sovereignty flows from the self-governance of Indian tribes before contact with European and American immigrants. (3) Indian sovereignty is interpreted as inferior to the ultimate "plenary" power of Congress.[11] Lastly, Justice Marshall wrestled with the legitimacy of the United States's settlement of Native-held North America. The fate of America's land hung on the Court's concept of aboriginal rights.

The federal response to the aboriginal rights of Native Americans hinges on a legal concept entitled the Doctrine of Discovery. The Supreme Court held that the European nation first landing on or discovering a land in the New World acquired ultimate title to the land and dominion over the original inhabitants, exclusive of any other European nation. With the signing of the peace treaty ending the Revolutionary War, the United States inherited ultimate title to the country from Great Britain, the preceding discovering power. However, the United States's ownership was clouded by the aboriginal rights of use and occupancy held by the

Native peoples of North America. Land could not be legitimately settled unless it was cleared of the Native aboriginal rights. Under the Doctrine of Discovery, aboriginal rights are viewed as lesser rights and can be removed by the negotiation of a nation-to-nation treaty, purchase, or by military conquest.

From these early Supreme Court decisions comes the United States's history of making treaties with Native American tribes throughout North America. The United States would negotiate a government-to-government treaty with the sovereign Indian tribes. The sovereign tribes would concede territory to the expanding frontier. In return, the tribes would receive medical supplies, provisions, or other forms of payment. The tribes usually would reserve a portion of their territory as well as hunting and fishing rights, which would be guaranteed forever under the terms of the treaty. Under the doctrine of the ultimate plenary power of Congress, however, Indian tribes were in an unequal bargaining position, and as they would learn, Congress could revisit the agreements and lessen or eliminate treaty-guaranteed rights.[12]

The treaty-making era solidified the fact that Indian tribes were recognized as sovereign governments with what is termed a government-to-government relationship with the federal government. Further, in an effort to balance Congress's ultimate power over Indian affairs, courts created the "trust responsibility" to Indian tribes. The trust responsibility requires that the federal government act with the utmost integrity when dealing with Indian tribes, and that laws and treaties be interpreted in a manner protective of Native rights.[13]

In the late nineteenth century, the United States government halted treaty making with the Indian tribes and instead adopted a policy of legislating laws to deal with Native aboriginal rights and Indian affairs. It was during this period that the United States's legal presence first came to the Native nations of the Tongass.

The Withdrawal of the Tongass

The Russian Treaty of Cession did not buy or extinguish Alaska Native aboriginal rights. Further, Congress passed the Alaska Organic Act of 1884, which cautiously chose to respect the rights of the Alaska Native peoples: "The Indians or other persons in said district shall not be disturbed in the possession of any lands actually in their use or now claimed by them."[14] However, as the course of Indian history has illustrated, this policy was not honored, and invading interests would not refrain from encroaching upon Native rights in the lands and waters they inhabited. The fishing, timber, and mining industries came to Southeast Alaska and directly trespassed on Native-held lands and waters. In 1897 the commander of the *Albatross*, a government fisheries survey vessel, told of visits by Tlingit and Haida chiefs:

> They are essentially fish-eating Indians, depending upon the streams of the country for a large amount of food supply. These streams, under their own administration, for centuries have belonged to certain families or clans settled in the vicinity, and their rights in these streams have never been infringed upon until the advent of the whites. No Indians would fish in a stream not their own except by invitation, and they cannot understand how those of a higher civilization should be—as they regard it—less honorable than their own savage kind. They claim the white man is crowding them from their homes, robbing them of their ancestral rights, taking away their fish by shiploads; that their streams must soon become exhausted; that the Indian will have no supply to maintain himself and family; and that starvation must follow.[15]

Despite the multitude of trespasses by miners and private fishing and timber operations, the most sweeping disregard of Native rights was at the hands of the United States government:

> Beginning in 1884 and continuing thereafter, these Indians lost most of their land in southeastern Alaska through the Government's failure and refusal to protect the rights of the Indians in such lands and waters, through the administration of its laws and through the provisions of the laws themselves; . . . a large area of land and water in southeastern Alaska was actually taken without compensation and without the consent of the Indians, through Presidential proclamations.[16]

In a series of presidential proclamations between 1902 and 1909, Theodore Roosevelt withdrew some seventeen million acres from the territory of the Tlingit and Haida Nations and formed the Tongass National Forest. The land was declared the property of the United States and was placed under the jurisdiction of the U.S. Department of Agriculture, Forest Service.

The Alaska Native Allotment Act

During this era, Congress made an ill-conceived attempt to slow the tide of Native land loss with passage of the Alaska Native Allotment Act of 1906. Modeled after Euro-American agriculture and private property concepts, the act intended to provide the opportunity for individual Natives to attain a private piece of their once exclusively held territory. It allowed any Alaska Native head of household to apply for up to 160 acres of unowned nonmineral land. An approved allotment would be transferred to the Native applicant as nontaxable Indian land subject to federal oversight.

Despite good intentions, the Alaska Native Allotment Act

proved to be a miserable failure in the Tongass for a number of reasons. First, the federal government failed to inform Native villages of the law and its legal requirements. This unfamiliarity with federal law combined with language barriers to make the Alaska Native Allotment Act inaccessible to the majority of people. Additionally, as we have seen, Native tribes held ownership to fish camps, streams, and bays according to traditional law, which is based on family and clan ownership. Implementation of the Native Allotment Act focused on individual ownership, and many allotment applications were rejected because Native use and ownership failed to resemble Western individual property ideals. Finally, land was not considered eligible for a Native allotment if it was previously appropriated or owned. When Theodore Roosevelt withdrew seventeen million acres in the early 1900s to form the Tongass National Forest, federal law held that all of that land was owned by the United States. Thus, within the Tongass, any Native allotment applicant must have personally and exclusively used the land as an adult, before the formation of the Tongass National Forest.

This dealt a crushing blow to the newer generations of Natives who became familiar with both English and the law, and wanted to apply for their family's lands under the Native Allotment Act. Natives born later than 1900 had little chance of qualifying because they could not have used land as an adult before the formation of the Tongass National Forest. Further, Native applicants could not claim that the land in question was always used by their ancestors, because the law was interpreted to allow only *individual personal use* before formation of the Tongass. Mention of ancestors or ancestral rights within the Native application led to rejection of the allotment claim.

The laws and policies of the Alaska Native Allotment Act directly contradicted traditional Native law and values. Despite the many obstacles, the applications of some Natives who predated the Tongass survived the many legal hurdles. Today their heirs or designees own inholdings within the Tongass National Forest, providing another interesting facet to the laws in the Tongass. With only a few successful applicants, the majority of Native lands continued to be lost to both federal and private interests in the Tongass. As individual outcries proved ineffective, the Native communities of Southeast Alaska organized to address the disregard of their rights.

The Tlingit and Haida Land Claims

In 1912, at a meeting in Sitka, Southeast Alaska Natives formed the Alaska Native Brotherhood (ANB). The ANB embarked on an effort to protect Native fishing and land rights, and to gain recognition of civil rights as citizens of the United States. Spearheaded by the ANB lobbying efforts, the Tlingit and Haida Indians secured special legislation to sue the United States for the taking of Southeast Alaska without compensation. Fifty years after the formation of the Tongass, the Court of Claims ruled in favor of the Tlingit and Haida. The court found that the United States directly took Tlingit and Haida territory with the formation of the Metlakatla reservation for the Tsimshian Indians from Canada, the withdrawal of the Tongass National Forest, and the formation of Glacier Bay National Park. Additionally, the Court of Claims found that the United States continuously failed to protect the rights of the Native people,

> [making] it possible for white settlers, miners, traders and businessmen, to legally deprive the Tlingit and Haida Indians of their use of the fishing areas, their hunting and gathering grounds and their timber lands and that is precisely what was done. These Indians protested to the Government and their protests went unheeded. . . . Whenever white settlers and businessmen entered their lands for exploitation,

the Indians were forced to move out . . . [and] the amount of salmon and other fish taken from the streams and waters by the new white fishing industries and canneries left hardly enough fish to afford bare subsistence for the Tlingits and Haidas and nothing for trade or accumulation of wealth. Thus it seems clear that the United States both failed and refused to protect the interests of these Indians in their lands and other property in southeastern Alaska.[17]

The Tlingit and Haida Indian tribes claimed $70 million in damages, including their lost property rights in the fish that were taken by the canneries and fishing industry. In 1968 the Court of Claims awarded the Tlingit and Haida $7.5 million for the taking of the Tongass, failing to add the interest that should have accrued over the sixty-year wait; the court also refused to recognize property rights in the migrating fish or the navigable waters of Southeast Alaska.[18] After debate about whether to accept the disappointing judgment or appeal, the Tlingit and Haida cautiously chose to accept the judgment award and set about improving the welfare of the Native people.

As might be expected, the small judgment did not solve many of the overriding issues facing the Southeast Alaska Native people. The full question of aboriginal hunting and fishing rights and their hampered ability to engage in the traditional subsistence way of life continued to affect the well-being of Tlingit and Haida villages.

In addition to forming the Alaska Native Brotherhood, Tlingit and Haida clans organized into federally recognized tribal governments under the Indian Reorganization Act. Incorporating all of the clans residing in a village into one tribe, they reasoned, would make it easier for the federal government to relate to the Natives of the Tongass in a government-to-government capacity. So while the Tlingit and Haida Indians maintained their complex clan system of authority and ownership, they began to relate to the federal government according to federal Indian law and the legal concept of a tribe.

LAND CLAIMS SETTLEMENT AND MODERN SUBSISTENCE RIGHTS IN THE TONGASS

The Tlingit and Haida lawsuit did not appear to settle the aboriginal hunting and fishing rights held in Southeast Alaska. Further, the Court of Claims did not speak to the aboriginal rights held by all the other Native tribes in Alaska. As industries moved into Alaska hoping to profit from extracting the rich natural resources, many of their efforts were frustrated because the legal title to the land remained clouded with Native aboriginal rights. With the discovery of oil in northern Alaska, it became clear that the issue of Alaska Native aboriginal rights needed to be fully settled. As oil companies sought to develop the oil lying under Alaska's North Slope, Native villages sat on top of the proposed right-of-way for the Trans-Alaska oil pipeline with claims of aboriginal title. The power of the oil companies demanded an immediate response, and Congress took direct action to resolve the aboriginal rights of Alaska Natives.

The Alaska Native Claims Settlement Act

Congress extinguished the aboriginal rights of Alaska Natives in 1971 with the passage of the Alaska Native Claims Settlement Act (ANCSA). The basic terms of ANCSA are as follows:

- "Aboriginal land title" was permanently extinguished.
- Aboriginal hunting and fishing rights were extinguished.
- Specially established Alaska Native "corporations" received qualified title to approximately 10 percent of Alaska.

- The Native peoples received $962.5 million.
- All monies and land were placed in the control of state-chartered for-profit Native corporations. Native lands were divided among twelve regions, each under the control of a Native-owned corporation. The Native people received shares of stock in this corporation and would receive dividends if the corporation made a profit.
- In addition to the twelve regional corporations, a thirteenth regional corporation was formed for Alaska Natives residing outside of Alaska. Further, each Native village formed a separate corporation. The village corporation maintained the surface rights to the land, but the subsurface rights were controlled by the regional corporation.
- Stock ownership in these new corporations was divided among Native peoples of each Alaskan tribe, with every living member sharing equally. Native people who did not live within a village received shares only in the regional corporations.
- All shares were to be held by Natives and were not transferable to non-Natives until 1991, after which time the stock in the Native corporations could be sold. The restrictions on the sale to non-Natives was eventually extended indefinitely, leaving it to the vote of corporate shareholders whether they want to sell stock shares in an open market.[19]

With the passage of ANCSA, Congress intended Native people to go into business and to participate actively in the economic development of Alaska.

ANCSA's Effect on Traditional Use

I believe that [the] Alaska Native Claims Settlement Act has divided our people. It has sown dissension between Native groups, families and individuals. The Act as it is has required our indoctrination into

Western society as a matter of corporate survival, adopting its ways of thinking of self, money power contrary to the native cultural upbringing, of thinking of family, the clan, the elders, living off the land.
JENNIFER BRADY, SITKA, ALASKA[20]

The Alaska Native people were never given the opportunity to directly vote on the ANCSA settlement. Gathered testimony indicates that most Alaska Natives believed that the land ANCSA conveyed to them would be secure and their way of life would be protected.[21] With regard to the land, this expectation is unfounded. Unlike the treaty-making era and previous Native settlements, the federal government chose not to negotiate with sovereign tribal governments, but to use the for-profit business corporation as the vehicle for land settlement. The cash settlement and land conveyed by ANCSA do not belong to Alaska Native tribes; they belong to specially created Native corporations. The land reserved for Alaska Natives is now a corporate asset. The corporate structure that was imposed offers no guarantee in perpetuity of Native ownership of land, nor does it explicitly protect the traditional subsistence way of life.[22]

The ANCSA settlement has done much to promote economic and political power within Native communities. On a fundamental level, however, ANCSA appears to contradict many traditional Native values. ANCSA disregarded the tribal way of governance and vested the settlement with Native companies incorporated under the laws of Alaska to conduct business for profit. The basic rules of business corporations dictate that they must produce income, show profit, and grow; these are the standards by which the market and shareholders judge a company. The primary assets of most Native corporations are the rich timber, minerals, and fossil fuels that lie within their lands. In order to remain in existence, show profit, or dispense dividends to shareholders, Native corporations must adopt Western corporate values of profit and conversion of natural resources to dollar-producing income. The profit imperative places traditional Native values in conflict with the economic mandate of the ANCSA settlement:

> In a sense, the gospel of capitalism has gripped the leadership of the regional corporations just as in another day, another kind of gospel was introduced for its educative and assimilative influence. The profit-making mandate has become a powerful vision, a powerful driving force.

> The corporate executives will be those who are willing to forego subsistence activities, to place a higher priority on board meetings than on salmon fishing, and to spend time talking to lawyers and financiers and bankers rather than the people of the villages.[23]

Many corporations in Southeast Alaska chose to clear-cut their forested land selections in an effort to show profit and dispense large cash dividends to their shareholders. The corporate land management decisions may have severely detrimental consequences to subsistence harvesters for generations to come. Additionally, ANCSA created procedures for village corporations to select their land settlement in areas outside their traditional territorial boundaries. Many corporations have selected lands rich in natural resources, which happen to be in the traditional territories of tribes from other regions of the Tongass. Corporate management decisions from afar have created divisive conflict between foreign and unconnected corporations and the peoples and tribal governments who are affected by their decisions.

ANCSA has greatly reduced the land base for traditional subsistence harvest. Moreover, the lands that have been reserved for Alaska Natives are private corporate assets and often are dedicated for purposes other than the subsistence life. Given the importance

of the wild foods and traditional subsistence harvests to the Alaska
Native way of life, ANCSA may have dealt a serious blow to traditional Alaska Native cultural values and economy. As one ANCSA
shareholder testified, "This act was done for our future benefit, but
it has hurt us, our children and grandchildren, and those that are
yet to be born."[24]

A REVIVAL OF SUBSISTENCE RIGHTS IN THE TONGASS

Although ANCSA was written to extinguish aboriginal hunting
and fishing rights, the drafters were mindful that the Alaska Native
way of life was threatened. Congress intended that after ANCSA,
the secretary of the interior and the state of Alaska would protect
the subsistence needs of Alaska Natives:

> The Conference Committee, after careful considera-
> tion, believes that all Native interests in subsistence
> resource lands can and will be protected by the
> Secretary [of the Interior] through the exercise of his
> existing withdrawal authority. . . . The Conference
> Committee expects both the Secretary and the State
> [of Alaska] to take any action necessary to protect the
> subsistence needs of the Natives.[25]

Unfortunately, both the secretary of the interior and the state of
Alaska failed to heed Congress and protect access to subsistence resources. Economic development in Alaska led to increased competition for fish and wildlife in villages throughout Alaska. Urban
and nonsubsistence interests dominated the state fish and game
boards, leading to decisions favoring sport and commercial users
over subsistence harvesters. After nine years of inaction, it became
clear that neither the state of Alaska nor the secretary of the interior was going to take any significant action to protect access to the
subsistence way of life.

The Subsistence Priority

In 1980, in response to the lack of protection for the subsistence way of life, Congress passed Title VIII of the Alaska National Interest Lands Conservation Act (ANILCA), which states:

> In order to fulfill the policies and purposes of the Alaska Native Claims Settlement Act and as a matter of equity, it is necessary for the Congress to invoke its constitutional authority of Native affairs and its constitutional authority under the property clause and the commerce clause to protect and provide the opportunity for continued subsistence uses on the public lands by Native and non-Native rural residents.[26]

Title VIII of ANILCA establishes a priority for nonwasteful subsistence uses of fish, wildlife, and other renewable subsistence resources on public lands in Alaska. Congress realized that the subsistence life required specific legal protection, stating that "the continuation of the opportunity for subsistence uses . . . is essential to Native physical, economic, traditional, and cultural existence" and that

> it is the intent of the bill in general, and the subsistence title in particular, so far as possible to allow the Alaska Native people to choose for themselves the direction and pace, if any, of the evolution of their own culture.[27]

Although Title VIII of ANILCA was originally conceived as Native legislation, in order to appease political concerns in the state of Alaska, ANILCA adopted a racially neutral approach to the subsistence priority. Thus ANILCA protects the subsistence activities of all residents of "rural Alaska," which includes most of the Tongass National Forest. Additionally, ANILCA provided the state of Alaska the option of maintaining management of fish and game in the federal lands and waters within the state's boundaries. ANILCA requires Alaska to establish a similar subsistence preference and management system under state law, in order to maintain its management authority over the immense territory of federal land in Alaska. This requires, at a minimum, that in times of scarcity, once conservation needs are met, rural subsistence harvesters would have first priority to the fish and wildlife, and that sport and commercial users would lessen their take. In addition, land managers are required to consider the effects development might have on subsistence resources.

Present-Day Controversy over Subsistence

The state of Alaska's implementation of the ANILCA subsistence priority has been a failure. State law and administration of subsistence have been the source of constant litigation and political strife. In 1989 the state of Alaska lost its option to manage subsistence hunting on federal lands, including the Tongass National Forest. In *McDowell v. State of Alaska,* the state supreme court found that the Alaska Constitution prohibits exclusive or special privileges to take fish and wildlife. Accordingly, the state was prohibited from extending a subsistence priority to rural residents of the state while excluding urban residents from the same privileges of access.[28] The end result of the *McDowell* decision was to extend subsistence hunting and fishing rights equally to all residents of Alaska, regardless of where they live. This placed state law out of compliance with the rural subsistence priority outlined in the federal requirements of ANILCA. In response to the *McDowell* ruling and Alaska's noncompliance with Title VIII of ANILCA, a group of federal agencies took control of subsistence hunting management on federal lands in 1990.

Unfortunately, this was not the end of the twisted path of

subsistence law in Alaska. The federal government interpreted ANILCA to apply only to federal lands, and did not extend federal subsistence protections to the fish in the navigable rivers and ocean waters of Alaska. A Native Elder named Katie John sued the federal government in an effort to extend federal subsistence protections to the precious fish runs that travel the navigable waters of Alaska. In the end, the federal courts held that the federal subsistence priority extends to all of the waterways that were reserved by the purposes of the original withdrawal of federal land. This generally includes rivers and streams that flow over national park lands, national wildlife refuges, and the Tongass National Forest.[29]

As federal agencies begin to extend their regulatory powers to manage subsistence fishing, they have extended their authority to fish destined for federal lands and waters. This creates the possibility of federal management of fisheries, even beyond the boundaries of federal lands. The extension of fisheries management authority is of extreme concern to the state of Alaska, which jealously guards its authority to manage the state's rich fisheries. The approaching federal interference has sparked an intense series of political and legal responses by the state to the implications of the Katie John case. So far, efforts to bring about changes in the law have proved unsuccessful, and political attempts at compromise have failed. Federal regulations designed to protect subsistence fishing are near completion, and the state of Alaska is in a position to lose ultimate authority over many of the state's valuable fisheries.

The subsistence controversy has become a source of political division and racial tension in Alaska. Many Natives are torn between loyalty to their home state and the fact that the state has failed to properly protect access to subsistence resources. As previously explained, Native tribes have a government-to-government relationship with the federal government. Further, under the federal trust responsibility, the subsistence priority should be interpreted in a way that is protective of Native rights. Thus, Native tribes have greater faith that the traditional way of life will be protected under federal management of fish and wildlife. Many non-Natives rigorously denounce tribal support of the federal takeover and view Native efforts to protect the traditional subsistence way of life as the seeking of "special rights." One thing is certain: subsistence is one of the central legal and political issues facing Alaska, and resolution is not in sight.

CONCLUDING THOUGHTS

At first glance, the issues concerning subsistence in the Tongass may seem interesting and almost curious in a region-specific way. In discussing the traditional subsistence life in the Tongass, however, we encounter one of the more pressing long-term issues facing human survival. In today's supermarket culture we have lost sight of the fact that at a fundamental level, the gathering of food has always been at the foundation of humankind. History teaches that the pain of hunger has moved all the peoples of the earth and collective cooperation in food gathering lies at the source of social interaction, language, and community. The different methods and traditions of food gathering are at the base of the world's cultures. When we speak of Native subsistence, we are talking about a unique and important way of life. Laws that either directly or indirectly separate Natives from their land, food, and culture will have grave consequences in the future.

Self-Determination

> *The great law of culture is to let one become what they were created to be.* DELBERT REXFORD, BARROW, ALASKA

These words of a subsistence whaling captain in northern Alaska capture one of the most fundamental of all human rights: the freedom to be who you are. In federal Indian law this concept is labeled

self-determination.[30] The human right of self-determination is gar-
nering acceptance in the world community, as evidenced by Article
27 of the United Nations International Covenant on Civil and
Political Rights:

> In those states in which ethnic, religious, or linguistic
> minorities exist, persons belonging to such minorities
> shall not be denied the right, in community with
> other members of their group, to enjoy their own cul-
> ture, to profess and practice their own religion, or to
> use their own language.[31]

Despite public rhetoric, disregard for Native rights and Native culture continues today in the United States and abroad. The importance of the traditional subsistence life cannot be overstated. When
the foundations of Native subsistence are weakened, other elements of the culture quickly deteriorate.[32] When governmental actions impede access to the traditional subsistence way of life, the
human right of self-determination is violated.

Today many Native communities are trying to strengthen their
subsistence economy and restore their tribal governments:

> It is their profound desire to be themselves, to be true
> to their own values. Far from deploring their failure
> to become what strangers wish them to be, we should
> regard their determination to be themselves as a tri-
> umph of the human spirit. Their determination to re-
> tain their own cultures and their own lands does not
> mean they wish to return to the past. It means they
> refuse to let their future be dictated by others.[33]

The Value of Cultural Diversity

Beyond the Native right to self-determination, the traditional
subsistence way of life has important implications for the overall

well-being of humankind. Natural systems provide a compelling message to humans: diversity is necessary for survival. Change is inevitable with the passage of time, and a healthy species has many different approaches to survival challenges brought on by changes in circumstances. Uniformity in attributes or approaches to a problem assures eventual extinction.

The economy and worldview of Western industrial society is based on the principle of ever-increasing consumption of land and resources. Western political institutions, economic policies, and beliefs are predicated on abundance and continuous growth. In a finite physical world, this approach to life will eventually meet limitations and scarcity. Western nations and their traditions for survival have continually outstripped local resources, and populations have outgrown their boundaries. "Progress" is then fueled by "underdeveloped" resources in other lands. This historical trend is evidenced by the age of imperialism and the European colonization of Africa, the Americas, and Asia.

The difficulty for Western governments in dealing with Natives in these colonized lands is that the Natives aren't always willing to give up their land to fuel Western progress. By either appropriating Native lands or introducing measures designed to assimilate Natives into the mainstream, Western governments are violating the human right to self-determination. Further, such measures are destroying human cultural diversity:

> Because of the ways in which cultures are eroded and destroyed, the world is rapidly becoming a monoculture in terms of agricultural systems, energy use, clothing, education, science, economics, mathematics, and ways of knowing....

> This is a dangerous situation for humans because this trend diminishes the potential for creativity at a time in our history when we desperately need to release our

creativity to address the daunting human problems in dealing with the environment.[34]

The pressures on tribal subsistence peoples have reached a critical stage. It is my sincere belief that it is time to slow the onslaught and begin a meaningful discussion concerning our collective future—a discussion in which all voices are heard.

The Still, Small Voice

Far beyond the points raised here, the most compelling advocates of self-determination and the traditional subsistence life are the Natives themselves:

> Us Natives, we should have the right to live out our culture . . . to take away our culture would be to take away our lives, everything we knew, everything our parents knew, everything our children should know.[35]

> Non-Natives don't understand how much these foods are a way of life. Your body craves them. . . . That's why we go to so much trouble to get them for elders and to teach young people about them.[36]

> I am concerned. What else do I have to give up? What else can I give up and still remain healthy culturally and psychologically? I can make a living in other ways, but they are attempting to destroy the very base of my culture—the most important ingredient. They wish to totally domesticate me. I won't let them. I have reached the point of no return. If I give away anything else, I will have given away my children's and grand-children's birthright. . . . We will lose too much of what is good in life.[37]

What God has put in our land and water, we revere it
so much that we work with it . . . we work for it. We,
The Tlingit people, are not giving up our ways. We are
going back to our ways. We know that our way of life
is very good to our people.[38]

If the land and wild foods are not available for subsistence purposes, major facets of Native culture will be in danger of atrophy
and disappearance. The tastes, smells, ceremonies, and language
that surrounds the consumption of these sacred foods will cease to
exist as they have for thousands of years. This will be a tragic loss
not only to the Native peoples, it will be a tragic loss to our collective library of human experience. It is my hope that this historical
accounting of subsistence law and policy in the Tongass will be a
helpful addition to avoiding such a tragedy.

NOTES

1. See "'Subsistence,' a Poor Word to Describe a Rich Way of Life," *Village Voices* 2, no. 4 (Fall 1998); "Crisis in the Last Frontier: The Alaska Subsistence Debate," *Cultural Survival Quarterly* 22, no. 3 (Fall 1998).

2. See Helen M. Drury, "Nutrients in Native Foods of Southeastern Alaska," *Journal of Ethnobiology,* no. 2 (Winter 1985): 87–100; Jeffrey L. Hartman et al. "The Role of Fisheries in the Alaska Economy," *Alaska Fish and Game* 20, no. 1 (1988): 4–5; George Gmelch and Sharon Bohn Gmelch, "Resource Use in a Small Alaskan City: Sitka," Alaska Department of Fish and Game (1985), 186.

3. David S. Case, *Alaska Natives and American Laws* (Fairbanks: University of Alaska Press, 1984), 275; Thomas R. Berger, *The Village Journey: The Report of the Alaska Native Review Commission* (New York: Hill and Wang, 1985), 57–58.

4. See Thomas R. Berger, *The Village Journey;* Hannah B. Loon, "Sharing: You Are Never Alone In a Village," *Alaska Fish and Game* 1, no. 6 (1989): 34–36; Gmelch and Gmelch, "Resource Use in a Small Alaskan City: Sitka," 150.

5. See Carol Jorgenson, "How Native Americans As An Indigenous Culture Consciously Maintained a Balance between Themselves and Their Natural Resources," *Eagle's Nest: Native American Fish and Wildlife Society* 6, no. 6 (December 1993): 6.

6. Mary Kancewick and Eric Smith, "Subsistence in Alaska: Toward a Native Priority," *University of Missouri-Kansas City Law Review* 59 (1990): 645, 648, citing "Medred, State, Tribe Work Out Subsistence Plan," *Anchorage Daily News,* June 16, 1989, A1, A12.

7. David S. Case, "Subsistence and Self-Determination: Can Alaska Natives Have a More 'Effective Voice'?" *University of Colorado Law Review* 60 (1989): 1009, 1012.

8. For a more in-depth understanding, see George Thornton Emmons, *The Tlingit Indians,* ed. Frederica de Laguna (Seattle: University of Washington Press, 1991); Ulli Steltzer, *A Haida Potlatch* (Seattle: University of Washington Press, 1984).

9. See Rosita Worl, *Principles of Tlingit Property Law and Case Studies of Cultural Objects* (Juneau: National Park Service, 1994); Nora and Richard Dauenhauer, *Haa Kusteeyi: Our Culture, Tlingit Life Stories* (Seattle: University of Washington Press, and Juneau: Sealaska Heritage Foundation, 1994), 22–23.

10. United States Constitution, article 1, section 8 (emphasis added).

11. See *Johnson v. McIntosh,* 21 United States Reports (8 Wheaton) 571 (1823); *Cherokee Nation v. Georgia,* 30 United States Reports (5 Peters) 1 (1831); *Worcester v. Georgia,* 31 United States Reports (6 Peters) 515 (1832). See also Felix Cohen, *Felix Cohen's Handbook of Federal Indian Law* (Charlottesville: Michie Bobbs-Merrill, 1982), 231.

12. See Edward Spicer, *A Short History of Indian Relations* (New York: D. Van Nostrand Co., 1979).

13. Felix Cohen, *Felix Cohen's Handbook of Federal Indian Law,* 220–228; *Seminole Nation v. United States,* 316 United States Reports 286 (1942).

14. Alaska Organic Act of May 17, 1884, 23 Statutes at Large 24. See also *Tlingit and Haida Indians of Alaska v. U.S.,* 177 Federal Supplement 464. (Use and occupancy rights of Tlingit and Haida were not extinguished by the Treaty of 1867. The negotiation of and language of the treaty show that it was not intended to have any effect on the rights of the Indians of Alaska).

15. As quoted, Robert D. Arnold, *Alaska Native Land Claims* (Anchorage: Alaska Native Foundation, 1978), 76.

16. *Tlingit and Haida Indians v. U.S.,* 177 Federal Supplement 468.

17. *Tlingit and Haida Indians v. U.S.,* 177 Federal Supplement 467.

18. *Tlingit and Haida Indians of Alaska v. U.S.,* 389 Federal Reporter 2nd 778 (1968).

19. Alaska Native Claims Settlement Act of 1971, 43 United States Code sections 1601 and following (1988). Also see Robert D. Arnold, *Alaska Native Land Claims.*

20. As quoted, Testimony before the Alaska Native Review Commission, Sitka, Alaska (Kettleson Memorial Library, Sitka, Alaska), 69.

21. Thomas R. Berger, *The Village Journey*, 26.

22. Thomas R. Berger, *The Village Journey*, 26.

23. Thomas R. Berger, *The Village Journey*, 41, quoting Professor Monroe Price.

24. Thomas R. Berger, *The Village Journey*, 6, quoting the testimony of Mike Albert, Tunanak, Alaska.

25. Senate Report no. 581, 92nd Congress, first session 37 (1971); also House of Representatives Conference Report no. 746, 92nd Congress, first session 37, reprinted in 1971 United States Code Congressional and Administrative News 5070, 5174-75.

26. Alaska National Interest Lands Conservation Act, 16 United States Code sections 3111-3126, 3111 (subparagraph 4) (1988).

27. 16 United States Code sections 3111 (subparagraph 1) (1988); 126 Congressional Record 29, 279 (1980), statement of Representative Udall.

28. *McDowell v. State of Alaska*, 785 Pacific Reporter 2nd 1, 2 (Alaska 1989).

29. See *Alaska v. Babbitt*, 72 Federal Reporter 3rd 698 (9th Circuit Court of Appeals, 1995).

30. Indian Self-Determination Act, 25 United States Code 450, 450a (1988).

31. As quoted in Thomas R. Berger, *The Village Journey*, 182.

32. "One of the chief causes of Indian decimation during the 19th century was the loss of the hunting grounds and the game on which the Indian tribes subsisted." David S. Case, *Alaska Natives and American Laws*, 276.

33. As quoted in Thomas R. Berger, *The Village Journey*, 182.

34. Larry Merculieff, "Establishing a Rapport between Indigenous Coastal Cultures and the Western Scientific Community," Fourth International Symposium of the Conference of Asian and Pan-Pacific University Presidents.

35. Testimony of Franklin James Jr., Ketchikan, Alaska, in Thomas R. Berger, *The Village Journey*.

36. Testimony of Bill Brady, Sitka, Alaska, in Gmelch and Gmelch, "Resource Use in a Small Alaskan City: Sitka," 150.

37. Caw Goo Woo, "An Eagle Speaks," *Alaska Fish and Game* 13, no. 3 (1981): 32.

38. Testimony of Ray Nielsen Sr., Sitka, Alaska, on record at the Sitka Tribe of Alaska.

I am deeply indebted to the elders of Sitka, Alaska, for sharing their heritage. In particular, I would like to thank Jessie Johnny, Mark Jacobs Jr., Ethel Makinen, Herman and Vida Davis, John Nielsen, Ted Borbridge, Daisy Jones, and Herman Kitka. I owe a great deal of gratitude to Robi Craig, the Sitka tribal anthropologist, for her review of the manuscript and her enduring support. I would like to thank Jude Pate, Sitka tribal attorney; Bob Sam, Sitka tribal graves protection and repatriation specialist; and Dr. Dolly Garza of the University of Alaska Southeast for their review and helpful comments.

DAVID AVRAHAM VOLUCK was born and raised outside Philadelphia and attended the University of Pennsylvania. Moving to the Pacific Northwest, he attended the Northwestern School of Law at Lewis and Clark College in Portland, Oregon. In the summer of 1994, David received a grant from the Public Interest Law Project to intern with the Sitka Tribe of Alaska. After this experience, he focused his studies on natural resources and Indian law. Upon receiving his J.D. degree, David moved to Anchorage to assist David Case with the revision of his treatise "Alaska Natives and American Laws." David then returned to the Sitka Tribe as a land and natural resources attorney and eventual director of their Department of Law and Trust Resources. In 1998, David rejoined David Case in the firm of Copeland, Landge, Bennet and Wolf LLP., emphasizing representation of Alaska Native Corporations, tribal governments, and rural municipalities. David returns to the Tongass often and enjoys visiting old Native fish camps, harvesting herring eggs on hemlock branches, and exploring the islands of Sitka Sound.

marbled murrelet, *Nancy Behnken*

Glacier Bay History

TOLD BY AMY MARVIN

Now this is the way I will begin telling the story
today.
Now,
at the beginning
of how things happened to us
at Glacier Bay.
the way things happened to us there.
This little girl was one of us
Chookaneidí.
It was she
who raised
the bird.
Its name was
(she would shorten up the name)
ts´ítskw.
Ts´ats´ée was its full name; these
tiny ones
that swim on the sea.
It was when
it came
out of its egg this little girl saved it.
She would say to it
as she was letting it go when it got strong,

as she was letting it go she would say to it,
"Don't go too far.
Don't go too far; you might blow away.
We are Chookaneidí.
We are Chookaneidí; I might lose you
So come back right away,
right away."
Maybe it was "Chookaneidí" that stuck in the mind of the bird.
Here it would
come back to her then.
This was how it got used to her.
It was this bird
that multiplied
there.
They multiply one generation after another over there.
It was then
they would say
"Chooooo-
kaneidí."
When they saw a boat they would say "Choooo-
kaneidí."
They're fun to listen to.
They say this even now.
People don't believe us when we tell this either.
The name of this little girl was Shkwáx´.
Shkwáx´
was her name.
She is the one who raised the bird.
Well,
from there
look at what's been happening to us,
to where this has led us.

Now
the time had come
for this young woman.
Very young
newly
put in confinement.
Today she would be called teenager.
This is what this young girl was.
Kaasteen.
This was when
they had her sit.
Not in the house.
But in an extension
of the house.
A room would be made.
It was like the bedrooms of today.
Someone who was in this condition would not be allowed inside
     the main house.
They would build a room for her
extending from the main house.
At the same time
there was a feast.
A feast was being held.
Everybody was gone,
everyone had gone to the feast.
But this young girl's mother
went to see her.
She gave her some sockeye strips.
"Here."
There was another little girl, a little girl maybe eight years old.
Her mother didn't want to leave her.
People didn't take their children out in public
in those days

because they respected one another.
This is how things were.
People didn't take children
even the babies.
This woman didn't want to leave her little girl.
She was weaving
a basket.
She brought her weaving out.
She wove.
They were all gone! It was deserted.
Then the little girl ran in by the one who had become a woman.
She sat with her.
Kaasteen
was eating the dryfish.
She broke them.
All of a sudden she bent down.
This is when she lifted the edge of her wall.
They say she held the dryfish out with one hand.
Then she bent down that way.
This is how the little girl told it to her mother.
"Hey,
glacier!
Here, here, here, here, here.
Hey,
glacier!
Here, here, here, here, here, here."
Hey,
glacier!
here, here, here, here, here.
Then she lowered the wall.
The little girl was surprised by this.
That was why she got up; she ran out by her mother.
"Mom!

Why is she saying this?
'Hey,
glacier!
Here, here, here.'
Three times she said this.
Mom!
Three times she said this."
"Don't say that! Go away!
You're always saying things,"
she said to her little daughter.
This woman was the witness.
This one who stayed home with her little daughter was the witness
about her,
about Kaasteen.
This is why
we tell it the same way.
We didn't just
toss this story together.
This is the way it's told.
My grandmother,
my mother,
my father,
were very old when they died.
This is why I don't
deviate when I tell it; I tell it exactly right.
At that time
the ice
didn't begin advancing from the top.
It began advancing from the bottom,
from the bottom.
That was why no one knew.
Not one person knew.
All of a sudden it struck

the middle of the land that people were living on.
Why was the land shaking?
Why was it?
People thought it was an earthquake; it didn't bother anyone.
Then another one,
then another one.
Why didn't it quit?
Here it was the ice crushing against itself and moving in.
That was why
they finally gathered together.
"What's happening?
It should happen just once.
Why is this?
Oh no!
It wasn't an earthquake, was it?
It's becoming stronger."
The people forgot about it again.
Then it happened again.
Here this woman finally said
"Oh dear! It's the one sitting in the room.
She called it with dryfish like a dog."
Where was the glacier?
There wasn't a glacier to be seen.
But that was what Kaasteen gave a name to; she named it "sít´."
What was it she named this?
There was a little piece stuck there.
That was what she gave a name to.
That was why the people who were wise gathered then.
"Oh!
I guess she said a bad thing."
When a person who is ritually unclean, you see,
mistakenly does something,
it turns bad.

That's the reason,
that's the reason
they gathered together.
Oh, she violated a taboo, didn't she?
I guess she mistakenly said things about the ice.
Oh, no.
They kept gathering.
They kept gathering.
They were really troubled by the way things were turning out on
    their land; people stayed in their homes.
It was becoming troublesome too.
But the young girl wasn't bothered by this anymore.
Perhaps it was changing her every moment.
It was because of her,
the glacier was doing this because of her.
Because of the way she called it over.
Here they said
"I guess she broke a taboo, didn't she?
Quick!
Let's get ready to get out."
Things weren't turning out right.
The house was already falling over on its side
from how strong the ice was getting.
    (Slap!)
It was behaving
like it was crushing against itself,
    (Slap!)
how strong the ice was.
And they knew.
It was the ice pushing the people, wasn't it?
It was pushing; it was pushing the village along.
This was when people said, "Quick!
    Quick! Quick! Quick!

Quick.
Let's move the people.
Quick!
Move the people.
It isn't right.
It isn't right."
This was when they said,
"Quick! Let's pack.
Her too.
It's OK to take the one who broke the taboo; it's OK.
Let her come aboard.
Let her come aboard."
People used to cherish each other, you see.
There was no way they could have left her there; she was a young
    woman
a young girl.
Yes, like the saying, "they had her sitting for seed."
This is when this happened to her.
This was when people said,
"There's nothing wrong with her coming aboard.
Let her come aboard."
That was why they asked her, indirectly,
"People will be getting ready now.
Quick!
Fix your clothes.
Fix them."
"No!
I won't go aboard."
Oh no!
Her words spread quickly.
"She said, 'I won't go aboard,' the one who broke the taboo.
She said she doesn't want to go aboard."
Oh, no.

Then it came to the opposite groups.
"This paternal aunt of hers should go to her,
her father's sister; Quick, quick, quick."
On that side of the village people were packing; it was already like a
    whirlpool.
The village was trembling constantly,
trembling constantly; it was as if they were expecting disaster.
Perhaps it was like the storm we just had.
It was very frightening the way things were.
They were trying to beat it.
"Yes, because it is like this, and because it is this way, my niece,
my brother's daughter
because things are this way, now,
let's go,
pack,
pack!
Pity your mother, take pity on your father."
They begged her.
"No!
No!
I won't go aboard.
I won't go aboard.
What I said
will stain my face forever."
She didn't deny it.
What I said will stain my face
forever; this is why
I won't go aboard; it won't happen.
That was why they gave up on her.
That was why they said
"Let's go!
But let's take these things
to her.

We can't just leave her this way.
Yes.
Let's go!"
It began to happen.
They began going to her
with things that would keep,
her paternal aunts,
all of them,
with all of us,
going to her
with things for her food.
"For Kaasteen to eat!
For Kaasteen to eat!"
In this way they brought
whatever
might keep her warm,
the skins
of whatever was killed and dried.
They were made into robes.
These, "For Kaasteen!"
("For Kaasteen!")
"For Kaasteen to eat!"
("For Kaasteen to eat!")
"For Kaasteen!"
In this way
they turned then and left her.
Now,
this is the reason it became a saying,
it will be a saying forever, for whomever is mourned, people
    relinquish
the ownership of things in their memory.
Only after this do we feel stronger.
And "for her to eat," is also said.

Only if the food which is given is eaten with another clan
can it go to her.
This is when she will have some,
the relative who is mourned.
When the opposite clan takes a bite she will also eat some.
This is the reason we call it "invitation to feast."
A feast is offered
to remove our grief.
Only when we give to the opposite clan
whatever we offer,
only when we know it went to her; only when this is done does it
    become a balm for our spirits.
Because of her,
Kaasteen.
And whatever we relinquish our ownership to,
for Kaasteen,
when we give them to the opposite clan,
only after this do our spirits become strong.
It's medicine, spiritual medicine.
Because of the things that happened to Kaasteen; this is what
    informed us.
When all the things were piled on her.
Yes.
Now.
They were gone.
They were all aboard the canoes.
That was when Shaawatséek´ got angry.
Yes.
She was already old.
She was already older than me at the time.
"Isn't it a shame," she said.
She started going there.
Yes.

The relatives who were going to leave her were standing by
    Kaasteen
in the house they were leaving her in.
This was when Shaawatséek´ pushed the door open.
Yes.
"Am I going to bring your next generation,
my brothers?
But take Kaasteen aboard.
Take her aboard.
I will take her place.
I'm expecting death
at any moment.
So I will take her place.
Yes.
Let her go aboard.
Let her go aboard."
This was when Kaasteen spoke, in a loud voice
"I will not go aboard.
I said, I will not go aboard.
I'm staying here."
That was it.
Shaawatséek´ couldn't persuade her either.
Now,
no more.
They gave up on her.
This was the last try
when Shaawatséek´ came for her.
This was why
they left her.
There was enough.
It measured up.
The food
from her paternal aunts,

from her paternal uncles,
from her mother's people
was piled high.
They were leaving her with almost enough to fill the house.
This is when they all finally
went aboard.
Yes.
They didn't paddle away just then.
When they were all seated in the canoes
they just drifted.
While they were packing, I guess, this song kept flashing on the
     mind of K̲aanax̲duwóos´.
It kept flashing on his mind.
He knew too
when they went to get her.
My!
No, she didn't want to leave the house.

Only when they were drifting out
they saw.
The house was rolling over.
And it popped out of their mouths
"It's rolling over!"
It fell over sideways,
and she with the house.
Yes.
That's when her mother screamed.
She screamed.
Kaasteen's mother screamed.
Yes.
The other women also
screamed with her.
While they couldn't believe it, it was sliding downward,

the house she sat in,
downward.

Their voices
could be heard from far away,
crying.

They had no more strength.
Today
death is not like that.
It's like something dropping.
At that time though,
if anything happened to even an infant, the grief would leave us
    weak.
The way we didn't want to lose each other.
The way things were.
Yes, this was why he stood up in the canoe.
The voices were still loud.
They were still crying.
She was dying before their eyes
as the house slid downward.
This was when he began singing, then.

FIRST SONG

Ahaa haa hei hei
ahaa haaa hei heiiiiy
ahaa haa hei heiiiiy
aa haa hei hei
ahaa haa hei hi.aa

Won't my house
be pitiful
won't my house
be pitiful

when I leave on foot?
hee hee aahaaa
hee hee aaa
ahaa, haaa hei hei hi.aa haa

Repeat first verse and vocables

Won't my land
be pitiful
won't my land
be pitiful
when I leave by boat?
hee hee aahaaa
hee hee aaa
ahaa, haa, hei, hei, hi, aaa

Repeat second verse and vocables

hooooo, hoo, hoo.

Now this is what happened to them.
This is how they were.
Now.
This is the song from there.
when they left Kaasteen.
This house became like her coffin,
this Chookaneidí house.
It went with her to the bottom of the sea before their eyes.
This is why the words are of the house,
when he first sang
this song
"Pity my house,"
he said.
Yes.
And when they left her, "pity my land."

Yes.
I guess they didn't put the comparison together
at first.
When one who was precious,
their relative,
this woman,
died before their eyes,
yes, no one else thought of songs.
They were just afraid.
They just trembled to go where they could be saved
because it was too much the way the land was shaking.
It wasn't letting up.
This was why they were afraid.
Even with all this he thought of the song.
Yes.
This is the reason it's everlasting, also for the generations coming
    after me.
I'm recording for them
so that they will know why this song came into being.
But no man volunteered
to stay with her.
But recently someone said that one did.
No!
No!
Well,
I will come to it,
the part of the story
why people were saying this.
After this
I guess it was
out from Pleasant Island.
When they were passing it,
Sdayáat,

a Chookaneidí,
also our relative,
stood up in the canoe.
Yes.
He also repeated,
"Stop for a moment.
Stop for a moment."

That was why they held those moving canoes motionless; yes.
"I too
cannot let
what I'm thinking
pass.
Please listen
to the way I feel too."
They began drifting; all the canoes drifted.

This is when he sang the song that flashed on his mind.

Yes.

SECOND SONG

Ahaa haa aaa haa
hei hei aaa hei hei
ahaa haaa aaa haa
yei hei hayoo
aaa yei hei
aaa haa haa

My land,
will I ever
see it again?
shei aanaa haa hayoo
aahaa yei hei hei hayoo

aanaa aaa haa haa
haa haa yei hei hayoo
aahaa haa haa haa.

Repeat first verse and vocables

My house,
will I ever
see it again?
shei aanaa hayoo
aahaa yei hei hei hayoo
aahaa aaa haa

Repeat second verse and vocables

a haa haa haa
hooooo hoo hoo.

Now, this is Sdayáat's song.
Yes.
This is how the two of them composed songs
when trouble came.
Well,
they didn't just abandon her carelessly.
Now,
not even the T´akdeintaan
searched their minds,
or the Kaagwaantaan,
or the Wooshkeetaan.
They just left.
It was only these men who expressed their pain.
They didn't just leave her carelessly.
Now
only then they began leaving.
The Wooshkeetaan

went to the place
called Excursion Inlet today.
But the Kaagwaantaan

went to Ground Hog Bay.
I guess it's called
Grouse Fort.
This is where they went, the group of Kaagwaantaan.
As for us, we continued away from them.
There is
a river called Lakooxas´t´aakhéen.
It flows there; it's still there today; where Frank Norten made his
      land,
a place like a cove.
It was there; we waded ashore.
Now
you know how tiring it is to be in a canoe.
It was then and there we waded ashore; this is where we prepared a
      place to live
at Spasski.
It's called Lakooxas´t´aakhéen.
It was there we waded ashore.
It was like
after a war.
There was nothing.
This is how it was.

*AMY MARVIN, whose given name in Tlingit is Kooteen, was born into the
Eagle moiety and Chookaneidí clan. Her mother's name was Sxeinda.át,
and her father, Shx´éik´—Pete Fawcett in English—was of the Yéilkudei Hít*

(Raven Nest House) of the T´akdeintaan clan of Hoonah, Alaska. Amy's mother married twice, and Amy is the youngest of fourteen children from those two marriages. She is of the Naanaa Hít, the Upper Inlet house in Hoonah, which was named for the house in the story told here, and she is a direct descendent of the two main women in the story, Kaasteen and Shaawatséek. She grew up in Hoonah and has lived most of her life there. She spent many years working in fish canneries and packing plants, beginning when she was twelve. Amy is a noted storyteller and orator, and is the family historian, keeping alive names, history, and music. She is also a basket weaver, song leader, and drummer. She shares the traditional Tlingit beliefs of most of her generation—that the land is the true spiritual and economic base of her people, rather than cash and profit. For her, the land and the spiritual history of the Tlingit people are inseparable.

Labrador tea, *Richard Carstensen*

Logging and Learning
in the Tongass Rain Forest

JOHN SISK

The diesel motor mounted on the log raft roared, and the cables
leading up the hill from the top of the log yarder groaned as the
entire mass of the Caterpillar engine and brine-soaked logs that
supported it were lifted out of the water. Dick throttled back
and released the tension on the cable pulley; the raft of great
logs swung back down and splashed into the water like a hinge
mounted to the beach. A cleared swath led from the beach up into
the infinite wet green of the forest. At the head of the swath, a massive, freshly cut log was hung up on a pile of branches and pole
timber, like a bull not quite able to break through a corral fence.

Curses and shouts echoed from the woods to the yarder and
back. Suddenly, from somewhere within the timber and jack-
strawed logs, a huge, wide man emerged, dancing in spiked boots
across the still lurching log, chain saw running, stooping to cut the
beast free. A bulging bruin in a hickory shirt, with the agility of a
deer, Ed jumped off, yelling a command as he disappeared into the
evergreen jungle. The diesel roared; the log popped free and came
careening down toward tidewater until it hung up again on something invisible in the runway of logging slash. Finally the log broke
free and let the cable slide it down to the beach and into the water,
where it was made fast to a dozen more logs, afloat in the bay.

A few minutes later, with the yarder shut down, Dick and Ed
sipped coffee on the beach as a light mist sifted out of the low

clouds, falling gently, soundlessly, through the windless air to become beading water on the boughs of the towering spruce, hemlock, and cedar. As coffee poured out of the thermos, steam rose from the cups, wafted in the cool air, and disappeared. Ed spoke, and a voice that moments earlier had bellowed from the woods like a bear was soft in the silence. "By golly, we're doin' this the hard way." Beyond, from across the steely sheen of Sea Otter Sound, came the call of sea birds—murrelets—keet . . . keet . . . keet, and the wingbeats of scoters slicing the air as they coursed over a sea that stretched all the way to Asia.

It was 1986, and Ed and Dick were indeed logging the hard way. Their several-acre logging "show" marked a tiny bite out of the edge of America's largest national forest, the Tongass. Beyond their small island was a much larger island where many thousands of acres of clear-cuts marked the cutting and peeling away of billions of board feet of timber—from the national forest and from the private land owned by Native American corporations. In this country logging is never easy, yet those extensive clear-cuts spoke of an industrial effort before which Ed and Dick's hard work seemed inconsequential. The logs removed from those hillsides had been rafted together and towed to a distant bay where clouds of steam billowed from a large pulp mill, centerpiece of the modern Tongass timber industry.

A big part of the regional economy, the pulp mill was also the market, the only market, for a lot of Ed and Dick's logs. It was also their biggest competitor, since it dominated the quest for Forest Service timber sales and set the price for Tongass hemlock logs. They knew the mill had the power to squash them like a bug, just as it had other small logging outfits, and they knew that when environmentalists put the squeeze on timber supply, the Forest Service would make the pulp mill, not Ed and Dick, top priority for log supplies. These things could not be changed, and therefore did not need to be discussed over coffee on a hard show on a beautiful spring morning.

Beyond the islands, and beyond the pulp mill, were more islands, more forests, and more clear-cuts, stretching eastward to the towering Coast Range, where mountains reared far above timberline into the realm of tundra, glaciers, and ice fields—a mighty wall of earth and ice separating Southeast Alaska and the Tongass from the rest of North America. Nestled in this seventeen million acre landscape of fjords, islands, clear-cuts, and primeval forests, about seventy thousand people live in communities large and small: cities, towns, Indian villages, logging camps, cabins, and boats are all homes for the denizens of Alaska's Panhandle. Surrounding every home, cloaking the shoreline and the valleys beneath the huge and humbling mountains, is the blanket of forest called the Tongass, a coastal rain forest composed of ecological communities of its own: muskegs, river bottoms, estuaries, and stands of spruce, hemlock, cedar, alder, and willow—habitats where a panoply of fish and wildlife find their own homes.

From before remembered time, the people who call the islands and waterways of Southeast Alaska their home relied on the luxuriant forests we call the Tongass. The deer, and the salmon returning to spawn in the forest's thousand streams, fed people for centuries. The trees of the forest provided then as they do today; log planks went into houses, cedar trees became canoes, and wood in every form was incorporated into the culture. Elegant bentwood storage boxes, awe-inspiring ceremonial masks, tough armor for warriors, spruce roots and cedar bark for basketry, the carved regalia of shamans—wood was integral to human life just as the living forest was integral to the lives of the deer, mountain goats, and fur-bearing mammals that also sustained the people. Wood fueled the campfires where meals were cooked and the smokehouses where salmon was preserved for the winter. Wood warmed the winter hearths in homes where families shared the long winter months.

When the Russians fortified themselves at New Archangel, now known as Sitka, one of their first endeavors was construction of a sawmill. After the sale of Alaska to the United States, the Americans followed suit, and by the time the Tongass National Forest was proclaimed in 1909, small sawmills cut lumber in settlements throughout the Panhandle. Mining timbers, fish traps, docks, boats, boardwalks, and buildings were all made from the trees of the Tongass forest.

The trees were cut by Ed and Dick's forebears, the hand loggers. They lived in camps, in cabins, and on boats, and they felled prime timber, the "big pumpkins" over three hundred years old, using springboards and axes, close to the beach where the logs could be floated and towed into town for sale to the local sawmill. A good hand logger could make a big Sitka spruce jump over a hill and dive into the water, or so the saying went. Expert in logging and hunting, handy at the helm of a boat, and all-round masters of wilderness living, the hand loggers were the kind of frontier people that city dwellers imagined and admired when they read about the wild forests of North America.

The Forest Service had much bigger plans for the Tongass. Beginning in 1899, ten years before the Tongass National Forest was established, the Forest Service began advocating a program of sustainable development in Southeast Alaska that featured hydropower for industrial factories, construction of pulp mills and logging roads, and sustained-yield forestry in which the annual cut did not exceed the annual growth of younger trees. Compared to forest devastation by unregulated private logging concerns in the contiguous forty-eight states, the Forest Service scheme was regarded as progressive and visionary. In 1951 the agency signed a contract with Ketchikan Pulp Company, a venture involving Puget Sound Pulp and Timber and the American Viscose Corporation, and a pivotal chapter in the story of Tongass timber began to unfold.

The 1950s and 1960s were halcyon days in Ketchikan, Alaska. A speaker at a recent timber industry meeting recalled: "We were just worried about putting logs in the water and making some money, doing it and having fun doing it." A retired Forest Service ranger explained that in those days federal foresters arriving in Ketchikan received a red-carpet welcome because they were "doing God's work," preparing timber sales for the pulp company. They were heroes, he said, and so were the pulp-mill workers and the men in the woods. The Fourth of July became the annual Loggers Day celebration, and the first of several generations of Ketchikan Pulp employees had the first year-round factory jobs ever in America's "last frontier." As Ketchikan boomed, another pulp mill was getting under way in Sitka, and hopes were high for additional mills in Juneau and Wrangell.

New jobs were established: building pulp mills, docks, roads, and houses. Engineers, chemists, foresters, attorneys, doctors, and accountants moved to town. Services for residents improved. There were new restaurants, bars, and stores. Paychecks arrived on time. Ketchikan and Sitka saw population and property tax revenues increase. Surely this was progress!

The forest in those early years seemed infinite. It stretched from one end of the Panhandle to the other in a vast wilderness of islands, mountains, coves, muskegs, and trees, trees in a rain forest thick and nearly overwhelming. The Forest Service promised that with scientific management of successive crops of trees— silviculture—it could guarantee a perpetual supply of timber from the forest. Is it any wonder that many Alaskans were confident and righteous about the new pulp industry? Wasn't this the beginning of a bright, sustainable future?

Approximately a century after the Forest Service's first vision of social and economic engineering on the Alaska coast, nearly half a century after the Ketchikan Pulp Company contract was drafted, the pulp industry has ended. Ed and Dick, along with many of their peers, hung up their spiked boots and chain saws years ago. The Forest Service has fallen from its pedestal and is struggling to regain public confidence, even with the timber industry it promoted. Southeast Alaskans wrestle with a legacy of social conflict, environmental damage, and dramatic economic changes.

The Forest Service's experiment with regional development had a zenith, but today many Panhandle residents are acutely aware of the pain of lost forests, lost opportunities, and lost jobs. The meeting rooms and coffee shops of Southeast Alaska echo with discussions of "community stability," "economic development," and "quality of life." Jobs, "sustainability," and even "ecosystem management" are the currency of debate. Alaskans want a second shot at the elusive dream of prosperity on the last frontier, of a thriving economy in the midst of a natural forest. That much we agree on.

But shouldn't we ask some hard questions before plunging off in the next effort at sustainable development? About how we arrived where we are today? What we have learned? About the possible role of logging and wood manufacturing in the future of Southeast Alaska? About how Southeast Alaskans can continue to live reasonably prosperous and responsible lives in the woods and communities of Alaska's great forest?

These are fundamentally political questions. They arise from the complex relationships among all who have a stake, an interest, in the Tongass National Forest. The logger, the salmon fisherman, the kayaker. The timber company shareholder and the government forester. The village deer hunter who puts meat on the table for family and neighbors. The builder with a small sawmill in a remote village. The Sierra Clubber. Politics permeates the web of life of the waters and forests. How many deer can be killed this year? Will we build tourist lodges in this pristine fjord? How much forest habitat shall we leave standing to shelter deer in winter? Will we leave enough old-growth forest along the salmon stream intact? Or cut it to the banks? Biology is politics, and politics is people, making collective choices.

Biology and politics are intertwined on the Tongass National Forest. Historically in Southeast Alaska, politics is remarkable in its frequent triumph over economics. Such a political triumph was the key to establishing the pulp industry envisioned by the early Forest Service leaders. Throughout the first half of the twentieth century, the Forest Service was unable to recruit investment capital to manifest the dream. Southeast Alaska was too rugged and too remote. Large-scale logging operations and manufacturing were too expensive there compared to other timbered regions. Markets were distant, and predicted shortages of newsprint and rayon did not amount to enough to sustain high pulp prices.

The message from the marketplace was clear and unsympathetic. The timber operations that made sense were the ones that locals had already discovered: lumber and logs for local use with export of high-grade spruce and cedar, all on a relatively modest scale. Dick and Ed were right on target. That strategy supported dozens of small Alaskan businesses, but the Forest Service was thinking big, swimming upriver against a strong economic current.

And so the Forest Service was frustrated until 1947, when the agency's most brilliant leader, Frank Heintzelman, established a partnership between political leaders in the U.S. Congress, private industry, and the Forest Service. That triad became institutionalized in the form of fifty-year contracts that spelled out the role of each player. Private industry would build and operate pulp factories and build a road system throughout Southeast Alaska. The Forest Service would design the timber sales to ensure a guaranteed wood supply to industry at affordable rates, and would allow the industry to charge road expenses off as payment for timber.

Congress would make sure the legal stage was set, and would appropriate money to fund the Forest Service. The economic problem was overcome by deliberate, generous government support.

This three-way relationship among Congress, a federal land management agency, and private interests has become known, popularly, as an "iron triangle." Iron is exceedingly strong, and a triangle is a stable geometric figure. The durability of such an arrangement is a tremendous asset when a desired public purpose must be carried out in spite of big obstacles. That same durability can become a dysfunction, however, when public priorities or economics change and the iron triangle of institutional commitments cannot adapt or innovate.

In the case of the Tongass, political careers and a Forest Service bureaucracy were built on pulp, and an industry that employed many Alaskans was dependent on both Congress and the Forest Service. The three corners of the iron triangle collectively controlled the flow of private and federal capital, along with much of the government and private employment in remote, sparsely populated Southeast Alaska.

How could such a powerful, durable political institution as the iron triangle of Tongass timber crack apart? In politics, the reactions to an initiative can become as powerful—sometimes more powerful—than the initiative itself; the Tongass pulp program is an excellent example. The Forest Service timber program was simply too ambitious, too exclusive, and too self-confident to accommodate the diversity of human cultures, enterprises, and values that depended on the Tongass forest. As a result, a rare mix of people, all in some way alienated by the Forest Service program, organized political coalitions with an objective of gaining, or regaining, what they considered to be their rightful place on America's largest national forest.

The first group of people to voice concern with the pulp program were Native Alaskans—Tlingit and Haida people who once called the entire region their homeland and in the 1940s advanced an aboriginal land claim to more than a million acres of the Tongass. The Tongass Timber Act of 1947, backed by the Forest Service and non-Native economic interests, postponed Tlingit and Haida land claims and allowed pulp company logging to begin on much of the forest the Natives considered theirs. It was not until the Alaska Native Claims Settlement Act of 1971 that actual land claims were approved by Congress. Approximately half a million acres of Tongass National Forest land were selected by the newly created Native corporations, which today operate their own timber programs and export unprocessed logs to Korea, Japan, China, and other destinations. The 1971 act did not, however, address rural Alaskans' use of fish, game, and cultural resources on the Tongass; these "subsistence" uses found no welcome in the Forest Service plan for the Tongass.

The Forest Service clearly considered logging and pulp manufacture to be the highest use of the forest: in the 1960s agency management plans called for the systematic clear-cutting of 95 percent of the Tongass's valuable old-growth timber in order to maximize pulpwood production, forever. This placed the agency at odds with everyone who believed, for whatever reason, that more than 5 percent of the forest should be left standing in its natural condition. Over time this drove hunters, fishermen, trappers, environmentalists, rural Alaskan communities, biologists, cultural and spiritual leaders, subsistence harvesters of fish and game, some union leaders, and even small logging businesses into various unlikely coalitions of Southeast Alaskans held together by a common threat. These were people who lived in the Tongass and depended on its natural wealth for their sustenance. Collectively, their coalition power was enough to signal significant dissatisfaction among Southeast Alaskans. Allied with the national environmental movement, they had enough power to challenge the iron triangle, toe to toe.

By the late 1970s scientific research in fisheries and wildlife biology began catching up with the silvicultural basis of the Forest Service timber management regime. Much of the research suggested that management of the Tongass needed to change in order to provide adequate habitat for salmon, deer, brown (grizzly) bear, and other species. Science contributed to a fundamental reassessment of how we manage forests for multiple purposes in coastal Alaska. The transition from tree farming to ecosystem management was under way.

In hindsight, the ensuing events seem inevitable, as public reactions against an entrenched Forest Service led to successive federal laws designed to protect some of the Tongass and provide for other users while continuing to support the pulp program. The Alaska National Interest Lands Conservation Act of 1980 addressed the entire state and included wilderness area designation for 5.4 million acres of the Tongass's most scenic and unique wildlands. The act also made subsistence use of federal lands by rural Alaskans a priority, even though the means for assuring that priority remains a controversial issue. On behalf of the pulp industry, the 1980 law also included a trade-off, advanced by pulp industry supporters, that provided a guaranteed subsidy and a mandated timber supply to come from the land not set aside as wilderness.

The Forest Service built roads and pushed timber sales with renewed vigor; detractors had their wilderness and it was time to get back to work. As the clear-cuts rolled across salmon streams and into local community hunting areas and municipal watersheds, many Alaskans found the Forest Service was even less willing to accommodate diverse uses of the "multiple use" forest lands than before the Alaska Lands Act passed.

Local opposition rekindled and grew, and in 1990 a monumental grassroots Alaskan effort culminated in passage of the Tongass Timber Reform Act. Buffer strips of standing timber were required along salmon streams, and the pulp mills' fifty-year logging contracts were changed. Approximately a million acres of land were declared off limits to logging, some as wilderness areas. In spite of the preservationist designation, one rural community leader explained: "I'm not sure that rural Alaska is really an advocate of wilderness. But I think they look at it as the only alternative."

In the 1990s, pulp markets ricocheted up and down erratically. The owners of the pulp companies began to wonder if they should call it good and close their pulp mills or hang on and hope for better times. A divisive political struggle that had lasted more than two decades was playing itself out, and the poor economics of manufacturing pulp in Alaska threatened to claim the day.

In 1993 the Alaska Pulp Corporation closed its Sitka pulp mill, and although Sitka weathered that closure better than expected, the smaller town of Wrangell was hit hard when Alaska Pulp shut down its affiliated sawmill there the next year. At about the same time, the Louisiana-Pacific Corporation, owner of the Ketchikan Pulp Company and other subsidiaries across the United States, found itself in financial and legal trouble. Soft markets, product liability suits, and alleged water and air-pollution violations cast a long shadow across the boardroom. Louisiana-Pacific made a major leadership change and began to restructure the corporation. The Ketchikan pulp division was a weak financial performer and relied on technology that could neither comply with new pollution control requirements nor compete with the plants of the future. In 1996 the company launched a knock-down-drag-out campaign to pressure the federal government into extending its commitment of Tongass timber through the year 2023, in order for the company to justify a major mill overhaul. Environmentalists and allied interests responded with an equally dedicated campaign to stop the extension, and succeeded. In 1997 Louisiana-Pacific held a press conference at corporate headquarters in Portland to announce its decision to close the Ketchikan pulp mill.

The politics were complicated. Senator Frank Murkowski and Representative Don Young of Alaska, both Republicans, were chairs of the Senate and House Resource Committees, and they struggled to expand logging on the Tongass and retain at least one pulp mill. Their opponents in Congress and in the Clinton White House, along with a surprising number of Alaskan voters, fought them to a draw. Alaska's senior senator, Republican Ted Stevens, chair of the Senate Appropriations Committee, cut a deal with the Clinton White House that directed $110 million directly to Southeast Alaska communities to help them weather the big transition in the timber industry. Louisiana-Pacific retained a portion of its timber contract sufficient to operate its two sawmills for three years.

The iron triangle of Tongass pulp mill development was broken. The fifty-year pulp-timber contracts were canceled. One company was gone and the other was out of the pulp business. The timber industry was changing, its future unpredictable. The Forest Service was in just as profound a transition as the timber industry. Politically, the agency was torn among local interests on all sides of the logging issue, a generally pro-environment Clinton administration, and a Congress dominated by the pro-timber Alaska delegation that controlled its budget and, potentially, its basic authority. The key agency leaders employed their considerable political skill to navigate the battlefield while preparing a new Tongass management plan that accorded timber a strong but smaller role and relied heavily on biological research, economics, and public comment to support an expanded commitment to other Tongass values. Predictably, many interests labeled the 1997 plan inadequate and filed formal administrative appeals. Yet the Forest Service clearly made a break, for the first time, from its historic and fundamental dedication to pulp production and made concrete commitments to fish, wildlife, subsistence, and recreation as management priorities.

What kinds of public discussions are occuring in the aftermath of the new Tongass forest plan? One discussion emphasizes a continuation of the struggle between those who, in effect, want to go back to the days when the whole Tongass National Forest belonged to the timber industry and those who might shut down Tongass logging completely if they had a chance. After decades of conflict, this polarization became part of the culture of the Tongass, and it reflects a forest landscape where over half of the best timberland is already clear-cut and significant acreage is off limits to logging. Too much has already been cut to sustain the ecosystem; too much is off limits to logging to sustain an industry. The persistence of polarized political wrangling is frustrating, and especially so for those who conceive of workable middle-ground approaches to living in the forest. But the persistent dichotomy is perfectly consistent with the fundamental design of American politics: polarize and debate, compromise, reassess. Nearly every important public policy issue in America that is elevated to national attention is tackled in this manner. It is an eternal, inevitable, and perhaps essential dance.

Yet this dance is fundamentally centrifugal, pulling individual people toward polar positions or dropping them out of the debate. In the case of a national issue over a national forest, where large international corporations are involved, this debate also pulls away from the forest itself. Strategies and compromises are hatched or hammered out in Washington, D.C., at a bank in Tokyo, or in a boardroom in Portland. A vacuum is left closer to the center, where a different and equally vital kind of discussion must occur.

That other kind of discussion begins with a search for common ground, and it needs to be connected, as directly as possible, with the forest itself. It needs to be open to all people who care enough about the forest to invest themselves in a principled discussion. This discussion is the anchor that keeps the more polarized political combat from inadvertently blowing us onto a rocky shoal. It is a discussion in which listening is as important as lobbying, respect for the long-term health of the forest ecosystem is paramount, and folks steadfastly refuse to dissolve friendships, neighborhoods, or communities, even though individually they may at times stand resolutely opposed over a very tough issue.

How much of this second discussion is taking place in the Tongass today? Not nearly enough, but more than ever before. After so many years in which the Forest Service and the timber industry excluded many from decisions about the forest, and several decades of spirited advocacy by those seeking fundamental changes in Tongass management, an open and respectful exchange of ideas is not a small proposistion.

What is being said about the future of the timber industry in Southeast Alaska? There remain half a dozen or so timber businesses hoping to be big players in the future, and dozens of smaller operations that have more modest goals. Market economics cannot be ignored; the federal government will not play as strong a role as industry booster and funding agency as it played in the past. In addition, the remaining unlogged timber on private Native corporation lands may become increasingly important as the Tongass harvest declines. Currently these corporations can export timber without processing, whereas Tongass logs typically must undergo at least primary manufacture in Alaska. Economic analyses suggest that the cost of sawing lumber in Alaska sometimes exceeds the value added to the wood by traditional manufacturing, creating an incentive to export unprocessed logs. This incentive appears to be diminishing, and private timber may play a significant role as the raw material for value-added wood manufacturing in Alaska.

At least three timber industry strategies for the future are apparent. Old guard foresters and pulp mill veterans want to reinstate some facsimile of the past: long-term contracts for Tongass timber, cheap stumpage rates, and protection from public appeals and lawsuits. They would emphasize the manufacture of fiber-based products like pulp, medium-density fiberboard, or oriented strand board in large, economy-of-scale factories that would place a big demand for raw materials on the forest. Solid wood products made from high-quality logs that don't get ground up would be a high-value by-product. This scheme would require much more logging than allowed for in the new Tongass forest plan. Advocates of this strategy are part of the generations of industry leaders who came of age working in a government-supported pulp industry. They believe the old way is the best way, perhaps the only way, to maintain a timber industry in Southeast Alaska.

On a very different track are Alaskan environmentalists who are pursuing ways to structure the timber industry to maximize social benefit—employment—and financial viability by adding more value to a smaller annual cut. Their goal is to manufacture finished products of solid wood—doors, windows, composite lumber, boat wood, craft works, cedar siding, and so forth—on a low- to moderate-volume basis. Wood waste and cull logs would be chipped for export or for use in heating, electrical cogeneration, pellet fuels, and specialty products like garden mulch and compost. Experience in the Pacific Northwest and Canada suggests that such an industry is possible and could employ large numbers of people for every unit of timber cut down and processed.

Research by the Forest Products Laboratory in Madison, Wisconsin, supports the notion that the future of the Southeast Alaska timber industry is in high-value-added solid wood products. According to the lab, wood supplies historically viewed as "low value" by mills in Southeast Alaska probably would be considered quite valuable by mills in other parts of the country. Researchers found that hemlock logs scaled as low grade in Alaska yielded excellent lumber.

Yet Southeast Alaska faces unique obstacles. Mills are scattered across an island archipelago with limited bulk transportation options, making it difficult to move logs, wood stock, and wood waste among distant, community-based manufacturing enterprises. The test will be in the marketplace, and for some of the new Alaska products and business strategies being considered, the marketplace remains untested.

A few lumbermen are trying to realize the high-value-added manufacturing goals cited by environmentalists, but in a more centralized manner at a somewhat larger scale that might allow for greater production economy. One project, for example, features a relatively small, state-of-the-art primary breakdown sawmill that will produce stock for finished products like furniture and doors while also producing planed and dried lumber, tongue-and-groove siding, and other solid wood products. Some of the players with the most private capital to invest, however, appear to be more interested in performing initial log breakdown in Alaska and exporting rough lumber or veneer to the Pacific Northwest where composite wood materials and finished wood products would be made.

Environmentalists are concerned that if all the proposed ventures move forward, their mill design capacities would add up to much more timber cutting than the forest can sustain. If all these ventures were capitalized, there would once again be strong political pressure on the Forest Service to allow more timber cutting on the Tongass than the forest and its stakeholders can bear.

Virtually invisible in the larger debate over the Tongass and the future of the timber industry are the most resilient and perhaps the most entrepreneurial businesspeople in the Alaska wood products industry. At least thirty small sawmills, located from one end of the Panhandle to the other, each sawing less than a million board feet a year, manage to produce a variety of products from rough green lumber to boat-building wood to music soundboards for guitars and pianos. These are people who, like Dick and Ed with their small, A-frame beach logging operation, know their forest and their home and are willing to do things the right way, even the hard way, in the course of making a life in the Tongass forest.

In addition to these businesses, there are dozens of small

construction, furniture, and crafts businesses that use local woods. Each contributes to family and community economies at a scale that is well within the capacity of local forests. These folks do not build great factories, nor do they employ lobbyists or make large campaign contributions. But these businesses rarely threaten the interests of other users of the Tongass forest.

A viable timber industry in the Alaska Panhandle can be one component of a diversified, and diversifying, regional economy. When the pulp mills were in their heyday, the Southeast Alaska economy was described popularly as a twofold resource economy: "fish 'n chips," or salmon and pulp. Later, it was described as a "three-legged stool" of fisheries, pulp mills, and tourism economies.

Today the economy resembles a wheel, its spokes made up of resource extraction, manufacturing, service, visitor, and information industries—each with increasingly specialized businesses targeting specific markets. An equally important spoke on the wheel is the noncash subsistence economy that provides sustenance for many Alaskans. At the hub of the wheel are the individuals and families living in the communities of Southeast Alaska, along with those who don't reside here but nonetheless have an interest in the Tongass forest. The timber industry has a place as a spoke on the wheel of the regional economy. To find that place, its leaders will need to engage the other businesses in the economy, community residents, and all the folks who have a stake in the Tongass forest.

How do real people with a stake in the Tongass forest engage together, constructively, in search of common interests and in affirmation of our own particular legitimacy? How might we advocate our interests while respecting those of our neighbors? How much can we take from the forest, how much can we enjoy the forest, without diminishing its capacity to provide?

This is the missing conversation that can stabilize conflict and reconnect us to the forest. It is a conversation that is—must be— rooted in the concept of community: the communities of Alaskans who live in the forest, the communities of people from all over who share particular interests in this great forest, and the ecological community of the Tongass ecosystem, of which we are only a part. Once we initiate and sustain this new discussion about our future and our home, we may be able to realize that elusive dream of prosperity on the last frontier, of a thriving economy in the midst of a thriving forest.

Born in Albuquerque, New Mexico, in 1955, JOHN SISK worked as a construction laborer and ranch hand before pursuing a career in resource conservation. He holds a bachelor's degree in biology from the University of Colorado and a master's degree in forestry from Northern Arizona University. He worked for the Colorado Division of Wildlife and the Colorado Open Space Council before moving to Alaska in 1983 to work as a community organizer for the Southeast Alaska Conservation Council (SEACC). John also served as executive director of SEACC and worked as a wilderness guide for Alaska Discovery expeditions. He received the Alaska Conservation Foundation's Olaus Murie award for conservation in 1992. He has worked for the Alaska Department of Fish and Game and currently works as a staff assistant for Alaska Governor Tony Knowles.

bald eagles, *Nancy Behnken*

Allowable Cut:
Fear and Transformation in a
Tongass Timber Town

DANIEL HENRY

We are out for three hours in my twelve-foot Lund before Skip spots a prime log leaning against a weatherworn root wad at the twenty-foot tide level. He stands up in the boat with the same keen vigor a hunter might save for a deer on the beach. "There's a honey," he rasps and points, stalking game. The forty-foot log still shows the orange burnish of a fresh spruce or hemlock. We cut the engine and drift in closer. A freshening southerly prompts dancing froth from seawater; lines of building chop murmur onshore, slapping a few feet short of our target. Skip crouches in the dipping bow until it scrapes in the beach shallows, then he grabs the bowline and leaps ashore.

We work quickly, spurred by the dying late-summer light and building seas. The log will yield a cord of firewood, more or less, which we'll share to fend off the winter that we watch creeping down craggy peaks on either side of the steep-flanked fjord. A few years back, logs like these lined the shores in such numbers that neighbors could build entire homes or put up firewood two years in advance. As the mills began to shut down, however, beach loggers around Southeast Alaska began searching for other sources of wood. During the flush of the timber industry in the 1970s and 1980s, beach logging was a way for friends and neighbors to bond: a six-pack rattling in the hull among peevees, ropes, pry bars, log staples, and chain saws meant half a day of jawing about local gossip and politics while we scanned the beaches for wood that had broken loose from the huge log booms headed for the mills. Ferocious storms once redistributed the logs destined to become cants or pulp. What wasn't shipped to Japan washed ashore for anyone with a boat to haul off.

Today, Skip and I complain about the lack of logs and what he calls the local "pinhead politics" that are probably pushing a mutual friend of ours, Bill, away from newspaper reporting, away from our town. He might have been out with us in the skiff if he wasn't going underground, retreating from the pressures of being an honest journalist in Haines. He is showing signs of wear that we have seen all too often among reporters here: bitterness, resentment, mouth-agape awe at the blatant disregard for civility. As we crumple our final beer cans and turn the skiff toward our home bay, we bet each other the next log that Bill will be gone before the snow flies. We were right.

Bill left Haines in mid-September with his beautiful Swedish wife and toddler son. After two years as the only reporter for our local newspaper, he was seething. As a veteran reporter in Minnesota and Pennsylvania urban centers, Bill had been used to investigating the smarmy details of local government decision making, domestic abuse, and corporate cover-ups. Duplicity, lies, and contradiction were the stuff of great stories, he maintained. The public has a right to know, he would chant like a mantra, especially a rural Alaskan community where the weekly newspaper may be the only shield between cold lies and the heat of truth.

Our town had never before tangled with a reporter possessed with such zeal for uncovering the truth. He had once brought down a Minnesota congressman who had spent public money on phone calls and favors for a secret lover. Bill's ardent belief in full and complete disclosure had brought him awards and attention. He moved his family to Haines for a "lifestyle change," but within a year of reporting in our small, isolated community of twenty-five hundred fiercely independent residents, Bill found that his mission was eating him alive. During the city council and borough assembly meetings, local leaders would extol the virtues of fairness while demanding special favors; local planning boards were ignored or gored; city fathers condemned the input of outsiders, visitors, and newcomers with name-calling, innuendo, and bluster. Elected leaders refused to allow their statements in public meetings to be quoted because they represented "ideas in progress" rather than considered positions. Anything less than a booster tone provoked tantrums, and Bill caught the brunt of them. He couldn't shop at either of the two grocery stores without being cornered for a cussing over that week's serving of the truth in print.

"Don't people know that their behavior is in absolute bad taste?" he marveled one night in his first winter of deep snow and darkness. "You can't just lie in a public meeting in America and get away with it." In principle, I agreed. The reality of living in a place like Haines, though, is that local truth is often determined by a clutch of citizens who are allowed to assert a position over and over again until it is accepted as truth. People who get in the way are ostracized until they shut up or disappear. Some of us come to accept this as one more thorny feature of communicating on the frontier. Some, like Bill, are driven back to the comforts of urban anonymity, to tell tales about towns that the facts forgot.

When counseling guru Scott Peck wrote that "community is a group that fights gracefully," he overlooked the dynamics of rural, resource-dependent towns in economic transition. The words that Tongass partisans use publicly to persuade each other prickle and burn with righteousness born in an oceanic region of ancient trees, young mountains, and tenuous human outposts. Words like *jobs, ancient forest, fish, endangered species, outsiders,* and *greenies* are lobbed like grenades in the rough-hewn arenas of discourse—fire halls, classrooms, bars, kitchens. Juxtaposed with the pervasive discourse of federal control in a state where freedom is worshipped on an altar of ideology, the war of words over the nation's largest national forest has captured the sentiments of an American public unwilling to submit their trees and taxes to another national sacrifice. The rhetorical blood, however, is shed among Tongass community members engaged in mortal combat over their visions of the good life.

What brings people together out here in the shaggy forest fringes of Southeast Alaska also sets us at odds with each other: beauty, wilderness, profound seclusion. In this sense, the concept of community that perseveres for perhaps seventy-four thousand people spread out over four hundred miles of shredded subarctic archipelago is this: a group that fights to survive, grace or no grace. We fight to establish even the barest niches in a place renowned for bad weather and bellicose temperament. The blind determination needed to sustain life here spills into our rhetorical efforts to attain dreams carved from wilderness. It is an unruly rhetoric that rankles people forced by topography and scarcity to rely on each other as neighbors or suppliers, lovers or friends. Codependent by necessity, we pull against the ties that bind us to each other, lashing out with persuasive volleys meant to justify our lifestyles and visions, only to find that we are inextricably connected. To some, like Bill, our contentious sense of community amounts to torture of the highest order.

In *The Rhetoric*, Aristotle defines rhetoric as "the art of using all available means to persuade." This definition anticipates the language of desperation that accompanied the drastic changes in Haines, Sitka, Ketchikan, and Wrangell in the recent years of mill closures of the 1990s. Residents and politicians did everything they could to convince each other and the nation about the best use of the rain forest, usually within the theme of survival: economic, social, ecological, ideological. The American bard of rhetoric,

Kenneth Burke, in *The Grammar of Rhetoric,* defines such persuasive activity as "the use of words by human agents to form attitudes or to induce actions in other human agents." He describes the range of persuasive devices as "a flat choice between a civilized vocabulary of scientific description and a savage vocabulary of magical incantation." An often volatile mix of Burke's incantations preceded each mill shutdown, followed by quirky, awkward lurches into whatever might come next.

The community and regional discourse before, during, and after the towns' mill closures followed rhetorical themes common to other towns in the real or imagined American frontiers. Early threats of closures were met with a righteous sense of outrage, followed in time by blame, denial, and, finally, capitulation. In my hometown of Haines, the drive to survive propelled citizens' persuasive language and actions as mills went down amid a prolonged and continuing battle for the soul of the Tongass. Long after the closures, swords still rattle over what is best for our forest, our future. As Bill discovered, out here the truth is relative from witness to witness, but, irrespective of the facts, a version may be locked in the public's imagination for years, perhaps generations.

I came to this corner of the remnant American frontier in 1979. For three years I worked with the Forest Service on missions throughout the Tongass. We flew in floatplanes around the vast forest to thin alders on Baranof Island, cut survey lines at Trap Bay on Tenakee Inlet, plant trees in Kake, repair recreational cabins in the West Chichigof Wilderness, carve canoe portages across Admiralty Island. We spread throughout the Tongass, backs bent to the work of the woods, minds reeling with myth.

In the early 1980s, I trolled for king salmon on a power-troller near Glacier Bay until the skipper's bottomless appetite for inebriants drove me to seek safer employment. There was an opening for a newspaper reporter in Haines, a friend shouted to me over the thunderous static of a satellite phone on the Pelican docks. I jumped ship, thinking that a news job could be no more dangerous than pitching drunkenly in the Gulf of Alaska.

I landed in a town built on the premise that eternal timber supplies are a right to those tenacious enough to withstand the rugged lifestyle. The mills pumped millions of dollars into isolated communities throughout the Tongass from the 1950s through the 1980s; they helped build schools, attract service industries, and supply a steady paycheck for locals. The public discourse was largely that of empire builders in a boundless frontier. Even as the mills in the Pacific Northwest began to choke for lack of supply after decades of strip-logging the public forests, mills in Southeast Alaska continued to devour Tongass timber supplied primarily by two fifty-year contracts. Markets had already begun to sag when a coalition of environmentalists, Natives, fishers, local businesses, taxpayer groups, and others gained purchase into some habitat protection with the Tongass Timber Reform Act of 1990. The Haines mill went down that same year, followed three years later by the Alaska Pulp Corporation pulp mill in Sitka, then by Alaska Pulp's sawmill in Wrangell, and finally Louisiana-Pacific's huge Ketchikan pulp operation in 1997. Each closure was characterized by its own rhetorical drama, which had little to do with truth and everything to do with self-preservation.

The decline of the timber industry at the time of my arrival in Haines was beginning to pull down wages and eject workers to other mills and forests. During the same period came tourists and other strangers who, if they weren't passing through, were looking for a home. I, too, came to settle among good folks in an idealized landscape. But the majesty of the scenery could not hide the escalating tension that would soon tear us apart.

As you cruise northward on the Inside Passage, the mountains grow loftier, glaciers become prominent, and the sea narrows into the deepest fjord in North America, called Lynn Canal. Exactly a century prior to my arrival in Southeast Alaska, naturalist John Muir, accompanied by a Presbyterian minister and three Tlingit elders from Wrangell, paddled a dugout canoe up the canal. Muir was eager to meet the fabled Chilkat and Chilkoot tribes who served as the gatekeepers and packers from the tide's edge over the mountains into the interior of Yukon and Alaska. These northern-most Tlingits were renowned for their fabulous artwork and aggressive defense of their homeland, and had mostly kept Europeans at arm's length. They were fascinated, however, by the fiery "Brotherhood of Man" oration issued by the craggy Scotsman upon their meeting in the village of Yendestucke near the mouth of the Chilkat River. In *Travels in Alaska,* when Muir had finished his talk about "the fine foodful country" God had given them, the shaman stood and offered this reply:

> It has always seemed to me while trying to speak to traders and those seeking goldmines that it was like speaking to a person across a broad stream that was running fast over stones and making so loud a noise that scarce a single word could be heard. But now, for the first time, the Indian and the white man are on the same side of the river, eye to eye, heart to heart.

A scant three miles from the portentous meeting site, a Presbyterian mission was erected in the early 1880s on a pasturelike isthmus called Deishu, or "end of the trail," by the local Tlingits. The Haines mission was named for a national officer of the presbytery who never made it to Alaska. Shortly after the turn of the century, half a dozen canneries sprang up in the area to process the salmon that returned in staggering numbers to spawn in the Chilkoot and Chilkat Rivers. The Klondike gold rush of 1898 brought thousands of dreamers up the Lynn Canal, but few of them paused at the bucolic Haines mission on their way to Skagway, a dozen miles farther. A decade later, Haines began to take on the appearance of a community with a future when the army built its first permanent Alaskan post, Fort William H. Seward. Not until the first full-scale sawmill was built by John Schnabel in 1939, however, did locals secure a sense of modern economic stability. Located on a point where the Chilkat River met seawater, the new mill was in view of the village site where John Muir won the approval of his Tlingit hosts. The mill would eventually become the mainstay of the town, a symbol of its entrance into the twentieth century and into regional and global timber markets. But the stability of the markets and the mill proved illusory.

After the Schnabel Lumber Company mill burned down in 1961, a number of small, portable mills kept processing lumber into cants until owner John Schnabel opened a new mill a few miles away at a deepwater port in Lutak Inlet. Cliff and Henry Reeves built a second mill—Alaska Forest Products (AFP)—at the original mill site on Jones Point; it opened in 1965. The new Schnabel mill opened in 1967. Both mills processed Sitka spruce and western hemlock logs brought up the canal from clear-cuts throughout the Tongass National Forest sprawling to the south of Haines. Faltering markets in Japan and Korea combined with higher prices for Tongass lumber led to the closure of AFP in 1976. The Schnabel Lumber Company, too, was dizzied by the roller-coaster economics of unstable foreign markets and an uncertain supply of logs. The "allowable cut," or timber supply offered by the Forest Service, became the focus of attention among community members enmeshed in a discourse about their particular visions of the future.

How many millions of board feet of rain forest does it take to keep a town alive? This became the key question asked by Haines residents who first faced the brunt of poor prices and dwindling supplies in the 1970s. Timber supply expectations became the subject of concern in 1972 when the AFP mill began to falter. Manager Tom Coiner, in the *Chilkat Valley News (CVN)*, blamed the slowdowns and temporary closures on the fact that the "easy timber" in the Tongass had been harvested, leaving the more expensive hillside stands. He also pointed to a previously reliable Japanese market now unwilling to pay the price for Alaskan lumber, forcing AFP to sell cants to British Columbia. "There is not enough timber locally for both mills under the present allowable cut," he complained. Something would have to give.

Since the establishment of the first Schnabel mill in the 1930s, locals had grown secure in their perception of Haines as a mill town. By the 1970s, the forest products industry was by far the largest employer in Haines: the related workforce amounted to nearly 70 percent of the adult population. Before the mill closures of the 1990s, Haines's relationship to the Tongass differed from that of other mill towns inasmuch as the community is surrounded by 229,000 acres of state land, some of which has been available for logging. Ketchikan, Sitka, and Wrangell mills, on the other hand, subsisted solely on Tongass timber harvest. Even today, John Schnabel speaks proudly of his company's restraint in keeping local cuts out of the town's view; the residents of other communities live with extensive deforestation as a visual backdrop. Nonetheless, nearly all timber processed by Haines mills at the time of their decline in the 1970s and 1980s came from the Tongass.

The Haines mills were also unique to the extent that, unlike mills elsewhere in the Tongass National Forest, their timber supply was not assured by long-term contracts. Wood came in when they could find it. According to Bob Tracy, Tongass regional forester at the time, of the 450 million board feet available for sustained yield harvest in the Tongass, 300 million were committed to Ketchikan Pulp Company and Sitka's Alaska Pulp Corporation, leaving the remainder open to bid. When U.S. District Judge James A. von der Heydt ruled in December 1975 that the massive clear-cuts on Prince of Wales Island violated federal law, the small mills panicked. "It is economically impossible to thin selectively in Southeast," said AFP manager Ed Lapeyri in the *CVN*. "You have to take everything. High lead logging requires clear-cutting, and most sales in Southeast require high lead. . . . We must find a way to maintain the economic base of our country without destroying the environmental habitat." A month later, AFP closed its doors forever.

The AFP closure prompted greater interest in local forestlands. At the time of AFP's demise, the timber shipped to Haines came solely from Hetta Inlet, a remarkable stand of old-growth Tongass trees four hundred miles away on south Prince of Wales Island, near the village of Hydaburg. The massive logs were corralled into huge rafts, then pulled north by a tugboat past four other mills. A small, independent sawmill in Klawock operated less than fifty miles from the site. Fearing a diminishing log supply, Schnabel began calling for a sustained allowable cut from the state lands closer to home. In a 1976 treatise published in the local newspaper under the title "The Forest Industry and the Future of Haines," Schnabel sounded the clarion call for a local harvest plan: "As owner and manager [for its forests], it is the State's responsibility to effect a harvesting plan in the Chilkat Valley. It is the industry's suggestion that the Chilkat Valley be offered to the industry as a management unit much like the industry in the Tongass National Forest operates." The mill could only be sustained, he argued, if a long-term contract arrangement similar to the ones procured by the Ketchikan and Sitka mills was forged between the state and the Haines mill.

Schnabel's declaration gave local millworkers an issue around which they could rally. It also initiated the unraveling of a community identity that for decades had been based on timber processing. After the dramatic tie-breaking vote cast by Vice President Spiro Agnew in the U.S. Senate, the mid–1970s saw a sudden influx of migrants passing through Haines on their way to build the Trans-Alaska Pipeline System in the far north. The population of fifteen

hundred nearly doubled, schoolchildren were packed into inadequate classrooms, families spent the winter in tents and truck
campers. Although many would move on, some stayed and
brought others, thus prompting a gradual erosion of Haines's
insularity. More would come, many of them were entranced by
the beauty of the forest and the abundance of wildlife sustained
within.

But the Haines-area forests are quite different from the great
stands of spruce and hemlock rising from Tongass lands to the
south. A map of our region depicts the Chilkat and Chilkoot
Valleys as narrow slices of green amid an immense convolution of
rock and ice. Unlike the furious froth that roars from glaciers balanced atop the enclosing peaks, the Chilkat and Chilkoot Rivers
muscle through verdant stands of cottonwood, spruce, and hemlock, many of which represent the greatest trees growing at such a
northerly latitude. Because of the severe winters and shallow soil,
the trees mature slowly to what foresters consider a harvestable
age. Haines trees need a century to reach the size necessary for
sawlogs. The marginal riverine forest provides habitat for brown
and black bears, lynx, beavers, moose, wolves, and the largest single
congregation of bald eagles in the world.

Before they were protected under the Endangered Species Act,
eagles in Haines supplied locals with idle entertainment and gas
money. A pair of talons would fetch a two-dollar bounty. Locals
would collect their "eagle money," then add their talons to a Main
Street barrel that, when it overflowed in spring, was dumped on
the beach, attracting squadrons of eagles to fight over the meager
remains. New people coming to town saw things differently—the
trees, bears, eagles, and the countless salmon runs that attracted
them meant more than the few bucks that could be gained from
stumps or carcasses. The dawning of ecological consciousness in
Haines gave loggers something else to fear besides diminishing

returns from the Tongass. It forced a reckoning that continues to this day.

John Schnabel's call for a long-term timber contract gave rise to community debate that had never before seen the light of a meeting hall. Local millworkers concerned about their jobs reiterated the position that the state should claim its ownership of the forest by allocating timber. According to the May 11, 1978, *CVN*, a small band of residents, organized as Lynn Canal Conservation, turned the ownership argument around to suggest that "as Alaskans, we are co-owners" of the land, thus presenting official habitat concerns for perhaps the first time in the area. When Governor Jay Hammond came to Haines for a hearing in 1978, he was told by Schnabel that "approximately 130 persons were without jobs because timber was not available locally" and that a state sale "must be long enough to assure loan agencies that investment is sound." The "Timber Report," written by a local economic development committee and published in the *CVN*, claimed that "the forests of Haines are overmature and should be harvested to allow for healthy regrowth." A long-term contract would provide a "Working Circle—an uninterrupted fifteen to twenty year timber contract designed in the interest of economy and efficiency.... The Working Circle concept should provide for watershed, wildlife and other ecological concerns" while taking the "first step to economic security." Industry's efforts to equate habitat protection with economic security played well to those whose jobs relied on a timber supply, but only inflamed the opposition.

Disagreements among neighbors became brawls over a few years of mill slowdowns and closures. The camps exchanged rhetorical gunfire over their visions of the future. When words seemed ineffectual, some mill partisans took to smashing windshields, slashing tires, and refusing service at local businesses to the "commie conservationists." Uncertainty about an adequate timber supply sharpened tempers and words. The need for a concrete determination of land use also forced the initiation of a public planning process, resulting in the Haines-Skagway Land Use Plan. For those who had settled here largely to escape government control, the plan was heresy. It did, however, allow for the governor to give the go-ahead for a fifteen-year timber sale contract, calling the annual harvest of 10.2 million board feet with a ten-year extension "a balanced approach." Approval of clear-cutting in the Haines forest did not, however, end the mill's dependence on Tongass timber. Along with the contract in 1979 came Schnabel's announcement in the *CVN* that he had signed a contract with Ketchikan Pulp for another eight million board feet of Tongass timber. This drew further attention from regional conservationists.

As the mill swung back into production, the Juneau-based Southeast Alaska Conservation Council (SEACC) entered the fray when spokesman Leonard Steinberg declared in the *Lynn Canal News* that "our primary concern is for protection of the Chilkat Valley fish, wildlife, and scenic resources, particularly the 3,500 bald eagles which show up there every winter. . . . SEACC is not opposed to logging in the Chilkat Valley, but this particular timber sale failed to adequately recognize other valuable resources such as salmon and eagles." SEACC filed a lawsuit to halt any contract for long-term logging in the Haines area, citing as examples the fifty-year contracts for Sitka and Ketchikan mills that placed "severe management constraints" on the Forest Service. In an article in the *Lynn Canal News,* Steinberg pointed to "new studies that have shown the need to maintain old-growth forests to maintain deer habitat, but the ability of the Forest Service to do that is pretty limited because of the long-term contract they entered into years ago before this new information was known about."

The rhetorical clash over survival, whether of the human or the ecological community, continued to escalate after the Haines forest contract was reality. Public meetings were packed by millworkers who often shouted down those supporting conservationist views.

The vitriol boiled over with the 1980 passage of the Alaska National Interest Lands Conservation Act (ANILCA), which protected millions of Tongass acres as wilderness. The additional "lockups" in the national forest meant fewer logs shipped to the Haines mill, fewer jobs, and, as the local newspaper saw it, more local paranoia. When the Schnabel Lumber Company closed its doors in October 1980 because of an inadequate supply of timber, tensions over survival further fractured the community. In January 1981, local journalist Jeff Brady editorialized in the *Lynn Canal News:*

> Haines reminded me of a small Southern town in the early 1960s. The South was forced to cope, and eventually learned to cope with and accept desegregation. . . . Haines is merely trying to cope with its own existence, just like every Alaskan town. But in Haines right now existence is looking people right in the face. People get mad easily. They bend the truth to their own satisfaction. Or they accuse others of misinterpreting the truth.

When the SEACC suit against the proposed long-term timber contracts was denied in court, local conservationists took their case to a national court of opinion. Standard-bearers of opposing truths were forced by publicity and changing values to sit at a table together and forge an agreement around a compelling national symbol.

The renewed focus on logging Haines land caught the attention of Colorado's Senator Gary Hart, who suggested that the federal government take extraordinary measures to protect the world-renowned Council Grounds eagle gathering site in the heart of the embattled state forest. Warm upwellings along this stretch of the Chilkat River reduce freezing, which sustains a winter run of chum salmon that may attract as many as four thousand bald eagles and thousands of other birds from as far away as the Columbia Basin, thirteen hundred miles south. A December view of the Council Grounds reveals throngs of powerful birds grappling for fish or waiting hungrily among the spectral mists rising from the Chilkat. An occasional wolf or wolverine may appear on the channeled river flats to seize its share of the winter bounty. Framed by the icy calm of deep winter, the image of thousands of screaming eagles fussing over salmon carcasses attracted attention among the national environmental organizations.

The threat of a federal takeover coupled with a series of Audubon studies showing a significant relationship between eagles and forest health prompted an uneasy alliance among state officials, biologists, local conservationists, and loggers whose goal was to work it out in favor of the birds. Governor Jay Hammond engineered a state moratorium on logging in the area that provided additional incentive for timber officials to resolve the question. An abiding concern over local control of resources resulted in the 1982 formation of the Alaska Chilkat Bald Eagle Preserve, a forty-eight-thousand-acre expanse preserving the biological integrity of the eagles' annual gathering place. In a 1996 address delivered at a bald eagle festival in Haines, Hammond (by then no longer governor) called the agreement to form the preserve a "mission impossible" that turned out to be "a crown jewel in the annals of cooperative resource management."

Ironically, it was the adamant refusal to accept outside control of local resources that forced combatant neighbors to approve the eagle preserve and, one year later, adopt a management plan for the Haines State Forest. Increased resource management, however, failed to quell the controversy about the local mill. Despite Department of Natural Resources commissioner John Sturgeon's assurances that the allowable cut in the Haines forest was part of a "multiple use document," others were dissatisfied with allowances for habitat protection. In the October 4, 1984, *CVN*, Lynn Canal Conservation president Vivian Menaker called it "a timber cutting plan rather than a multiple use plan" and said that the "consideration for fish and other uses are not fair."

In the final analysis, community furor over the timber supply had less to do with protecting habitat than did economics. Depressed market conditions in Alaska and the Pacific Rim pushed the mill over the brink. As the refurbished old Schnabel mill— called Pacific Forest Products in its next incarnation—slowed to a halt in late 1984, tensions in Haines soared. Conservationists were blamed for the reduced supply in the Tongass and in the local forest. As the sole reporter employed by the *Chilkat Valley News* at the time, I witnessed the frustration and denial that bubbled up like lava from the tectonic schism dividing my neighbors from one another. Letters to the editor ran red with rhetorical blood. Those who openly applauded the industry's decline were cast as dissemblers; mill supporters were called anachronistic. In a February 14, 1985, letter to the *CVN* editor, local logger Al Gilliam offered his perspective of the inherent conflicts:

> Many people have been labeled all sorts of things because of a misunderstanding by the public on the true volume of timber here. Public figures actually led smut campaigns against "greenies" in order to bolster their position of apple pie and the American Way. I find it a bit ironic that these same people have supported the largest welfare deal to the logging industry that I have ever heard of. Personally, I'm proud to be a timber faller, and I'm also proud to know the difference between right and wrong. I'd also like to see the industry stand on its own two feet.

Through the remainder of the 1980s, the mill struggled to sustain itself, often pitting neighbor against neighbor in a battle of blame and denial. Former Alaska Forest Products manager Ed Lapeyri took over the mill, called it Chilkoot Lumber, and supplied it largely with logs cut from Prince of Wales Island. Any threats to its survival were met by high-pitched anger from millworkers and their families. In other Southeast Alaska mill closures following Haines's, the tenor of arguments over jobs and habitat grew more shrill as shutdowns loomed ever nearer. When local schoolteacher Richard Buck contacted the state's Department of Environmental Conservation in 1989 about mill emissions, workers paraded down Main Street in public protest. Millhand Richard Phillips carried a sign that said "If the mill dies, Haines dies." The protesters entered the elementary school and demanded to see the teacher. "One man's complaints shouldn't put a lot of people out of work," Phillips told a *CVN* reporter. Within a year, Chilkoot Lumber shut down for the last time. The teacher stayed; the millworkers moved on or found other jobs. Instead of blaming locals, however, the mill owners discovered that timber giant Weyerhauser had schemed to deny the smaller mill its fair share of promised Tongass timber. A successful lawsuit ensued, but the Haines mill's victory was pyrrhic: the doors were closed forever.

The mill attempted to recoup its losses, and local conflicts temporarily flattened out as a new industry swept through Haines. The long arm of Walt Disney reached up the Lynn Canal to select our town for the filming of Jack London's classic tale of northern survival, *White Fang*. Even the cash flow generated in the heyday of Haines's mills couldn't match the money Hollywood pumped in over the winter of 1991. Indeed, the year saw the highest receipts in the town's history.

The early 1990s also brought to Haines the prospects of a massive copper mine, Windy Craggy. Eager to make up for the mill closure, John Schnabel and other development advocates claimed that the mine, located on the Tatshenshini River a hundred miles up the Haines Highway, would provide stability to our town and to the nation. "All this can be accomplished in a few decades," Schnabel wrote to the *CVN* on March 14, 1991, "if we set aside the emotional aspects of debate and through a rational exchange of concerns and ideas find solutions that will enable us to overcome the hurdles in any new major concept. We must do this or perish."

While arguments around the familiar theme of survival cropped up during the Windy Craggy controversy, residents were beginning to see that their existence did not necessarily depend on extraction of raw materials. The growing influx of tourists coming to see the eagle preserve and the surrounding natural beauty pro-vided the economic incentive for a cautious approach to develop-ment. A 1991 *Los Angeles Times* editorial portrayed the copper mine debate as another struggle over our community's identity: "How does a town achieve progress without destroying the things that made people want to live here in the first place?" The answers for Haines residents since Windy Craggy have weighed in favor of tourism and steady residential settlement.

The proposed copper mine became part of the largest protected wilderness in the world, including not only the Tatshenshini-Alsek Wilderness, but also Glacier Bay, Wrangell-St. Elias, and Kluane National Parks. By 1992 the Alaska Chilkat Bald Eagle Preserve Advisory Coucil declared that the preserve provided "habitat for a subsistence, sport, and commercial salmon fishery worth $15–$40 million per year." The council suggested that the bald eagle preserve "propelled the site to one of Alaska's top ten tourist desti-nations." Far from being stable, however, our marriage with tour-ism, fishing, and real estate has raised other questions among locals about our future. Questions about land use planning, resi-dential development, new roads, new mines, and the impact of tourism still prompt heated debate about our ultimate survival. Concerns over allowable cut have been redirected to the parade of newcomers—gawkers and speculators—eager for a piece of the Alaskan myth.

While he was writing his novel *Alaska,* the late James Michener once said to me during an interview in Haines that "the world will soon come to this place to rediscover what it once was." As visitors continue to stream into our community in record numbers, residents still grapple with reshaping our identity. The truth is still just as hard to discern, and just as maligned as Bill claimed before he left town. In one of the first articles Bill wrote after leaving Haines, published in the *St. Paul (Minn.) Ledger,* he said that Haines was "hell" because of the "impossibility of reason—because of a culture that celebrates dissent in defiance of the law, historical fact and any coherent value system outside of self-interest." Like the other former mill towns of the Tongass, we are left to forge new relationships with ourselves and the rugged land we choose to call home.

A hundred and twenty years after John Muir crossed the cultural river to his Tlingit brothers, Haines people still strain to hear what we have to say to each other over the roaring glacial chasms between us. This place—like much of Alaska—has drawn so many fiercely individualistic folks together that we sometimes have trouble agreeing on the weather. But the one thing we can all agree on is that tourists in growing numbers will continue to toddle off their ships and out of their motor homes to squint at the stunning spectacle: four mountain ranges, two rivers meeting the sea, and a forest that is home to grizzly and black bears, wolves, moose, goats, porcupines, five species of salmon, and attendant squadrons of bald eagles.

It was market demand, after all. Following the prolonged decay of the mills, our community has lurched into the next (and most obvious) means to survive. Especially after the formation of the eagle preserve, locals are forced to agree that we live in a place that outsiders will pay good money to see. John Schnabel opened an RV park; Ed Lapeyri bought the best motel in town. Whether they are in a bus creeping up on jaw-dropping numbers of eagles or peering out of a chopper clattering past sheer rock towers rising out of stark ice fields, visitors stare, starved for experiences in what may well be the last place that America once was.

DANIEL HENRY *teaches high school English, debate, and drama in Haines, Alaska. His essays and poetry have appeared in* Northern Lights, Connotations, The Bloomsbury Review, Explorations, Chronicle of Community, The Redneck Review of Literature, *and* Undercurrents, *among other publications. He has received grants from the National Endowment for the Humanities and the Alaska Humanities Forum to complete a book on the rhetoric of American land use conflict. Henry lives with his wife, Jeannie, and son, Charlie, on the roadless side of Mud Bay in a house they built with the help of good friends.*

western sandpipers, *Katherine M. Hocker*

The Independents: Hope All Over

TIM BRISTOL

To fully appreciate what it's like to be an independent wood products business owner in Southeast Alaska, you first have to know a little about the Ketchikan Pulp and Lumber Company (KPC), the staggering, but not quite fallen, giant of the Tongass timber industry.

A good place to start would be at the mill site itself, located four miles north of the city of Ketchikan at Ward Cove. For over forty years, the mill turned trees from the Tongass National Forest into high-quality dissolving pulp, a versatile product used in everything from diapers to explosives, cellophane to food filler. In a way, this mill ruled Ketchikan—and most of southern Southeast Alaska, for that matter. It was Ketchikan's largest private employer and nearby Prince of Wales Island's as well. On adjacent Annette Island, KPC's Metlakatla sawmill provided nearly all of the town's good-paying, year-round jobs. The closure of the mill launched skyrocketing unemployment, now hovering near 80 percent for the small Native community.

KPC provided more than jobs at the mills and in the woods. Its millions of dollars in paychecks, contracts, and investments coursed through the entire economy of the region. From bush air carriers to grocery stores, business owners came to count on KPC. The mill also sponsored baseball teams and community functions like picnics and parades. Its dominance, its reach into almost everyone's life, made Ketchikan the ultimate mill town.

Several generations of Ketchikaners did their time at the mill, and quite a few ended up liking the hard, dirty, dangerous work—or maybe it was the paychecks. For many, a summer job became a full-time job, and a couple of years at KPC became a couple of decades.

Wayne Weihing is one of those people. He spent twenty years as a maintenance man who worked his way up through the union to a supervisory position at the Ward Cove mill. As he often points out, he has "walked though every square inch of that mill." And worked just about every job, from driving log bronc to fixing the hog fuel burner. As he looks back, Weihing recalls that danger and discomfort were "a part of the job description." But thanks to his union, he was well paid and backed up with good benefits. In the mid-1980s, Weihing found himself in the thick of the fight with management over wage and benefit concessions. As one of the leaders of the union, he tasted bitter defeat when the workers caved in to management threats that the mill would close if its demands weren't met. You can hear anger in Weihing's voice whenever he speaks of KPC. Over time, he became one of Southeast Alaska's most vocal critics of both mill owners and the Forest Service, the government agency that provided KPC with huge amounts of Tongass timber—about 190 million board feet annually.

Despite his animosity toward KPC, Weihing is the first to admit that the big mill was a large part of his life and the lives of many of his peers. As he drives by in his big pickup, he can't help but shake his head—the scene at Ward Cove is so different now. The big, red-brick buildings are being demolished, the waste pits capped and cleaned. Smokestacks lie dormant. The air smells good. All that's left running at one of Alaska's largest industrial sites is a sawmill.

To get a little more perspective on KPC's hegemony, head downtown and grab a stool at the Fo'c'sle bar. *Evergreen* magazine, a pro-industry publication, sits in the rack, free for the taking. The Fo'c'sle isn't the friendliest bar in town, but it's worth stopping in since it still has a little authenticity and a lot of history. Ask the bartender about the thousands of dollars kept in a cigar box behind the bar. Having cash on hand guaranteed that timber dollars would flow into the bar even faster than the beer and whiskey flowed out. Loggers in from the camps often didn't have bank accounts, and the owners of the Fo'c'sle, with their box full of money, made it as easy as possible for workers to wash away the aches and pains of a hard week in the woods.

But even the toughest old-timers won't deny that the days of big timber in the Tongass are nearly over. Ward Cove and the Fo'c'sle are glaring reminders. Day by day, piece by piece, the mill is falling to the wrecking ball. And downtown, what was once one of Ketchikan's toughest bars, full of hickory-shirted, chain-smoking, hard-drinking loggers, is now half filled with tourists in plastic ponchos.

Still, the pride prevails. And the anger lingers. A bumper sticker on the mirror behind the bar asks "Do you work for a living or are you an environmentalist?"

In addition to the pervasive timber culture in Ketchikan, there's the pressure from well-moneyed, long-established business owners to attract another large-scale "smokestack" industry for Ketchikan. Getting all those laid-off pulp mill employees back to work will be extremely difficult. Pulp mill jobs—which in many cases paid $45,000 to the average working stiff with no more than a high school degree—don't really exist in America anymore. The push for more blue-collar manufacturing jobs will continue in Ketchikan, spurred on by those who hold power and, for the most part, who tied their fortunes to what is now commonly referred to as the "old" timber industry. Any new wood products industry jobs will require more skills, greater flexibility in order to deal with volatile timber markets, and, in many cases, some entrepreneurial flair.

This transition has already occurred in other timber-dependent regions of the country, but for now, Alaska lags behind. In one more way, Alaska really is the last frontier.

There have always been other players in the Tongass timber industry—they've just been in the shadows of the big mills. For this small, diverse, and notoriously individualistic group, the end of an era marked by the closure of KPC may be cause for cautious optimism. Lost in the smoke and the heat of the Tongass timber wars were these independent timber operators. According to a recent report from the Southeast Regional Timber Industry Task Force, there are forty-one independent timber businesses operating in the forests of Southeast Alaska right now. Those forty-one cut a combined total of 99 million board feet of timber per year. For reference, remember that it takes about 10,000 board feet to build the average two-story, three-bedroom home. Compare that 99 million board feet to the 120 million board foot annual appetite of Ketchikan Pulp's two remaining sawmills, add in the 160 to 200 million board feet of timber that used to go to the pulp mill every year, and you start to get an idea why many of the small sawmill owners shed no tears for Ketchikan Pulp.

Mike Sallee's place is only a twenty-minute skiff ride from the pulp mill, but it's a world apart. A lifetime Ketchikan resident and the owner of a small sawmill, Sallee is one of those rare people who was able to speak out against KPC logging yet avoid the dreaded preservationist label. In a place where one's years "in country" are worn like a badge and folks are always attempting to prove who's more Alaskan, Mike Sallee is the real deal.

Sallee, as he explains it, "works in a broad spectrum of resource development jobs." He long-lines for black cod, works as a commercial diver harvesting geoducks and sea cucumbers for Asian seafood markets, and runs his little mill on Gravina Island, just across Tongass Narrows from Ketchikan. Sallee says that he and his brother Dave between them have "held just about every job in the timber industry."

The fifty-one-year-old Sallee says he learned at a young age that working for the big timber outfits wasn't what he was looking for over the long term:

> I started out working for two years as a choker setter
> at Fire Cove and Neets Bay on Revilla Island. It was a
> long time ago but I do remember quite a few hot,
> sweltering days. I remember the wet, clammy days,
> too. Superimposed on both kind of days were the
> buggy days. It wasn't much fun.

A choker setter is the low man in the hierarchical world of the timber industry. He's usually a young guy with lots of energy. Choker setters run the steep slopes, attaching cables to the fallen logs. They signal to the rigging slinger when the cable is cinched (choked) around the log. The cables snake up the slope to a landing where a machine known as a yarder collects the wood. The yarder is a mobile tower to which the cables are attached. The logs travel up the cables to a central location below the tower. For Sallee, two years of crashing though logging slash, dodging logs, and battling bugs was enough. He decided quickly that he was more interested in sawing wood than in logging:

> I've been sawing wood for a long time, although I
> don't remember doing anything for sale when I first
> started. I started out working at my brother's mill. He
> was part owner, but both he and the other guy were
> busy logging, so I started . . . rolling logs onto that
> sawmill and started cutting one-by-fours, one after
> another. I don't remember if it was a high-quality log
> or not, but I sure turned that piece of wood into a lot
> a sawdust along with these weird little boards.

His first sawmilling experience may not have been entirely successful, but Sallee was hooked. He's been running his own mill for nineteen years now, usually working for friends and acquaintances. He operates what's known in the industry as a mobile dimension mill, a small, movable, circular sawmill that can be found in front yards and cleared lots all over Southeast Alaska:

> The idea was they could be packed back into the forest or a remote location and turn trees into lumber. The mill has two independent blades. The first pass cuts a piece of the tree into a slab. Then after that slab is cut, with each pass of the blade you're slicing boards. The real strength of this mill is [that] it can saw any type of wood from a twenty-foot diameter tree down to a tiny thing.

He cuts a pittance, forty thousand board feet a year, probably equaling the average amount that breaks loose from a log raft as it's towed to the KPC sawmill. Actually, it just may be Sallee who ends up sawing some of those wayward logs:

> Beach salvage logs are a major part of my operation, but I guess I'm getting a bit into the renegade stage since I don't have a salvage permit. It sounds like easy pickings, but there are a finite number of quality sawlogs out there. A lot of times you see a log on the beach, lots of logs on the beach, and you're thinking there's enough wood [lying] there for several houses, but then you cut into them and most of them have defects. I guess my dream log would be a three-foot-diameter, eighty-foot-long yellow or red cedar that's totally sound.

Gathering wood is not a high-tech operation. Sallee hops in the skiff, keeps his eyes peeled and his axe handy. When he locates a good-looking log, he takes a cut out of it, bends over, and breathes deeply, hoping to detect the scent of yellow cedar, the most valuable of the four tree types found in Southeast Alaska. A lot of grunt work later, it arrives back at his sawmill. It isn't a fancy business, but it keeps Sallee busy. He cuts cedar into siding, mills construction-grade lumber out of spruce and hemlock, saws logs into stair treads and windowsills, cuts wood for decking and doorways.

"It's mostly a word-of-mouth business," he says. "I've sold wood to about seventy-five people throughout the years, and most folks are repeat customers."

Sallee not only provides an alternative vision of timber use of the Tongass, he backs up his beliefs with low-key activism. He serves on the board of directors of the local conservation group, the Tongass Conservation Society—not the most popular bunch in Alaska's top timber town.

"I'm not sure how I ended up going to TCS meetings. I think I was more interested in knowing what was happening rather than making some political statement," says Sallee. "I don't feel particularly adept at public debate or public speaking. It's like you need a drill sergeant in this country if you're going to get yourself heard and get things done."

Whether he considers himself an environmentalist or not, there's no denying that Sallee has a strong conservation ethic:

> Even when I was working out at Fire Cove all those years ago, back when you didn't hear any kind of environmental talk, I remember one of the hook tenders mentioning that the industry was not operating on a sustained yield basis. . . . That got me thinking. I also worked on an itinerant produce boat as a teenager. We went around delivering fresh produce all over, so I got to see quite a bit of country. As I've gone back to a lot of these places, I've seen them changed into major tree

farms. I was also an avid hunter as a teenager, and a lot of those places just don't have the wildlife anymore.

So how does a man who makes his living from wood get involved with a conservation group?

"I don't have a problem with logging as a practice," says Sallee. "It's a question of scale. When corporations log, they change the whole face of the land."

There are a few more folks like Sallee around Ketchikan, but it's still the stronghold of industrial-scale loggers—not just Louisiana-Pacific but Alaska Native corporations as well. Native corporation logging is so extensive that the Forest Service has actually erected signs denoting where federal cutting ends and the still larger Native land clear-cuts begin.

Despite all the pro-timber sentiment, Ketchikan remains somewhat insulated from the excesses of the industry it loves so much. If you want to capture the essence of the Tongass timber industry—its blood and guts, the sounds and smells—you need to climb on a bush plane and get out of Ketchikan. Fifteen miles away lies a landscape of sawdust and stumps, where the industry's past and its future come together. While you're traveling the thousands of miles of logging road on Prince of Wales Island, you have the opportunity to visit many more sawmill owners, people like Pete Smith and his wife, Valery White. You might get a chance to talk with Ginny Tierney and Elaine Price, the movers and shakers of logging camps that turned into towns. And if you've got the gumption to keep going after the road ends, you might consider stopping by and sharing a cup of coffee with folks like Joe Sebastian and Joan Kautzer. Or maybe fisherman Don Hernandez or storekeeper Sylvia Geraghty—people who have battled Ketchikan Pulp for years. Ketchikan is a good place to start educating yourself about timber issues, but you need to spend some time on Southeast

Alaska's largest, most heavily logged island in order to comprehend more fully the industry's problems and its promise.

The short flight to Craig, Prince of Wales Island's biggest community at just over two thousand people, is truly awe-inspiring. It's hard to believe so much forest could disappear in forty years. Most folks sit back and relax on the plane, the best way to get on and off "the rock," as the island is sometimes called. But it always seems like there are one or two people on board who aren't from the area. They're easy to spot because they tend to stare out at the landscape below, some shaking their heads, perhaps wondering where all the forest went.

Once you're in Craig, one of your first stops should be to see Jerry Jones, the owner of J and M Salvage. All it takes is a few good questions to get him warmed up to the subject of the timber industry and the Forest Service. Once Jones gets involved with an issue, he's like a pit bull: he bites down hard and doesn't let go. There is no easy conversation with this man, no happy chitchat. Jones challenges you, questioning your assertions and assumptions. Bring up environmental issues and he'll often frown. He has a strong conservation ethic and has been a passionate and powerful advocate for a smaller, more sustainable timber industry on Prince of Wales Island, but he is not an environmentalist. Still, conservationists who spend time on the ground, especially in timber communities, believe many other loggers feel like Jones. They know things have to change, but they either dislike or distrust environmentalists—maybe both. A man like Jones serves as a bridge, helping people of differing viewpoints come together, coaxing them to focus on what they have in common, not what separates them.

Jones, who has been in Southeast Alaska for over a decade and in the timber industry for twenty-five years, started out with big outfits like Silver Bay and Phoenix Logging, subcontractors to the Sitka and Ketchikan pulp mills. Working the big logging shows, living the camp life, made Jones good money, but he wanted to be his own boss. After witnessing firsthand the waste associated with the road-building and clear-cutting operations of Ketchikan Pulp, Jones realized there was money to be made cleaning up the giant's mess:

> I knew I could make money because there was so
> much waste, so much good wood just left behind to
> rot. Now I just go back into the units highgraded by
> KPC, clean up the logs left behind, and export them.
> I was able to salvage twenty log trucks full of timber
> this year alone from units that had already been
> logged. What I'm doing here is further utilizing the
> resource. Talk about value-added—this is the ultimate
> in value-added. I'm getting value from something
> most people think is worthless.

Although Jones depends on KPC's excess, he has no love for the company, or for the agency responsible for managing the timber program.

"As I got into business for myself, I became a lot more aware of the political situation, the roadblocks that kept me from getting wood. The Forest Service nearly got rid of the small sales program for local timber operators," says Jones, ticking off his complaints with the agency:

> Then they got rid of green sheet sales where a person
> could go out and pick their wood. The Forest Service
> cruised it, and then you went and bought and logged
> it. Even today the local demand is probably only 3 or 4
> million board feet, and the Forest Service is barely fill-
> ing the demand. For so many years KPC tied up all the
> Forest Service resources. They were the big bully on
> the block.

Jones is still waiting to see how much things have really changed here on the island. For a long time, Prince of Wales has been a KPC colony, and Jones knows the old ways will die hard. Under KPC's long-term contract with the Forest Service, the mill was to receive 8.25 billion board feet of timber over fifty years. Most of that wood came from Prince of Wales Island. There are over two thousand miles of logging roads there, and tens of thousands of acres of clear-cuts on public lands, along with many thousands more on adjacent private lands. It's almost impossible to stand anywhere on this third-largest island in the United States and not see the impact of industrial logging.

Jones's skepticism about the Forest Service and its ability to change is well founded. The Forest Service plans to sell hundreds of millions of board feet of Tongass timber in the next several years, but hardly any of it is tailored to the needs of small operators. With the pulp mill closed and local demand only a few million board feet a year, Jones wonders where all this wood is supposed to go:

> Look, I believe this forest is big enough to accommo-
> date all of us who want to really live here. I also believe
> that the forest belongs to everyone and we all should
> be treated equally. But the small, local businessman
> has not been treated equally. Look at all the big tim-
> ber operators left in Southeast Alaska. They're getting
> handouts. I never got a handout for my business.

While they may not quite be "handouts," Jones is correct when he asserts that the large-scale operations, regardless of their environmental and economic track records, continue to get most of the breaks. For example, Steve Seley, a timber industry maverick, just secured a $4 million guaranteed loan from the U.S. Department of Agriculture. Seley has pledged to commit to the concept of value-added, the process of adding stages of processing to the wood here in Southeast Alaska. Each step—kiln drying, sawing, resawing, and possibly even finished-product manufacture—extracts more of the potential value from the wood and presumably employs more people for each piece of wood worked. The goal is to capture for Tongass timber the jobs and revenue that traditionally have been created in overseas markets. Seley also has stated publicly that he doesn't want to build roads and clear-cut. He says he would like to move his operations toward selective cutting methods and rely heavily on helicopters, which can pluck individual trees, or small groups of trees, out of the forest below. It's a more environmentally friendly, albeit much more expensive, way to log in the Tongass. All these promises won him unprecedented support from the region's chief conservation organization, the Southeast Alaska Conservation Council (SEACC).

"The goal is to harvest timber within the region, manufacture it within our region, and make it available for Alaskans," says Seley. "Once we do that, our industry is going to get the support it needs."

Now SEACC and Seley will have to figure out whether they can live with each other. Seley says he hopes to avoid logging in sensitive areas of the forest; SEACC says it will try to stay out of Seley's way as much as possible.

Some who have watched Seley throughout the years remain skeptical about his long-term commitment to a value-added sawmill and manufacturing facility. Still, one has to be impressed with his new Ketchikan facility. "I know I've got things to prove to some folks out there," says Seley. "This is for the long term; this is my dream. This is the last time I'm starting over."

Then there's Silver Bay logging, the old Alaska Pulp Company logging contractor. Silver Bay secured itself a long-term, low-interest loan from the state of Alaska in exchange for reopening a sawmill in Wrangell. Silver Bay's boss, longtime logger Dick Buhler, is a cagey businessman who not only has survived, but has thrived for years in a harsh Southeast Alaskan business climate. In his comments on an old Forest Service timber sale plan, which included helicopter logging to minimize road building, Buhler wrote: "Helicopter logging is a joke, please remove all proposed helicopter units from this sale." But last year, Silver Bay was able to coax a $400,000 loan from the city of Juneau in order to build, of all things, a huge helicopter hangar.

And Frank Age, owner of Pacific Rim Cedar in Wrangell, was able to convince his city council to front him money to bid on Forest Service timber. Armed with other people's money, Age has been an active buyer of Prince of Wales Island timber sales—sales that Jerry Jones thinks should be scaled down and set aside for people running wood products businesses on the island.

Actually, Jones is right: there was at least one "handout," and it was a big one. It went to none other than KPC. After a period of long and tortuous negotiations between Louisiana-Pacific and the U.S. Department of Justice, a deal was struck, and it amounted to a closeout of KPC's long-term contact. In exchange for shutting the mill and giving up its sweetheart deal with the federal government, KPC received three hundred million board feet of timber and $143 million in contract claim damages. It was a tough pill to swallow for folks like Jones, who believes KPC has actually stolen timber from the public throughout the years, but if it means they're really gone, it's probably worth the price.

As he talks about the future of the timber industry and of his island home, Jones wavers between hope and skepticism. He's seriously thinking about buying himself a small sawmill, hoping the closure of KPC will free up Forest Service resources:

> I think we'll have to wait and see if the government is
> going to be a help or continue to be a hindrance. They
> need to make some more land available. It's too ex-
> pensive to lease or buy land, and there are very few
> places you can go to set up any kind of timber opera-
> tion. The government could also consider low-interest

loans for businesses already here that may be thinking about expanding. Maybe that money could come in the form of low-interest loans, with the money tied to a job target. Another thing they could do is change the way they offer timber. So many of the sales are too large or too far away and have too much road building for someone like me.

There are plenty of challenges and changes in store for Prince of Wales, but Jones says he plans to hang around and see what happens: "I expect to stick around as long as I can make money, and I've always been able to make money in the timber industry. Besides that, I love getting value out of things that some consider worthless. I get a lot of satisfaction out of that. I also get to work outdoors and set my own schedule and keep a lot more of the money I make, since I do all the work."

In contrast to his high, if cautious, hopes for the Prince of Wales Island timber industry, Jones worries about the rest of the economy:

> Most of the Native corporation timber is gone, and I have no idea what they're going to do next. And everyone's into tourism, but I can't see why anyone would come to an area that's already been logged off. Although there are tourists coming here, I think a lot of the opportunities have already been lost. You're fighting through a jungle in the few inaccessible places or you're driving a gravel road. I also think we're going to see a pretty serious restriction in our hunting opportunities due to loss of habitat.

But Jones is a can-do kind of guy, so talk of failure never lasts long: "I guess the bottom line is, despite all the obstacles, there's a lot of opportunity here that just doesn't exist anywhere else."

The unique thing about Prince of Wales Island, at least from an island-bound, mountain-straddled Southeast Alaskan's standpoint, is the road network. Just about every place else in Southeast, the road ends before your trip really begins, but not here. Prince of Wales is ribboned with over two thousand miles of road—about fourteen hundred of them considered drivable. You can drive north for a long time, pulling off on hundreds of side roads. Those roads lead to hundreds more—a spiderweb of gravel spurs that usually dead-end at the bottom of a clear-cut.

One place worth checking out is Coffman Cove, a big logging camp on the east coast of the island. Coffman, with a population of somewhere around 260 people, was established in the 1960s by Ketchikan Pulp and served as one of its major logging camps and road-building hubs. In 1989 the camp decided to incorporate and become a small city. Now the little town, which depended almost entirely on KPC, wonders if it can survive. One person who thinks it can is the mayor, Elaine Price. She has ideas—lots of ideas. They tumble from her lips as she drives her pickup around town, showing off its potential. Where the untrained eye sees a pit filled with black water, the ugly remains of an old oil tank farm, Price sees prime real estate being freed up for a new use. A bare spot on the beach is the soon-to-be-completed site for a new hydraulic boat lift. Across the cove from "downtown" is the future home of a new boat maintenance and storage facility. Price also has ideas for small sawmilling operations, a furniture plant, and, possibly, a log home kit manufacturer.

There are at least a dozen more projects she's tracking. A new community center and ferry service for Coffman Cove are two of her high priorities. Although Price is only on the payroll half-time, she'll drop everything to give a visitor the sales job. Whether you're a serious business owner or the most reluctant tire-kicker (or even the occasional environmentalist), Price is proud to take you around town. Her focus is on the future, and her pitch is always punctuated with hope.

If Price can secure just a few of those economic development projects for her beleaguered town, she'll be able to retire from office a hero. These are, without a doubt, the toughest times ever faced by this community. Ketchikan Pulp was, and still is, Coffman Cove, and KPC is closed. The mill still has two years of timber nearby that its owners plan to cut and ship to their sawmill in Ketchikan, but after that, no one knows if the company will keep much more than a skeleton crew in town. Most aren't very bullish on their future with KPC. The signs of decline are everywhere. Nearly new yarders, worth hundreds of thousands of dollars, are being cut up for scrap. Plenty of pink slips have already been handed out. Families have moved away. Even the Forest Service, which has never shown a penchant for downsizing, recently closed its local staff bunkhouse.

It's true that almost all the people living and working in Coffman Cove came from someplace else, just like the rest of the population of Alaska. Many of them grew up with the timber industry in Oregon and Washington. Picking up, starting over, and following the work is a way of life they are familiar with. But KPC offered them something more: a home base, steady employment, and a sense of security. True, the KPC empire on Prince of Wales was built on the assumption that the American public would continue to hand over its money and trees, but that kind of big-picture thinking is far removed from the day-to-day work in the woods. KPC gave these folks good jobs in a great place, and now that's gone.

The funny thing is, most of the timber workers don't blame conservationists for their problems. While most are of the mind that the typical urbanite "greenie" wouldn't know the difference between a hemlock and a spruce (and they're probably right), they know there's truth to the environmental arguments. Ketchikan Pulp got away with too much for too long, and it finally caught up with them. Most waver between gratitude and anger when it comes to KPC, but here, unlike in Ketchikan, where too many still spend their time posturing and pointing fingers, people are busy getting on with the future. Today.

"I know they're gone," says Price about KPC as she bumps the truck over ruts in the road. "But a lot of us want to stay here. It's our home. We don't really want to grow here in Coffman Cove. We just don't want to die."

A forty-five minute drive farther north is another logging camp, this one abandoned by KPC. Whale Pass is now populated by an eclectic blend of lodge owners, retirees, independent timber operators, and assorted hangers-on who pick up work with KPC whenever they can. Whale Pass is where you can find Pete Smith and Val White. If you're looking for a profile of the do-it-yourself Alaskan pioneer type, take a picture of Pete and his family.

Smith and White own Wales Waterworks, a small custom-cut sawmill operation that's gaining a reputation for quality work. Smith cuts roughly fifty thousand board feet of timber a year and sells it to customers as far away as Hawaii and New York. He mills mostly red and yellow cedar. Custom boat builders, who love the rot-resistant properties of cedar, have proven to be some of Smith's best customers. Smith and White, who started the business in 1992, have wholly embraced the value-added concept. When conservationists began the search for a constructive alternative to large-scale, industrial road building and logging, they ended up finding Smith and White.

"I could make a lot of money, I guess, from exporting round logs, but I choose not to sell any unprocessed timber. I take a lot of pride in processing all my timber," says Smith. "We go through several stages of processing, from cutting down the tree to milling it and resawing it. We end up marketing a product that doesn't need any more manufacturing. We produce things like siding, boat lumber, and finished flooring and decking."

One thing that immediately strikes you when you sit down to talk with Smith and White is how quiet they are. Yet anyone involved with resource development issues in these parts has heard of Pete Smith, and probably Val White as well. The two of them have been tireless advocates for protection of the remaining old-growth timber around their village—especially since so much is already gone.

"Old growth is a one-shot deal, and once it's cut, it's cut," says Smith:

> Old growth provides the higher quality wood fiber that isn't going to be reproduced for another five hundred years. It's a finite resource. I have absolutely no market for a second-growth, wide-grained tree. Old growth is only here once in our lifetime, and cutting it too fast endangers our future. I'm basically getting this thing set up to pass it along to my kids. I want them to have the same opportunities I had, to live this lifestyle and carry on in my shoes if they like.

White, following up on her husband's comments, criticizes the Forest Service timber management policy, which calls for cutting the area's timber every hundred years.

"Trying to manage forests around here on a one hundred-year rotation is a ridiculous idea," she says. "Maybe you can do that in Louisiana or Texas with a pine tree plantation, but you can't do that in Southeast Alaska."

Walking around their homestead, it's hard not be amazed at this couple's energy and talent. They have a huge garden, which they believe to be one of the largest on Prince of Wales Island.

They're also the proud owners of "Godzilla" and "Son of Godzilla," two army transport trucks they use to yard and haul their timber. Smith is constructing a new truck storage and repair shop as well as a new house. The family also generates their own electricity with a small hydroelectric system on a nearby creek. And for his next project, Smith hopes to tear apart and rebuild a 1920s-vintage log yarder; he needs it to get to a stand of timber he recently purchased from the state.

That's enough to keep anyone busy, even this family. Yet they always manage to find the time to send in comments on timber sales, to oppose bad resource legislation, to attend meetings, and to spread the word on conservation issues in their neighborhood.

"Oh, part of it is our own selfish interest," says Smith. "But it's also the right thing to do."

One thing is certain: the answers to the difficult questions surrounding Tongass timber management aren't in some politician's head or government report. The best ideas, the credible, doable solutions, are coming together out there in the communities. Maybe that great idea is taking shape right now, right there in Whale Pass, in the mind of a man hunched over a sawmill. Or perhaps someone is dreaming up the answers while cruising timber in an old clearcut. And maybe, just maybe, consensus is being crafted in the KPC cookhouse at Coffman Cove.

In Southeast Alaska, there's hope all over the place.

TIM BRISTOL works as a grassroots organizer for the Southeast Alaska Conservation Council, a coalition of seventeen conservation organizations, headquartered in Juneau. Before coming to SEACC in 1995, he lived in Anchorage, where he worked as an organizer at the Alaska Center for the

Environment and as an editor and reporter at the Anchorage Press. *Born and raised on the banks of the Niagara River in North Tonawanda, New York, Bristol moved to Alaska to escape the environmental hazards of Love Canal, contaminated fish, and Buffalo-style chicken wings. He studied journalism at Buffalo State College and writes for* Native Americas *magazine, published by Akwekon Press at Cornell University.*

bumblebee on cow parsnip, *Richard Carstensen*

Forest Management:
You Can't Stand Still

STEWART ALLEN

The wheel is turning and you can't slow down,
You can't let go and you can't hold on,
You can't go back and you can't stand still,
If the thunder don't get you then the lightning will.
ROBERT HUNTER, "The Wheel"

On May 23, 1997, regional forester Phil Janik signed the Record of Decision approving a revised plan for the Tongass, ending a ten-year, highly contentious process for managing the nation's largest national forest. The debates will continue, but everyone involved breathed a collective sigh of relief.

The plan is a blueprint for how the Forest Service will manage the Tongass National Forest for the next ten or so years. Although many other factors greatly influence the people and resources of Southeast Alaska, the Tongass Land Management Plan is probably the single most important document charting the region's future. As steward of seventeen million of Southeast Alaska's twenty-one million acres of land, the Forest Service has a profound effect on the landscape, the seventy-four thousand people who live here, and the Tongass's national and global audience.

This chapter takes a closer look at the new plan and the agency that developed it. Nationwide, the Forest Service came in for much criticism over the past thirty years as it wrestled to achieve a balance among the many uses of national forest lands. Many critics argued that the agency had become a slave to large-scale commercial development of the forests—and especially to the powerful timber industry. The agency fell behind a shift in public values: environmentalism moved toward the mainstream; recreational use of the forests exploded; concern about endangered species evolved into concern about ecosystems. New legislation preserved large tracts of land and protected resources, but left the Forest Service wondering about its mission, which had once seemed so clear.

The debates included differing views of the agency's role in promoting community well-being. The Forest Service's mission always addressed the health of rural communities located near the forests, as well as cities that depended on water that flowed from forestlands. Previously, policies were designed to maintain community stability by pumping large volumes of timber into local mills to fuel local and regional economies. The emerging wisdom questioned not only whether this practice was sustainable, especially when the trees being cut were old-growth forests, but also whether the long-term effects on communities were really beneficial. We have learned, for example, that mill towns are economically vulnerable; their reliance on a single industry turns out to be maladaptive when timber prices fall, when supplies wane, or when competition increases.

While many communities in the Pacific Northwest have been forced for decades to cope with new policies that turned off the timber spigot, the small, remote communities of Southeast Alaska are just now dealing with the change. Mill closures in Haines, Wrangell, Sitka, and Ketchikan in the 1990s have had profound social and economic effects in Southeast Alaska. Communities throughout Southeast are in a time of transition, adopting a wide range of strategies to thrive under changing conditions.

The long struggle to revise management of the Tongass must be considered against this social, economic, and environmental backdrop. The new plan is noteworthy for many reasons, but two in particular indicate that the Forest Service is entering a new era of land management for the Tongass. The first is what the plan says: its resource allocations reflect the Forest Service's movement toward an ecosystem-based approach to managing public lands. The second is how the plan was created: the agency reexamined how its scientists (biologists, sociologists, and others whose job is to provide a better understanding of ecosystems) and land managers (whose job is to make decisions about what kinds of activities and land uses will be allowed on the Tongass) can work together to overcome past abuses by each camp.

These features represent the agency's attempt to improve stewardship of the Tongass. Will it be successful? A closer look at each reveals a complex blend of opportunities and barriers that will only be sorted out over time. Yet one cannot help but feel that the groundwork is being laid for a sustainable future for Southeast Alaska, with the Forest Service playing a key role.

AN ECOSYSTEM APPROACH

Public debate over the Tongass has always centered on timber, a fact demonstrated when the *Juneau Empire* labeled the Tongass Land Management Plan a new "harvest plan." Industrial-scale harvest began on the Tongass during the 1950s; annual timber sale volumes rose from sixty million board feet in 1952 to over two hundred million in 1956 and nearly six hundred million in the early 1970s. The mechanisms were long-term contracts; the two largest, with the Alaska Pulp Corporation and the Ketchikan Pulp Company, committed some two hundred million board feet a year for fifty years. The long-term contracts had been actively sought by the Forest Service, which believed that a guaranteed flow of timber was necessary for industry to set up business in the remote region.

Another long-term contract, this one for 8.75 billion feet of timber with the provision that another pulp mill be constructed by the winner, was purchased in the 1960s but fell through as a result of high costs and environmental concerns. Tongass historian Lawrence Rakestraw points out that during this period of intensive harvest, effects on visual quality, water pollution, and fish and game were considered. Yet although scenery was preserved along many ferry and cruise ship routes, it was apparent that timber was the goal, and protection was just mitigation.

By the 1980s, public opinion began to make a dent in Tongass logging practices. But even the new laws designed to recognize the national and nontimber values of Alaska lands contained provisions consistent with pro-timber policy. For example, the Alaska National Interest Lands Conservation Act (PL 96–487, December 2, 1980) specified that the Tongass would provide 4.5 billion board feet of timber to the "dependent industry" and authorized expenditures of at least $40 million annually to ensure this level. The law also established loans to purchasers of national forest materials so they could increase use of wood products.

Society's outrage and emotional reaction to the clear-cut timber harvests in Southeast Alaska was typified by the 1987 book *The Tongass: Alaska's Vanishing Rain Forest*. Viewing the past timber harvests on Prince of Wales Island from the air and from logging roads, Robert and Carey Ketchum wrote:

> What has not been cut and dragged away has been crushed under the weight of the fallen trees and heavy equipment. Everything has vanished. Prisoner of War Island is left only with root wads, debris piles, and splintered, unusable timber strewn like slivered toothpicks across a vast landscape. The ecology has been irreparably undone. We drove on in silence and anger. With each bend of the road, further vistas opened and the destruction continued to unfold before us. Miles of roads connect nothing to nothing. Spurs loop off

to nowhere. Lakes, once beautifully rimmed with trees, sit at the bottom of denuded valleys and hillsides like remnant puddles in a post-holocaust landscape.

Changing societal values were reflected further in the Tongass Timber Reform Act of 1990, which replaced the mandated output levels with direction to "meet market demand" for timber on both an annual and a forest planning cycle basis. The act also specified that economic factors need not be considered in identifying lands not suitable for timber production. Established in reaction to increased risks to values other than timber, the act symbolized the public's increasing concern about ecosystems. This concern extended to lands owned by Native corporations, which were being harvested even faster than public land. Since the early 1980s, more than half of the timber harvested in Southeast Alaska has come from these private lands, a fact often overlooked in the debate over federal policy.

Enter the 1990s and the Forest Service's adoption of ecosystem-based management as its policy for national forests. The Tongass is a candidate for ecosystem management if ever there was one. Containing 14 percent of the world's temperate rain forest biome, it is the largest remaining piece of relatively undisturbed temperate rain forest on earth.

Ecosystem management, in the eyes of former Forest Service chief Jack Ward Thomas, is the "next intelligent evolution of multiple use." Rather than focusing on a given set of results, ecosystem management concentrates on overall health and productivity through an understanding of how different parts of the ecosystem function together. It acknowledges that humans, whether through science or through centuries of experience and local knowledge, don't have all the answers. We have much to learn not just *about* nature, but also *from* it.

More a philosophy than a concrete strategy, ecosystem management is a "concept of natural resource management," according to a memo from the chief. The agency is still struggling with how to carry out its ecosystem-based management philosophy. One problem is that this strong swerve in resource policy has not been institutionalized through legislation. As a result, Congress, the administration, the agency, and the public are left to define and debate exactly what ecosystem management means. To the environmentalist, ecosystem management may connote simply a new way for the Forest Service to justify cutting trees. To the timber industry, it means a way for the agency to justify far lower harvest levels.

The movement toward ecosystem management for the Tongass is described in the remarkable document called the Record of Decision. The ROD, as it's known, is just forty-four pages long (plus a short appendix on wild and scenic rivers). It is written in plain English, not bureaucratic jargon, and in the first person, the voice of the regional forester. The text exudes responsibility and accountability on every page. And it is honest, clearly acknowledging not just the intended benefits of the new plan, but also the risks of adverse effects to humans and other species who use the Tongass. It recognizes the need for more information and better science.

The ROD describes a land management strategy that differs markedly from that portrayed in the original Tongass Land Management Plan published in 1979. The new plan sets aside nearly fourteen million acres to remain as natural settings. Just over a million acres are included in old-growth habitat reserves, compared to none in 1979. Wildlife habitat reserves incorporate 70 percent of the existing productive old growth on the Tongass. Beaches and estuaries are now protected by thousand-foot-wide buffer zones without scheduled timber harvest.

As a result, the timber available for harvest drops substantially. Of the 5 million acres of productive old-growth forest that remained in 1997, 4.2 million acres were withdrawn from timber production entirely. The average allowable sale quantity (ASQ), the ceiling for how much timber can be harvested, was cut by nearly half, from 520 to 267 million board feet. The 267 million figure is close to half of the previous ASQ, but is actually more than the amount harvested in recent years. Standards and guidelines that apply to portions of the Tongass where commercial timber harvest is allowed (about 22 percent of the forest) are designed to maintain nearly 70 percent of current productive old growth within those areas, even if maximum permissible timber harvest occurs over one hundred years. The silvicultural system was changed from one relying exclusively on clear-cuts to a mixture of techniques, although clear-cutting is still the dominant method.

Shortly after the revised plan was issued, one benefit of the reserve system and other conservation measures was realized when the U.S. Fish and Wildlife Service, the federal agency charged with listing and recovery of endangered and threatened species, ruled on petitions requesting the listing of the Alexander Archipelago wolf and the northern goshawk. The agency determined that the species did not merit listing because adequate habitat protection would be provided on the Tongass. Avoiding listing is to everyone's benefit. Lest you think this is just one federal agency supporting another, rest assured that no love is lost between the two. These agencies are often at odds despite their common federal lineage.

The revised plan also is expected to increase protection for streams used by anadromous fish, though factors other than Forest Service management have provided the bulk of the variability in fish populations. These include ocean cycles, fish market characteristics, and climate. For example, recent record salmon runs have not necessarily led to greater prosperity because they have been accompanied by sharp drops in value per pound. As a result, the revised plan is not expected to affect the fishing industry significantly. The fishing industry has always been a mainstay in

Alaska, and fish harvesting and seafood processing together are the largest natural-resource-dependent industry in Southeast.

The tourism industry is the fastest growing of the natural resource industries, and continued growth is expected. A main source has been an increase in the number and size of cruise ships making the voyage up the Inside Passage, Alaska's most popular tourist destination. In Juneau, for example, cruise ship passengers increased from just over two hundred thousand in 1990 to over five hundred thousand in 1997. An increasing number of ecotourists are also traveling more off the beaten path in search of adventure, wildlife, and solitude.

The plan attempts to support the tourism industry through management of federal lands for scenery, recreation, wildlife, and a variety of activities and experiences. Despite these efforts, the amount of what are called semiprimitive, motorized opportunities may not be adequate to meet expected participation rates in some places on the forest. Access to many recreation places on the Tongass is limited to flying, boating, or walking; there just aren't many roads in an archipelago where the human population density averages two people per square mile (compared to a U.S. average of over seventy). The relative absence of roads except in a few places like Prince of Wales Island creates an interesting recreational mix of motorized access to remote locations.

The new plan's effects on subsistence are likely to generate a good deal of discussion. Assuming a maximum permissible timber harvest over one hundred years, the revised plan forecasts an impact on subsistence harvest of deer in upcoming decades in some areas of the forest. Subsistence use of resources located or dependent on the Tongass provides Southeast Alaska residents with a variety of social, economic, cultural, and related benefits. Subsistence is a major component of the lifestyle and culture of many Southeast Alaskans, as well as a definite contributor to economic well-being. Subsistence use is substantial; over half of the households in rural Southeast obtain more than one-third of their meat from subsistence harvest. Subsistence is protected by federal policy, which establishes it as a priority over other uses in times of scarcity.

The plan's effects on the timber industry, and associated effects on many Southeast communities, remain at the forefront of the debate over ecosystem management. As has been the case in the Pacific Northwest, the timber industry in Southeast Alaska has declined dramatically, with employment down well over 40 percent since 1990. The plan allocates nearly 4 million acres to various types of development, including about 1 million acres open to moderate development and just under 3 million acres open to more intensive development such as timber production, mineral projects, and transportation and utility systems. Timber harvest is scheduled on about 670,000 acres (including 200,000 acres of currently young or second-growth forest) over the next one hundred years. This compares to the 400,000 acres of primarily high volume old-growth forest on the Tongass that were clear-cut during the last half of the twentieth century.

The ASQ, like many "magic" numbers, tended to acquire a life of its own, serving as a rallying point for both support and opposition. During the lengthy planning process, everyone had a preferred number, which shifted with the political winds. Numbers like this tend to alter the debate from meaningful discussion to lines drawn in the sand, as though where, how, or when the timber gets harvested is unimportant.

The lower ASQ of the revised plan is more than adequate to meet demand for timber as calculated by Forest Service economists. Yet estimates of demand are subject to many assumptions and tend to bounce around. The demand for timber estimated in the 1997 final environmental impact statement was about 320 million board feet per year; a new analysis by the same economists later in the year lowered estimated demand to somewhere between 113 and 156 million. The drop was attributed to new competition for the Japanese market from other countries, closure of the last pulp mill in Southeast and the loss of a local market for manufacturing residues, and industry changes in the Pacific Northwest and Canada.

All acknowledge that the closing of the pulp mills may greatly change the configuration of the wood products industry in Southeast Alaska. It will take some time for the industry to shape itself, and estimates of demand vary based on assumptions. However, the ending of the long-term contracts provides an opening for smaller operators. A new, smaller mill planned to open near Ketchikan (with an estimated sixty employees, compared to some five hundred associated with the pulp mill), and a company is negotiating purchase of the sawmill in Wrangell, which had closed in 1994.

In the world of commerce, one firm's problem is another's opportunity. Dick Buhler of Silver Bay Logging, for example, has poised his company to take advantage of the changing timber industry picture in Southeast Alaska. Interviewed for the October 1997 *Loggers World* cover story, Buhler said his success resulted from the ability to recognize and adapt to a changing social environment: "It hasn't always been easy for us. The logging here has seen a lot of changes and most weren't good for logging. Most of the companies aren't around any more. . . . The future of logging is helicopters. We're getting sales just because we have [helicopters]."

Thus, in an era in which companies have gone out of business, Buhler employs some four hundred people across seven logging camps and offices (not all in Southeast Alaska). He's confident that his company will be around a while longer: "Logging is becoming a lot more environmentally sensitive today and I think the helicopter is the way of the future. I've always been in logging and I plan to keep on logging." His aviation division is building a new hangar near the Juneau airport, with help from a City and Borough of Juneau loan through the Southeast Alaska Economic Fund. Silver

Bay will be able to maintain its helicopters in Juneau, adding twenty or thirty high-paying jobs to the local economy instead of using contractors from the lower forty-eight.

To be sure, there are many who feel that the amount of timber coming off the Tongass is still too high. A look at the Ketchikan area's schedule of proposed actions for the first quarter of 1998 suggests why: Port Stewart timber sale, 75 million board feet; Control Lake timber sale, 90 million; Sea Level timber sale, 40 million; Chasina timber sale, 40 million; Luck Lake timber sale, 13 million; Staney Creek timber sale, 30 million; Cholmondeley timber sale, 37 million. The reason for cutting this timber is not to accomplish ecosystem management objectives, but simply to support the timber program. Thus, while the timber industry is claiming that the agency is running it into the ground, others are aghast at the volume being sold, cut, processed minimally, and shipped across the Pacific. Maybe times have not changed so much after all.

The effects of the revised plan will vary by community, because the thirty-two communities in Southeast vary significantly in how they benefit from management of the Tongass. For example, of the twenty-three community groups in Southeast Alaska (the smallest scale for which detailed employment information is available), ten have 1 percent or less employment in wood products, twelve have 1 percent or less in seafood processing, and six have 1 percent or less in tourism-related employment categories. (Government employment, in contrast, is substantial nearly everywhere in Southeast Alaska.) Effects on communities also will depend on how projects are scheduled and carried out, because the Forest Plan is more of a zoning device that specifies what activities are allowed on what lands than it is a site-specific plan that describes exactly what will occur where, and when.

Regardless of one's perspective, the revised plan did draw attention. When a draft version became available for public comment in

1996, over 21,000 comments were received, including 14,000 on form letters, 4,200 questionnaires, almost 2,000 letters, and 500 comments at public hearings. About 4,000 came from Southeast Alaska, 1,750 from the rest of Alaska, and almost 14,000 from outside Alaska, especially from California and Washington. This national interest reflects the value of the Tongass to the nation as a whole, perhaps more than any other national forest. Alaska's resources, in fact, are typically cited by economists and others demonstrating how resources can have value even to those who never see them in person.

To summarize the responses, people's values and beliefs were coded into one of three common interest categories: greater environmental protection; multiple use/ecological protection (which turned out to be people who believed that logging is an acceptable multiple use but who were opposed to the pulp mills and long-term timber contracts); and greater emphasis on wood products.

As is often the case, the views of local residents differed somewhat from those of the rest of the public: 48 percent of the total comments were classified as favoring greater environmental protection, compared to 28 percent of those from Southeast Alaska; 28 percent of the national comments favored greater emphasis on wood products, compared to 37 percent from Southeast. The middle category—multiple use with ecological protection—somewhat surprisingly was favored by just under half of the Southeast Alaska respondents and about one-fourth of the national respondents. What is most interesting about these comments is that they suggest that a high proportion of the public could be satisfied with the new land management plan. The forty-some entities that filed legal appeals when the ROD was published were not pleased, however, and they represented a wide range of interests, including communities, tribes, environmental groups, and the timber industry. Subsequent rulings in 1999 on the appeals further

lowered the scheduled timber harvest—not enough for some, too
much for others.

SCIENCE-MANAGEMENT PARTNERSHIP

During development of the new Tongass plan, a unique partnership clarified and integrated the respective roles of scientists and
managers. Not all within the agency welcomed this shaky marriage,
yet it provided important checks and balances for both parties, to
the benefit of all.

Forest research in Alaska, first authorized in 1928, did not become a reality until 1948 with establishment of the Alaska Forest
Research Center. The first director, Raymond Taylor, believed that
research organizations are most productive when they have "small
staffs, simple quarters, and are hard up for money." The science-
management relationship was tested early when regional forester
B. Frank Heintzleman believed that the research center should be
under his control, rather than being under the Branch of Research
in Washington, D.C.

Scientists participated on the Tongass planning team as full
members, but with specific responsibilities. They were responsible
for developing credible, value-neutral scientific information, including likely levels of risk to resources and society associated with
various decisions. Managers considered this information along
with legal mandates, societal desires, public comments received on
the draft environmental document, and other factors to make the
decision on a preferred alternative for managing the Tongass.

This arrangement is hardly earth-shattering, yet you would be
surprised how frequently it has been violated. Scientists have had a
difficult time separating their role from that of the decision maker,
as though science, not society, has the answers. Abuses by management also have occurred; managers have ignored, misinterpreted,
or selectively applied information when it did not support the decision they wanted to make. The key to the science-management

relationship on the Tongass was mutual acceptance of the respective roles: don't tell me how to do science, and I won't tell you how to make decisions.

A new method of determining how well the arrangement worked consisted of scientists writing a formal evaluation of whether managers used science findings appropriately in making decisions about how to allocate Tongass lands to various uses. Scientists who had provided key information to managers rated how the final decision (as documented in the ROD) used available science findings. Did the regional forester consider available data and analyses? Did he interpret them correctly? Did he use them to identify any risks associated with the decision? If the answer was yes to all three, then science was used appropriately.

Note that this does not mean that the manager had to select a course of action that minimized the risks to a particular resource, whether it was species habitat or economic opportunity (or both); he simply had to demonstrate that the risks were considered, and to provide a rationale for the decision. As an added check on the process, the scientists' evaluation was peer-reviewed by other scientists not involved with the Tongass.

The evaluation was useful not only as a product, but also as a process. The first draft of the use of science report was developed after the first draft of the ROD, allowing room for managers to respond to and incorporate initial inconsistencies regarding use of scientific information. All told, the evaluation and the Record of Decision underwent more than a dozen drafts that led to a decision that could be defended as scientifically credible.

Formalizing this relationship provided many benefits. From the regional forester's perspective, the plan was better protected from appeals accusing the agency of using faulty science or selective use of science to support predetermined outcomes. From the scientists' perspective, the process ensured that data and relevant analyses were considered and consistently applied by managers.

The science-management partnership is continuing beyond development of the new plan. One example is a groundbreaking study of alternatives to clear-cutting, currently well under way. This experiment compares the effects of eight different levels and types of timber harvest to a no-cut control area. One of the other seven treatments leaves 75 percent of the timber standing; another leaves 25 percent. The study is scrupulously designed and carried out, with on-site field teams ensuring the integrity of the study by working side by side with the logging crews.

Scientists are measuring many types of effects that result from each type of harvest, such as use by wildlife, quality of habitat, stream sedimentation, soil erosion, and regeneration (what types and density of species result from the cutting "disturbance"). Social scientists and economists are measuring people's perceptions of visual impact, the feasibility and economics of alternative timber sales, and the central issue of acceptability. How do people feel about the selective cuts? Is any harvest too much for some people, regardless of the social, economic, and biophysical effects or benefits? How do people make judgments about the effects on scenery compared to effects on stream erosion? What factors do people consider most important when they evaluate whether timber harvest is acceptable to them? What are some of the barriers facing more widespread use of select harvest, and what are some of the opportunities?

The agency's willingness to conduct such studies and, presumably, to apply the results to management practices, reflects another facet of ecosystem management—the heightened role of science. We learn more, and we adapt our plans accordingly. In this case, the learning is not just about biology but also about people and their perceptions of forest practices. This use of social science, while it is not new, demonstrates how ecosystem management incorporates people as part of the ecosystem.

Ecosystem management requires increased understanding of

social and economic systems and their links with biophysical systems. The assumption is that over the long term, healthy social conditions contribute to healthy biophysical conditions, and vice versa. Ecosystem inventories thus require inventories not just of flora and fauna, but also of such conditions as past and present use of natural resources, economic and noneconomic values associated with those uses, and people's beliefs, knowledge, and attitudes regarding national forests. It is equally important to understand how public values and expected benefits from public lands change over time.

CONCLUSIONS

The Tongass is a paradox, a land of seemingly limitless vistas, resources, and opportunities. Yet we have limited-entry fishing for salmon, individual fishing quotas for halibut, season and bag limits on Sitka black-tailed deer for both sport and subsistence hunting, competition for guiding permits, a patchwork of clear-cuts on private and public lands, conflicts among uses, allocations of land for special purposes. At times, it does indeed feel like this vastness has limits, and that resources, uses, and values are carved up and distributed like meat on a platter.

An ecosystem-based approach to managing the Tongass certainly doesn't have all the answers—but it does seem to ask good questions. How can the Forest Service better collaborate with local communities and others who have a stake in the resources of the Tongass? How can scientists work with managers in clearly defined roles to avoid past abuses? How can the agency do a better job of providing goods and services desired by society over the long term, while maintaining options for the future based on changing societal needs and values?

The Tongass Land Management Plan's effects will unfold over time. As for now, at least the Forest Service, residents of Southeast Alaska, and others who care about the Tongass have a blueprint to follow, adapt, and shape over time into a socially acceptable, sustainable plan that attempts to meet the needs of the present without compromising the future.

If there is one thing we know, it is that management of the Tongass will always generate controversy. There's nothing inherently bad about controversy as long as there is a good forum to promote understanding and discussion. Lots of good ideas get generated during arguments, if people remain willing to listen and consider opposing views.

The new blueprint for the Tongass comes complete with a new framework for conducting what we hope will be a more civil dialogue and debate—collaborative stewardship. Recognizing the past failure of many public-involvement efforts, the Forest Service now intends to open up the process of managing the Tongass. The vision of collaborative stewardship is a lofty one in which the agency, local communities, and others who care about the Tongass sit at the table together, developing projects both on and off the forest for the benefit of all. The line blurs between the agency and the public, changing the management mindset from "us and them" to "we." The public is not asked simply to review and comment on potential agency actions or programs, but to help design, create, and monitor them.

Collaborative stewardship faces many barriers in Southeast Alaska. Some are legal, such as the Federal Advisory Committee Act that regulates how collaborative groups can be formed. Some are practical, such as the limited time already overextended Southeast residents have to put into the long discussions required for true collaboration and consensus to emerge. Some are philosophical, such as national environmental groups' concerns that local communities will dominate the discussions. And some are organizational, such as the Forest Service's will and ability to engage in truly collaborative processes—thereby giving up control over the eventual outcome. Some Forest Service line officers view collaboration as a normal way of doing business, while others see it as a threat. In Southeast, collaborative stewardship has a true champion in Acting Regional Forester Jim Caplan, but the downside is that many employees resent the program as just another top-down management initiative.

Collaborative stewardship has the potential to dramatically alter and improve the way the Tongass is managed. But it also could fade away like other buzzword philosophies, in vogue only as long as a few champions are at the right place within the agency. The success of the new Tongass plan and of the Forest Service could well depend on which path is taken.

As one steps back from the rhetoric and views the changes being made by the Forest Service and others, the potential for consensus over the Tongass emerges. There appears to be reasonably strong support for a smaller-scale timber industry with benefits accruing to local residents rather than distant corporations, and with fair competition and fewer subsidies. There is certainly widespread support for conservation of the Tongass rain forest and the many species that depend on it for survival. And there is support for the communities of the Tongass, as well as recognition that preservation of the forest means preservation of the people, too, and of lifestyles that are inseparable from the land and water. Perhaps the time for discussion to take place is now, while Southeast Alaska does not suffer from the depletion of resources that has changed so many other places. The Forest Service is at the table, waiting.

STEWART ALLEN is an environmental psychologist who has worked for a variety of federal and state agencies, including the U.S. Forest Service, the Tennessee Valley Authority, the U.S. Fish and Wildlife Service, and the Montana Department of Natural Resources and Conservation. He also taught at the University of Montana and the University of Idaho for four years and owned a consulting firm for eight years. He has written more than fifty professional papers and presentations on relationships between people and natural resources. He is married, has three sons and two yellow Labs, and is probably out skiing or sea kayaking as you read this.

brown bear with salmon, *Nancy Behnken*

Love, Crime, and Joyriding
on a Dead-End Road

JOHN STRALEY

Crime and nature writing are, for most people, worlds apart, and for that reason I've often considered giving up my life of crime and becoming an ascetic wilderness poet. Not because of any talent for poetry, but for the smaller reason that drives people toward solitude: I get tired of human beings doing things I just don't like.

Once, I was standing in the dark looking at a forest beyond a parking lot thinking how easy it is to get along with trees. A tree has never pointed out that I am a liar and a hypocrite, a tree has never referred to me as "scum," and, come to think of it, a tree has never stolen my car.

I had come home from a trip and discovered that my car had been stolen from the Sitka airport. This is strange for two reasons: first, Sitka is on a rain-forested island with only about twelve miles of main road, and second, my car is incredibly ugly. It's been rolled several times and has been painted in green house paint. It lists to the right and has moss growing in the molding around the windshield, and although it is legal, it has to be push-started 30 percent of the time. Not the kind of vehicle I would think of as attractive to someone looking for a ride to boost. I walked around the football-field-size parking lot, and every single car I looked at with increasing alarm was not mine. I sat on the curb in the dark. Drops of rain lit up in the runway lights. The lovely trees flung their arms around in the wind.

For more than thirteen years now, off and on, I've worked as a defense investigator in Southeastern Alaska. I've worked on hundreds of crimes, mostly serious felonies, and all of them for the defense. It is wearing work, full of doubt and ambiguity. When I'm introduced as a private detective, people often ask, "Is it just like TV?" and I usually say, "No. It's much sadder than that." This disappoints them, but I say it anyway because it feels good to tell the truth about crime every once in a while.

I work in the cities and villages of Southeastern Alaska: island towns, mostly, or mainland towns shut off by the mountains. Deer will cross busy streets in the middle of the day and bears might come around to snuffle through the garbage set out behind the diner. The towns are peaceful and relatively quiet, yet people drink and lie and hurt each other just as in other places, but it seems harder to ignore here. We are neighbors, and we know each other as doctors and loggers, fishermen and nurses, teachers and waitresses, but also as punks, liars, bullies, and con men of all stripes. On these islands you are daily confronted by civilization and wildness in stark relief.

I am not, by any stretch, a nature writer. I write about human beings living in particular places, and about the crimes they commit. But it was nature writing that first inspired me to consider how close attention to one creature might give important clues to the health of an entire community. If the nature writers are right, then human beings must surely be an indicator species. But indicators of what? And which humans are the ones most worthy of study? Looking at different individual humans might well lead to wildly different conclusions about the health of their "habitat" taken in the largest sense. A prosperous and emotionally healthy person might give one impression; an examination of jail inmates might give another. But couldn't the same be said of falcons? Is every one equally as successful as another? I just don't know. But I am curious what the examination of some of the men and women in jail might indicate about the relative health of the Tongass.

So, I'm choosing to write about a homicide. This homicide never happened, but the story is substantially true. The rain where the body is found is real, the bloodstain on the steps, and the personalities of the witnesses, all of those things are true, and it doesn't matter if this particular murder never happened.

A lawyer from the public defender's office in Ketchikan calls me on a Sunday night saying she has a new client from a remote logging camp on one of the islands near Prince of Wales. He was arrested twelve hours ago and is accused of shooting his girlfriend in their trailer. The trailer sits in a remote rock pit surrounded by a clearcut. It's on a logging road system some six miles from the main camp. Our client was from Washington and had been promised a job building road a couple of months ago, but because of a last-minute lawsuit, work had stopped. "He'll be assigned to me in the morning." The attorney's voice sounds tired. "He hasn't worked in months. He can't afford a murder defense. He's going public so we better get on it." I can hear the evening news on a radio in her office.

The client's blood alcohol level was .36, more than three times the legal limit for driving, when he was taken into custody. The victim's was nearly the same. There is a history of violence in the relationship. I will have to fly out to the crime scene, but the public defender wants me to go there after I talk to the client in jail. He's being held in Ketchikan.

"Has he made statements to the police?" I ask, and she says she doesn't know, but adds almost as an aside, "My bet is he spilled his guts."

"Other witnesses?" I ask. She doesn't know, but thinks there was a party at the trailer earlier so there may be some witnesses to whatever it was that led up to the shooting.

"Any priors?" I ask, and she says she's not certain, the client's name is vaguely familiar, but it is too soon to get his criminal history. She will find out as soon as she gets to the office.

I tell her I'll fly to Ketchikan in the morning to meet our client at the jail.

When I go into a jail to meet a client for the first time, I never ask him to tell me the whole story of what happened. It's been my experience that people in jail often lie to their lawyers and their investigators. They lie when it would be better to tell the truth. They lie against their own self-interest. They lie because they are deeply afraid and would do or say anything to get past the door of the jail. But mostly I think they lie because they don't really believe I'm there to help them; they think I'm there to judge. Generally, I seem rich and they are poor. They are locked up and I am free. I am white and often they are not. I use a legal jargon that, frankly, we both only partially understand and I never tell them what they want to hear. Why should they trust me, or their lawyer?

But on that first visit I have a litany of rehearsed questions: What have you told anyone else about what happened? Is there anything that is going to disappear if someone doesn't get to it fast? Was there a witness who actually saw something important who is going to leave the state sometime soon? I avoid questions of guilt or innocence. Guilt and innocence will come much, much later.

On this Monday morning I check through security at the jail and go to a full-contact visiting room. I can talk to the prisoner and show him papers without being separated by a wall and bullet-proof glass. They bring him into the interview room.

His name is Bob. A white male thirty-six years old. Born in Oklahoma, a recent resident of Spanaway, Washington. He is washed and smells like shampoo. He's in a red jumpsuit, and his hands and feet are in manacles. This means he's been kept in isolation for the night, which is fine with me because it gave him less of a chance to talk to anyone.

The officer chains him to a bar across from me. I shake his hand awkwardly and explain very slowly who I am, who I work for, and that I'm here to help him in any way that I can. He nods his head and says he understands. His eyes are rimmed red from alcohol and tears. He tries to back away from me but the chains stop him.

"She's not really dead," he blurts out.

"No," I tell him. "She is dead."

"I didn't kill her," he says. I hold my hands up and tell him to stop talking. Then I slowly and carefully take him through the litany of questions.

We know Jody was shot. Who saw it happen? Who was there when the gun went off? Where is the gun now? He shrugs his shoulders, the chains tinkle, and he starts to cry again. He answers each question the same: "I don't know."

Then I ask him one of the closing questions. "Do you know if there is anyone I should talk to today who can tell me who shot and killed Jody?"

His chest heaves. "No. Not right now." He is shaking his head and he won't meet my eyes. "I can't think of anybody."

"That's all right," I say. "I'll come back again and we can talk more. This is just the beginning." Bob nods at me, uncomprehending.

I call the guard on the phone and we arrange to get photos of my client's body. Head to foot, naked, all angles. The guard insists that it's already been done, but I insist that I have to do it again. I have my own camera checked through. My client holds a ruler next to his bruised temple and I snap the shot. I photograph his hands and note the slightest cut or bruise. I take pictures of his knees and his butt. He is covered with old scars across the knees and one particularly nasty one up the chest where a snapped choker cable slashed him six years before.

After we are done the guard takes Bob's elbow and starts to take him away. We are in the hall. I signal the guard that I need just one more thing and the guard moves away. He talks to another staff person on the other side of a reinforced grill. He doesn't want to eavesdrop because he doesn't want to end up a witness in court.

I tell Bob for the third time not to talk to anyone about the incident. Not a soul. Not his cell mate and not officers. No one. Bob nods. He is starting to listen. He is beginning to understand that he is going to be in jail for a long, long time, even if the best happens. Even if he goes to trial and is acquitted, he will be in jail for almost a year. We talk about bail. He says he has a trailer in Aberdeen, a three-quarter-ton pickup, and his tools. His mother has her place in The Dalles, Oregon, but he is not going to ask her. The bail is $200,000.

There is one last question. "Who are your friends?" I ask him. "You are going to be painted as a monster. Who will tell me good things about you? Who likes you?" I ask.

"Jody . . ." he says reflexively and then, turning pale, he stops and looks as if he is going to gag.

"Who else?" I move on quickly.

And he gives me names. A bull buck from an old job. The wife of his old boss. An aunt and a sister back in Oklahoma.

I take their names and then I shake his hand again, telling him to take it one day at a time. "We've got a lot of work to do before all this . . ."—and I gesture around to the prison and his handcuffs— ". . . before all this is resolved. I will come back in three days. I will tell you what I know."

The door behind me buzzes, the heavy lock clatters, and I walk out. Bob turns toward the guard who will take him back to isolation.

Later I learn that Bob was in isolation because of death threats made by some of the other inmates. He had gotten into a fight in jail, which also helps explain the manacles. He had been fighting with old friends of Jody. I make a note to track some of them down and find out what they know.

By the time I get to the public defender's office I have a stack of messages. I talk to the lawyer. She wants me to talk to Jody's family before they leave the state. I don't want to but she says I should. They are at the Juneau airport. They are taking Jody's twelve-year-old son out of Alaska and back to Seattle. It may be the only chance we get to talk to them in person. Before I leave for the airport, the lawyer tells me that Bob had indeed made a full confession to the arresting officer. She says, "Yeah, it looks like he tells the whole story—i's dotted and t's crossed. It might be suppressible. I've got to listen to it. We'll have to see the circumstances, check the Mirandas and his status of custody when he talked. But . . ." She lets out a breath. "We still need to go ahead with the full court press." She walks into her office and I head for the airport.

Jody's family is easy to spot. They sit in a corner, pale and not speaking to anyone. A man and a woman somewhere in their sixties. A twelve-year-old boy. The grandpa wears a flannel shirt and a hat with a chain saw logo. He's holding a carry-on bag. His wife wears a nylon windbreaker and clutches a handful of tissues. The boy holds a brand-new computer game. It's turned off. He's staring at the ground.

I introduce myself slowly. I tell them I work for Bob's lawyer. I avoid the term *investigator.* It's distracting and easily misunderstood. They are friendly at first. The old man smiles and accepts my condolences. I ask them what happened, and when they start to answer the old man stops himself.

"Now just a minute. You work for his lawyer?"

"That's right," I say.

"We're not talking to you. We don't have to. The district attorney told us we didn't have to."

"That's right, you don't have to talk to me."

The grandmother says something under her breath. "Scum," she says.

I try to hand my card to the grandfather and he stands up and slaps my hand away.

"You keep that goddamn card," the old man says. "He took her from us. He's not going to slip out of that. Who's going to raise this boy, for God's sake? You? You and those goddamn lawyers?" His wife grabs his hand and the old man shucks her off.

"You better get the hell out of here," he says.

"Please." The old woman's voice is trembling. The boy pulls his ball cap down over his eyes and sinks deeper into his chair.

"I don't know you," the old man says, and he stands on the balls of his feet. His hard, old hands are balled into fists. I back away. "You got one hell of a job," he says. "You must be sick." He turns his back on me.

"That might be true," I say to myself, and walk away.

Later I learn that Jody's son was a witness to the killing. He had called the logging camp on the VHF radio and hid under his bed waiting for a crew of men to come over the road from the main camp. They locked Bob in an empty toolshed and waited for the troopers to arrive from the detachment in Klawock.

The next day was rainy. I took a cab to the flight service so I could take a floatplane to the old logging camp; from there I could get a ride to the crime scene.

Every time I fly it's the same: the soggy wooden buildings of Ketchikan fall away under the wings of the plane. The steep coastal mountains stand like a stone fence and the plane veers to the west toward the heavily timbered islands on the outside coast.

The islands are bristling humps of timbered rock and moss. Streams from the ice fields cascade down hundreds of feet to the salt water. There are large clear-cuts threaded together by shot rock roads. Logging debris lies parallel to the direction of the landing where the ancient trees were yarded up to the road. There are old roads grown over with alder trees in the middle of even-aged second growth where all the trees try to grow to the same height at the same time. The wind buffets the plane from the southwest, and I wedge my hand up on the ceiling of the cabin to steady myself. There are a woman and a boy in the back seat of the single-engine plane. The boy must be about six years old, and he's asleep. His mother looks tired and doesn't say a thing to me.

The plane lands on the water of a quiet bay. There's a ramp running down from a stone bulkhead. The bulkhead is held together by spruce logs cabled together. A single tree some eight feet in diameter acts as the float for the dock. The boy wakes up and scrambles up the dock to a waiting pickup truck.

Bob's old boss picks me up. He has a battered pickup truck. Mechanic's tools and piles of receipts litter the cab. He shoves a socket set off the seat and onto the floorboards. "Don't mind this stuff," he says and then shakes my hand in a hard grip. His name is Carl, and I have met him once before, long ago, but Carl doesn't remember.

Logging camps are relatively safe places to live. Safe from crime. But the wildness of alcohol and physical abuse is as present as it is in any of the small communities. Sitka, Ketchikan, and Juneau each has more homicides than all the logging camps, and by far the greatest majority of homicides in rural Alaska are committed by family or friends of the victim. The murder of strangers is rare. Murder for profit or in the commission of another crime is relatively rare as well. Alaska is a leader in domestic violence.

"Bob was a hell of a hand," Carl says. "You know, when he wasn't drinking. We had worked a helicopter sale in the Cascades. He was a good hand." Carl's voice trails off.

We drive past the school yard, where a girl is chasing around with her arms spread wide and a little brown-haired boy is frolicking in front of her like a loose-limbed colt. Carl's wife waves us down and hands him a sheaf of messages through the window of the truck, and she offers us slices of warm bread. Carl eats his immediately, and I balance mine on my knee as we drive off up through the camp.

There are trailers with sheds and metal garages. It is a tidy community with pickup trucks and crab pots stacked next to the skiffs hauled out on their trailers. Shiny fat ravens hop around the side yards near the garbage cans. There are bundles of trees, spruce and hemlock, stacked in a yard next to the road. Their bark is sloughed off in spots, and the flesh of wood has been gouged by cables. The air as we pass is sweet with the smell of sap. Carl asks if I can stay for salmon dinner tonight. The run has been strong this year. He smiles as he drives away from camp and down the gravel road to the crime scene.

There is a single wide trailer in a rock pit, yellow crime scene tape across the door. A trooper is there and waves as we stop. There has been a black bear coming around and nosing into the garbage all night. The trooper has been there to protect the crime scene until he gets the okay from the crime lab to release the scene back to Bob's landlords. I look up to a point just beyond the edge of the rock pit where a cedar tree droops down in a delicate arch. The limbs sparkle slightly. When a breeze comes by, these branches swing easily, causing fat raindrops to fall. At the door of the trailer is a dark bloodstain that has cascaded down all three broken stairs. About a dozen garbage bags are piled outside the trailer. Some food scraps, meat tins, and scraped-out cans of chili, but the bags are predominantly stuffed with beer cans and whiskey bottles. I look carefully at the garbage. This is usually the best evidence I find on my own. The trooper sees me, and before I open another bag he tells me to stop. "I think they want the garbage," he says. "I mean the lieutenant wants it. I think." I nod and step away from the garbage bags. I hear a rustle in the woods. The black bear sits on his haunches, watching us.

Ten months later, Bob pleads guilty to second degree murder. At his sentencing, he makes a statement to the judge. He says he is not afraid of the consequences because, as strange as it sounds, he really loved Jody and he didn't mean to hurt her. He never would have done it if he had been sober. He's got his drinking under control now. He hopes the judge knows that. "I'm not a monster," Bob says. He is standing up as he says these things. The judge thanks him for his comments and asks him to be seated. Friends and family members from both sides will make statements to try to give the judge a complete picture of both Bob and Jody. Police officers will testify. So will an expert on the effects of alcohol. The judge asks Bob to stand again, and this time the judge gives a short speech. The judge says that Bob did not heed the signs of danger in his life—the alcoholism and the increasing violence. Hence the judge believes that the chance of rehabilitation is slight. The judge reviews the reports of domestic violence that led up to the murder. He reviews the complaints and the restraining orders. "There were clear signs that you were headed for trouble and you chose to ignore them. Your substance abuse was prolonged and reckless." He stares at Bob directly and adds, "And your drunkenness on the night of the killing clouded your intent, but it did not change the result. Drinking doesn't explain everything about this young woman's death." Bob shakes his head and stares down at his lawyer. Bob had been prepared for the long sentence, but, strangely, this is the first time he has been officially reproached for his actions. This is the first time that he has been told publicly and sternly that what he did was wrong. He is not prepared for that. His face turns pale, his hands shake.

The judge ticks off a list of other criteria he must consider in sentencing. He must consider the "affirmation of societal norms" as well as the defendant's prospects for rehabilitation. Here the judge looks up over his glasses. "A young woman's life has been taken, tragically and unaccountably, without concern for the consequences. And while I see your prison record has been good, it appears that it took this substantial tragedy for you to confront the destructive patterns in your life. Sadly, this self-awareness came too late and only after the most extreme circumstances." He gives Bob forty-five years to serve.

Bob sits down. Jody's parents cry and hug each other. Bob's mother stares down at her hands and tears roll from under her glasses. As Jody's parents leave the courtroom, her father puts his hands on Bob's mother's shoulder. She acknowledges him but does not speak. Bob shakes his head and will not look at his mother. Realistically, he will be eligible for parole when he is sixty-six years old.

Jody's family buried her in a little cemetery in eastern Washington. The cemetery looks over the Columbia River. Jody's son passes it every day going to school. Sometimes his friends tease him about his mom being dead, and he pretends it doesn't matter.

After the sentencing I go out for drinks with Bob's lawyer. We order microbrew and make small talk. Her eyes are rimmed with dark circles. She had been getting by on three hours sleep for the last few days, getting ready for the hearing. She is disappointed in the forty-five-year sentence and we talk about appeal points. Still, she is relieved that she was able to save Bob from a life sentence. We talk about some of our other cases and then have another beer. She leaves early to go to the gym and I go for a walk. Rain slants down through the streetlights. The reflected lights of passing cars smear like lipstick on the storefronts. The bars clatter with congenial laughter. I want to go in and drink, but I go back to the hotel and sleep.

The truth is that most real crime, in actual places, makes a soul weary. Sometimes I'm laid low by a sadness that puts me down in a chair and won't let me get up. Some criminal investigators drink, some burn out and get cynical, others head south to look for a higher class of criminal. As I said, I've been tempted to throw in the towel in favor of the hermetic life of a wilderness poet. I fantasize about a rustic hut situated in an ice-scoured valley. There would be a crude plank table with a bench and a bowl of ink. I could sit at this table and nurture my own exquisite vision of the nonhuman world.

But I always come back to the feeling that I'm linked somehow to Bob and Jody and this whole sad business. I love the icy purity of the alpine world, I love the long-limbed trees dancing in the coastal storm, and I realize that my sanity depends on them somehow. But if I have a relationship to these granite rocks, then surely I must be linked with these flawed and complex mammals who work and drink and love and, mysteriously, kill one another. I am, after all, the same kind of creature and I share their habitat.

I spend a lot of time telling stories now, reworking what I've seen, people I've met: the brutal men and their victims, the sad-eyed angels, and the dispirited con men, trying to sneak or steal a piece of the good life. I do this reworking in order to make sense of things, and I bump my head on the fact that there is always more to say about crime. There is more to say about race, class, gender, and the acceptance of violence in our culture. There is more to say about poverty and alcohol and the question of who deserves the good life in America. Who gets to be the indicator species when it comes to the creation of public policy? I walk around these island towns and look for solutions but eventually I remember there is no "final solution" to crime. We all live on islands of some pre-scribed dimensions, and everyone among us has worked the edges. If there is any sense to be made of crime in the Tongass it might be as simple and as complex as this: there are no roads out.

So I sat on the airport parking lot curb, watching the windblown trees until my wife picked me up and took me to the police station where I filled out the report about my car. The officer on duty knew me and seemed amused that I was the victim of this particular crime. "Stolen," he said. "What's this world coming to?"

I laughed and handed him back the form. My car was found at three in the morning the next day, parked on a well-lighted street up near the elementary school. It was almost out of gas. The high school girl who stole it had been drinking and dug around in several cars left at the airport. Mine was the first key she found. The police officer stopped her for driving erratically and she tried to lie about where she got the car. A friend riding with her had never been in trouble before. She burst into tears and spilled out the whole mess for the officer.

It was raining when I got my car home. I backed it in under an alder tree that half-sheltered a narrow lane near my toolshed. The tree was losing its seed pods, which crunched under the bald tires. The interior of my car seemed strange and out of sorts. There was a faint smell of perfume and cigarettes. Someone had spilled beer next to the transmission hump, and the smell reminded me of so many of the crime scenes I had walked through, where so many lives had flown apart in the rages of brutality. I felt lucky then to have gotten off so lightly in my life.

Then I thought of the girl who had taken my car. What would become of her? I noticed that the knob of the radio had been torn off and thrown away. It's a clue, I thought, and wondered if it told me anything about her or the relative health of our community. I watched the trees, still waving wildly in the wind, then looked up to the mountains hunched in their green robes around this isolated little town, and I imagined that drunken girl driving twelve miles of road in this ugly stolen car—the windows down, rain spattering on her cheeks as she yells and cries and pours her soul out to the music before coming to the irrevocable end of the road, where she throws the radio knob into the forest, then turns the car around to head back home.

JOHN STRALEY is a private investigator and the author of five Alaska mysteries featuring Cecil Younger. The latest of these is The Angels Will Not Care *(Bantam Books, 1998). He lives in Sitka, Alaska, with his wife, Jan, and his son, Finn.*

killer whale, *Nancy Behnken*

Naatsilanéi

TOLD BY WILLIE MARKS

He was married to the sister of those young men.

Naatsilanéi
was what they say his name was.

He would tell stories to his brothers-in-law
about how well he could use those crampon snowshoes.

They didn't think
he could get on
the sea lion rock.

That was why they prepared.
"Well! Let's let you all take me out!" is maybe what that man said.

He already had
those crampon snowshoes.

They took him out there by boat.

They took him by boat.

When the boat got there—
wow! there were a lot of sea lions
on the island!

The waves
reached high.

When he thought the time was right—
my! he leaped to shore.

He stuck to the spot there.

They thought he would slip into the sea.

Maybe that's what they wanted; if he fell into the sea they wouldn't
    help him.
But then he outsmarted them.
He ran up to the top.
To the top, I guess.
He ran through the sea lions.
When he had speared about four or five of them

he said,
"Bring the boat over now!"

Just as he said that they pulled in their oars.
Which way was the wind blowing? Maybe it was blowing
    southeast.

The wind was taking them.

He could only watch them.
It was their very youngest brother,
the youngest of the brothers, his brother-in-law.
It was he, who while he was crying, grabbed an oar to get him.
Maybe he was rowing
to his brother-in-law.
But they tore it from his hands.

That was how they started to blow toward shore again.
When they were blown far enough out that's when they sat up.
They began to row to shore.
But he sat at the top of the island.

When it began to get dark maybe he wrapped himself up, pulling
    his blanket over his head
on that sea lion rock.

Maybe they were saying he was swept into the sea by the waves.
On the mainland though
they couldn't rescue him.

It was getting dark when he heard that thing in the roar of the
    waves while he was trying to sleep.
"I'm coming to get you!"
He pushed the wrap from his face.
It was a beaver robe he wore.
There was nothing there.
Nobody there.

The fourth time, the third time,
the fourth time.
The third time when he didn't see anything he prepared for the
    fourth one.
He watched through the hole where the eyehole was.
Maybe his thoughts were "What's going on?"
It stood up right before his eyes, at the lip-edge of the waves, this
    huge man.
Before it could speak Naatsilanéi asked it, "Where to?"
"Under this rock."

"How am I going to get there?"
he said.
It lifted the edge of the sea like a cloth.
"Go under this," it said to him.
He didn't even feel the sea.
Oh!
It's a village,

a house.
He went there, down there.
As he was entering the house, he saw that man lying there.
A harpoon point was stuck in him.
It was a harpoon point.
He had been harpooned.
But they, the sea lion people,
couldn't see what the human had made.

"How will we pay you?"
they asked him. "How much do you want?"
He had only to think,
"Something I could reach my village with."
"You've got it!"
they said to him.
"You will be paid with it."
They could read his mind,
whatever he thought.
Then he probably just put on an act.
He went by the sick man.
While he was feeling around him
he pulled the bone spear head
out of him.
That's where the proverb comes from
"he was like the man who had a spear removed."
He sat up without feeling pain.

That's why they gave that thing to him,

that big balloon,

a motorized rubber raft, I don't know what to call it.

They probably took him to the surface again, to the reef.
"Get into this thing.

Don't think of this place again; think only of your village.
Okay," they said to him.
Then he went inside of it.
They probably tied it shut with him.

One,
two,
three,
four,
they tossed it up in the air.
They moved over the waves the fourth time.
Then the wind gusted, that southeast wind.
The bubble was blown with him.
After the wind had been blowing for a while he thought, "Oops,
what if it blows back there with me again?"
He felt the waves pounding him on the shore.
It probably had a zipper for an opening.
They opened it.
"We told you not to think like that!" they said.
"So now think only of that place! Don't let your thoughts return!
    Go right straight to your home!"
He tried it again.
The wind began to carry him.
When the waves were pounding it on the beach,
I wonder how he got out.
There was probably an automatic button.
Well, it was on the other side of his village.
He recognized it.
He had bad feelings
about what they had done to him.
That's why he went up right away.
It was probably getting dark already.
Maybe he was sneaking

toward this wife of his,
toward this village of his.

Was it like now? People don't cry for each other any more.
On that little point, sitting on top of the rock was his wife.
She was crying over there.

He went up to her. "Hey, honey!"
"Oh, yeah," she answered.
He told her what had happened to him.
Maybe this is how she turned against her brothers.
The thoughts of that woman turned against them.
That was why she helped her husband.
"Get me my adze."
Probably some food, too.
"Be sure there's lots of rice."
That's how she brought them to him, perhaps during the night.
Maybe he knew where they usually passed
when those brothers-in-law of his hunted.
He adzed out those things.
Those sea lions had probably instructed him on what he should do.
That's why he immediately worked on those things.
They were Killer Whales he adzed.
Killer Whales.

I don't know what kind of wood.
He made them from any old wood.
He made them
just the easiest way.
They were ready to go.
He had them in the water.

Probably at midnight; when the night turns over all things
are evil.
Midnight.

Maybe that's when he told them to go.
One, two, three, four.
Those creatures immediately ran into the sea.
No! They floated up out there.
There was no spirit in them.
There was no trace of it inside
the wood anymore.
That was why he tried a different kind; he tried all kinds of things.
Only when he finally carved yellow cedar
he carved for the last time.
When he finally told them to go into the sea
they glided through the sea.
When they stood up out in the water they had many things in their
    jaws.
He got
seal,
halibut.
"Well, come over now!" he said to them.
"The boat will pass through here.
I will tell you when to go for them."
That's what he probably said to them.
"But you put the youngest one
in a safe place.
Throw him on a broken piece of the boat."

All right, they would paddle early in the morning.

The boat was passing through there.
Okay,
he had them ready then.
He probably talked all the time to the fish
he had made.
When they were right for him he told them to go.
Shhhhhhhhhhhh.

They stood up around the boat.
They crunched the boat between their jaws.
Those things he carved were doing this.
But the smallest one the one who had picked up the paddle toward
    him,
fell on a piece of the boat.
Maybe that was what the young boy
paddled to shore.
That's why he, that young boy,
was able to tell about it.
Probably Naatsilanéi told him too.
Probably he came to him, I guess; that little brother-in-law of his
reached shore.
He went home.
That's when
Naatsilanéi talked again to those fish he had carved
that had crunched the boat in their jaws.
"Next time
you will not do this again,"
is what he told them to remember.
"Whatever you'll eat is what you will kill."
That's why those things don't do any harm to humans,
however large they are.
That's when Naatsilanéi went into the forest,
maybe to wherever he would die.

*WILLIE MARKS (1902–1981), whose Tlingit names were Kéet Yanaayí,
Tl'óon, Yaduxwéi, and Wáank´, was a respected Tlingit elder of the Eagle
moiety and the Chookaneidí clan. He was the survivor of two houses, the
Brown Bear Den and Brown Bear House of Hoonah, Alaska. His father*

Jakwteen was Lukaax.ádi from Yandeist´akyé in Chilkat. His mother's name was Tl´óon Tláa, a Chookan sháa from Hoonah. He was the youngest of six children. From the time he was born, Willie and his family lived a subsistence lifestyle, following the seasons of the resources. He was an excellent hunter and a fisherman all his life, fishing both commercially and for his family's food. He had eclectic interests: he enjoyed eating Chinese food with chopsticks, and he learned to play the steel guitar and to dance the Hawaiian hula. Still, he remained true to his Tlingit heritage. He was a well-known carver of traditional totem poles and masks, a skill he taught to several family members. From childhood he was trained to be a ceremonial leader and shakee.át dancer, and, upon his brother's death, inherited the position of house leader of the Brown Bear House of Hoonah. This story was recorded in October 1972, when he was seventy years old.

Sitka black-tailed deer, *Richard Carstensen*

Heart of the Hunter

RICHARD NELSON

The secret.
and the secret hidden deep in that.
GARY SNYDER

The deer's hoofprints, keen edged in wet, black sand, couldn't be more than a couple hours old, but the brown bear's tracks look even fresher. Deeply dished indentations of its hind feet, twelve inches from splayed heel to scimitar claws, obliterate several of the deer's imprints, proving the bear came afterward. Pushing her muzzle into each depression, Keta savors a feral scent as dense and pungent for her as burned toast would be for me.

I unshoulder the rifle and kneel down to put my nose beside hers, but detect nothing except the salty tang of kelp and tide. Then, hunkered shoulder to shoulder with the dog, I carefully scrutinize the way ahead, a lazy curve of beach ending in a bedrock point heaped at its edges with seaweed. But I see no trace of shaggy flank, no furred hillock of shoulder and back, no glint or blink of eye—only a batch of crows above the tide's reach, pecking and flapping and gabbling.

The long windrow of seaweed, five feet deep and thirty feet wide, washed ashore in massive swells kicked up by our latest North Pacific storm. Clambering onto it, I find a series of broad pits dug into the snarl of composting eel grass and kelp, with the posthole depressions of bear's feet leading from one excavation to the next. Beside the last and biggest crater is a mound of droppings the diameter of a medium pizza, bright tan, moist, and gleaming. It looks something like dog scat, but appropriately scaled for a creature weighing six hundred to eight hundred pounds.

I make no claim to fastidiousness or refinement, having occasionally eaten things most people from my own culture wouldn't touch with a long stick, yet when I lean close to inspect these droppings, their feculent, curdling aroma takes the breath right out of me. The odor, which outclasses anything of this sort I've ever encountered, does eloquent justice to an immense, churning digestive tract. Its contents include a goulash of plant seeds, grass, and seaweed, along with bits of gravel and shell—evidence of the bear's shoreline foraging.

To find out if this scat is as fresh as it looks, I poke two fingers far down into the glutinous melange. And sure enough, from the surface to the very core, there's not a hint of cooling. In fact, a thermometer inserted where I've stuck my fingers would probably register close to a brown bear's normal body temperature. Information like this should never be taken lightly. I fasten my eyes on the shoreside forest just beyond a batch of driftwood logs about forty feet away—the direction in which Keta is presently sniffing and peering. I suspect the animal saw us coming, hesitated just long enough to deposit this organic calling card, and then took off at a dead run. On the other hand, it's only prudent to assume the bear is lurking back among those shadows deciding what to do about us.

Perhaps we should get out of here, but I choose instead to follow Keta up toward the trees, pausing for long intervals to watch and listen, trying to ignore the heartbeats thrumming in my ears. This is not blind foolishness, however, because I trust Keta's judgment. If she sensed the bear nearby, she'd fix a burning border collie stare on one spot in the underbrush and her whole body would tremble excitedly. But now, although on full alert, she acts like the place has been abandoned.

As we ease into the forest, I can't stop thinking of what we found in this same place a few months back. Beneath an enormous spruce, in a game trail worn raw by the previous winter's deer traffic, lay a bloodstained shoulderblade neatly punctured with a single tooth hole. Not far away we found a patch of matted grass and trampled earth ten feet in diameter thickly strewn with gray-brown hair plucked from a deer's hide. Then we discovered the four scattered legs, their bones still articulated, hide and meat stripped away, tendons shredded, hooves intact. A wafting smell of decay indicated several days had passed since the blacktail—a full-grown adult—had been killed or scavenged by a brown bear.

I imagined the deer feeding just outside the woods, and the bear stalking meticulously into the wind, hunching behind bedrock mounds much the same color as its fur, lifting its head to watch when the deer leaned down to nibble seaweed, then cringing back when she snapped to alertness; and the bear drawing shallow breaths, neurons flaring in the maelstrom of its brain, muscles coiling and hardening; and the bear, unleashed like a boulder on a steep slope, pitching against the deer's late flight; and the collision of muscle and bone, the shearing of flesh, the two animals twisting together and becoming still; the unraveling violence lapsing to serene quiet, broken by the bear's heaving chest; and fog bursting from the bear's nostrils, warm blood rivering down its tongue; and the deer's body yielding and relaxing, its heartbeats subsiding, its eyes staring absently into the sky as night came down and down.

I trust these imaginings because I've stalked deer in this same place and watched them with the same predatory intent, drawing from the part of my mind that is purely and passionately a hunter. In this sense, the bear and I differ little from each other, or from our fellow island predators—flicker and robin, mink and shrew, marten and river otter, great blue heron and bald eagle. We all have the gifts of canniness and guile, we share a common hunger, and our bodies are made from the flesh that feeds us.

And here, on this wild island at the continent's far northwestern edge, a human hunter must accept the possibility of also being hunted.

When I found those deer remains I was keenly aware that a brown bear, after killing its prey and eating until satiated, often buries the leftovers under dirt and brush, beds down nearby, and keeps watch. Anybody who stumbles onto a cache risks unleashing the big animal's protective fury, so rather than dawdle around, I motioned Keta to my side and we quietly deserted the place.

But today's situation is clearly different. Although the bear couldn't be far off, there is no sign of a kill and no indication the animal hung around to protest our arrival. Most important, Keta now seems more interested in a winter wren scolding from a thicket than she is in the bear's cooling scent. Of course, bears are always somewhere nearby on this Alaskan island and they must occasionally watch us without letting themselves be seen, so, except for the fresh reminder, this day is no different from any other.

The morning's events remind me of what a Tlingit Indian man once told me about bear country etiquette. "The elders taught us," he recalled, "that if we didn't bother bears then bears wouldn't make trouble for us either. And if we come upon a brown bear, we should talk to it like this: 'My grandfather, forgive me for trespassing on your land. I'm just a poor man hunting for my food, the same as you are.' According to the old people, if you do this, bears will leave you alone."

During my years as an apprentice hunter in Koyukon Indian villages, I heard much the same thing. Elders advised that someone who comes across an aggressive bear should act unthreatening and say in an easy voice: "I'm not bothering you, so you might as well go away." A woman can shame and quiet the animal by uncovering what is most female about her while saying, "My husband, it's me." This harks back, I believe, to the ancient story of a woman who married a bear and had his children, a history that links our two species and still affects the ways Koyukon people behave toward bears. In Koyukon tradition there is a powerful feeling of affinity between humans and other animals, and one of the most important moral virtues is avoiding arrogance toward any part of nature.

With these lessons in mind I motion Keta to my side and head on past the spot where we found the punctured scapula last spring. I've walked this path hundreds of times over the years and have a pretty good mental map of the surrounding terrain, with its puzzlework of forest and muskeg, stream and pond, hillock and swale. Of course, blacktails and brown bears have also used this path, perhaps for centuries, and they know the landscape far more intricately than I do. Nevertheless, I've poured my heart into this island, I have a strong sense of belonging here, and I think of myself as a member of its living community. In common with the other animals, I take food from this place to nourish my body, and I come here to nurture my spirit as well. The trail, inscribed with tracks from last night's deer, leads me back into a familiar and beloved world.

Taking a few steps, then hesitating for long minutes to watch and listen, Keta and I move at a pace only slightly faster than no pace at all. My senses become increasingly engaged, warming up like a runner's muscles. Beside the trail I notice that most of the dainty twigs on a huckleberry bush are pruned to nubs—evidence of deer browsing during last winter's heavy snows. Faint chitters reveal a mob of white-winged crossbills among the boughs high overhead, prying seeds from spruce cones and unleashing a shower of flaky brown scales.

Today's excursion started at first light when I stashed camping gear and enough food for several days into the skiff, eased away from our home shore on Anchor Bay, and set a course across Haida

Strait. I felt a bit lonely going off without Nita, my partner and usual hunting companion. Although she doesn't carry a weapon, Nita has an impeccably sharp eye for deer, loves being outdoors in the patient and meditative way of "still hunting," and enjoys participating in the work that provides our staple foods—most important, venison, as well as salmon, halibut, lingcod, rockfish, berries, and other edible plants.

Given her penchant for seasickness, Nita was lucky to miss this morning's boat ride. Like an afterthought from the fifty-knot storm two days ago, a hefty swell ran in from the ocean, setting up a fracas on Haida Strait. Here in the North Pacific, October's burly gales and constant rain are just occasionally interrupted by a day like this, when the beast of autumn sleeps. As I approached the island, a gap widened among crumbling colonnades of cloud, spilling out the first sunshine I'd seen all month. Blue water sparkled like shattering glass and the island stood out in crisp detail: driftwood logs stark as bones on black rock, the land sweeping away in long ridges serrated with trees, and above it all the chasmed face of Kluksa Mountain—enormous, snow covered, and ethereal—half hidden amid gauzy webs of fog.

I felt as if the island were imbued with a pervading, indecipherable power that both frightened and compelled me. Then I gazed out over the Pacific stretching off to the horizon's brink, and I recognized how minute and vulnerable I was, alone on this remote shore. But I willingly accept the risks, and regardless of consequences, I'd rather be here than anywhere else on earth. Many times I've yearned to own some part of this island, although it's public land that rightfully belongs to everyone, and this morning I realized the equation is in fact reversed, that the island owns *me*. To this I freely yielded myself as I anchored the skiff in a cove sheltered by reefs and islets.

Partway through the woods, Keta abruptly halts and stares ahead as if she's spotted a deer—or is it something bigger?

Momentarily I realize the object of her interest is a red squirrel about the size of a kitten, perched on a fallen tree trunk six feet away. The squirrel should dash off like a lizard on a rock, but she hesitates, acting almost tame, then crabs awkwardly along the mossy bark, her body strangely crooked. Easing closer, I notice the fur on her right shoulder is creased and soiled. Perhaps she fell off a high branch, but more likely the squirrel escaped from an eagle, marten, or mink. In any case, wobbling gait and dazed behavior make her an easy mark and I doubt she'll survive for long out here. Nature is not fed by mercy, after all.

Daylight glimmering between mazy tree trunks reveals the muskeg just ahead. We inch past a saturated swale crowded with enormous skunk cabbage that look like they belong in a tropical forest, their broad, spatulate leaves standing as high as my waist. Hungry blacktails have scalloped some leaves to about half their normal width, and several others have been torn right out of the ground, their stems eaten and their roots excavated. Bear work, probably earlier today.

I stop at the muskeg's edge, half hidden by the trunk of a cedar tree, and hold my open palm toward Keta—our hand signal to sit. She folds back her ears, obeys, then pricks them up and watches as I kneel quietly beside the cedar for a long look at the surrounding landscape.

Back in August, Keta and I came to this same place to watch just as we're doing now, and she picked up a strong scent indicating a deer close by. We began moving slowly upwind, stepping noiselessly on wet grass, concealing ourselves behind a copse of shore pines. During our approach, I never once glimpsed the deer, but from Keta's growing excitement I knew it wasn't far off. Bucks, except when they're addled by the rut, have an almost preternatural sense for danger, a mind entirely different from the less cautious does and adolescents. This thought came to me as I heard a sudden thump of hooves. And then I saw him—a buck with sprawling antlers, their beams almost as thick as ax handles. He bolted across the muskeg, never once hesitating or stopping to glance back as blacktails often do, and within seconds he vanished into the far woods. Although I'm not interested in trophy hunting, I'll admit keeping a sharp eye out for that deer ever since.

The same boggy meadow stretches before us now: autumn-sere grass patched with stunted pines and brushy junipers, a few small ponds and streamlets, and Kluksa Mountain's timbered flank rising steeply behind. The broad sweep of land looks inviting and fecund, as if it should be alive with animals like the Serengeti plains. But the island has only two large mammal species, brown bear and blacktails, and our deer usually take shelter in the woods during full daylight.

This muskeg is separated from another by a narrow isthmus of pines, but there's a short break where you can see into both—an ideal spot to try the deer call. Because we've had weeks of constant rain, the moss and duff squish loudly underfoot, but I pick each step carefully and reach the opening in about ten minutes. There, I lean the rifle against a pine, gesture for Keta to sit, and give the call a few short blows. Its thin, reedy sound, similar to blowing on a grass blade pinched between your thumbs, makes a fair imitation of a bleating deer, or a fawn's voice if it's pitched very high. Bears may also come rumbling toward a call, apparently hoping to find easy prey, so the prudent hunter carries a powerful rifle and uses the call near a good climbing tree.

Knowing a bear is around, I keep a close watch both on the muskeg and the inscrutable radar dog. A few minutes later, Keta locks her ears and eyes on the woods about fifty yards away. Crouching down, rifle braced against the tree trunk, I strain to pick out any movement. It seems as if there's nothing . . . until I spot a doe well out into the muskeg, as if she'd somehow materialized there. The deer comes deliberately toward us, moving in the stiff, mechanical way that telegraphs her anxiety, switching her tail, reaching out for a scent, leaning from side to side, honing her ears in our direction. Keta stays put, although she can't help quivering with desire.

The doe stops forty feet away, facing in our direction, more inquisitive than afraid, and for several minutes there's a petrified stillness, as if we were all snared in an unbreakable gaze.

Koyukon people say animals offer themselves to those who have shown respect toward all members of their species, and there is no shame or guilt in taking what is given, so long as it is done properly, never in excess, and used without waste. I haven't forgotten that I am here to hunt. This island has a healthy population of blacktails, does are legal game, and I am not unwilling to take female deer. Of course, a buck would be in prime condition now and probably heavier than a doe, but this female looks very large and very fat. What constrains me is the possibility that last summer's fawn, although well past nursing and fully capable of living independently, could be tagging along somewhere nearby, still learning from its mother. Part of me urges doing what I came for, but another part is tangled with ambivalence, wondering if a fawn might eventually appear.

While I'm knotted by indecision, a raven soars out from the woods, circles overhead, and lands in a dead tree not more than thirty feet away. The hawk-sized bird clutches a bare, whitened branch, tilts down his head, and unleashes a clamor of gurgling, sonorous croaks. Shading my eyes against the corona of sun, I watch his beak open and close, the feathers on his throat ruffle and flatten. He looks like a midnight phantom etched on a screen of molten light.

I remember sitting on a bluff in northern Alaska with Grandpa William, a Koyukon elder, while he scanned the valley below for moose. A raven appeared, gliding low enough so he could have heard our whispers. Grandpa William watched for a moment, then spoke earnestly to the bird, as if he were imploring divine help in our search for game, which indeed he was: *"Tseek'aath,* Old Grandfather, I wish the animals would come our way easily." The raven drifted on without giving a sign—no aerial somersault to "drop his packsack full of meat for us" and no yodeled *Ggaagga!* (the Koyukon word for "Animal!") to assure us of luck and show the way toward game. A few days later we went back to the village empty-handed.

Above me now, the raven inflates his body, bends his spindly black legs, turns his shining beak this way and that, and spills his convoluted chant into the forest. It was the Great Raven who created our world, Koyukon elders say, and his living descendants still have extraordinary powers that can benefit people. For example, the raven will sometimes lead hunters to game, although it isn't simply out of goodness, because he knows he'll get scraps from the kill.

Still, I can't help wondering why a raven has appeared at this moment. Is he laughing at this man, so distant from his earthly roots that he's paralyzed with indecision when a deer presents herself? For generations beyond reckoning, our ancestors lived free from such dilemmas, accepting what was given in the hunt, moving in the embrace of an inspirited natural community, surrounded by wild creatures who listened and understood. But in modern societies, the old order has lapsed and we're beset with moral confusion about our dependence on the living world.

So here I stand, befuddled, the raven's voice echoing in my ears, the doe looking on. She comes nearer until she finds an eddy in the breeze laden with scents of man and dog. At this she flinches back, raises her head and flags her tail, then struts off. Near the center of the muskeg she stops behind a juniper bush and looks back for a long minute, as if she's presenting herself one more time. But I have lowered the rifle and watch as she melts off into the woods.

Grateful for Keta's partnership and patience, I stroke her silky black fur and whisper "Good girl!" in her ear. The deer's exit has triggered Keta's roundup instinct and she's all afire, looking eagerly into my eyes, begging me just this once to let her chase. When we first started training a few years ago, I used to pick her up and aim her snout in the direction of a deer because otherwise she'd never see it. I also tied a light cord about twenty feet long onto her collar, and if she charged after an animal I'd yank back when she reached the end. Startled and amazed, she quickly learned to stay put.

These lessons had another important purpose: in wild country an uncontrolled dog is liable to chase after a bear, harass and anger it, then come running back to you with the enraged bruin on its heels.

Over the next few hours Keta and I track through a series of boggy muskegs separated by strips of forest—lofty Sitka spruce, western hemlock, and yellow cedar growing mostly along stream courses and steep-sided ravines. The sharply whetted concentration of hunting brings on a relaxed, almost hypnotic state that I've never experienced any other way, even while stalking animals with a camera. It's as if the primal mind becomes wholly engaged and nothing matters except this footstep, this tanglework of brush and trees, this muddy track or nibbled leaf, this moment's interweaving of birdsong and rustling leaves, this touch of breeze, this flutter of moth's wings, this patter of falling spruce needles . . . and always, the possibility of a soft brown shape moving at the margin of sight.

By late afternoon thickening overcast blankets the sky, the air becomes dense and clammy, and the breeze increases. During this season, when storms charge in like Brahma bulls from the Pacific, anyone with a lick of sense pays close attention to weather signs. Knowing that the waters in our little cove degrade into chaos during heavy weather, I hurry back to camp, load everything into the skiff, and head several miles up the coast to a well-protected anchorage close to muskegs favored by deer. Right now the sandy shore of this anchorage is inundated by a full-moon tide, so it's impossible to tell if bears have passed here recently. There's no time to worry about it, because evening's coming on and deer should be moving into the open.

We make our way through a dim gallery of spruce and hemlock giants, with sapling trees growing atop long-fallen trunks and a plushy cloak of moss laid over the earth. Keta knows the deer trail that takes us into a narrow, boggy muskeg that eventually broadens to a sweep of semiopen terrain with ample cover for deer but also good visibility for hunting.

She follows a river of scent toward a small patch of trees—just the sort of place where you'd expect to find deer. Perusing every nook through binoculars reveals nothing, so I move ahead very cautiously—but not, as it turns out, cautiously enough. While we're still a fair distance off, a doe unwinds in flight from the trees' edge, tail high and ears pinched back, punctuating each suspended leap with a snort. When I snort back she stops, mistaking us for other deer, but the ruse only works for a few seconds.

Meanwhile, Keta begs desperately to chase, fairly crazed with herd-dog impulses. In this we're much alike: I would love to sprint alongside that deer, to savor at close range her dazzling agility, to watch the flex and spring of her sinewy legs, the moss flying from her hooves, the boughs parting against her neck like water cleaved by a dolphin's prow. Perhaps only a person who hunts can penetrate the seeming paradox of loving a creature that you also stalk and kill and eat.

After the doe, we pass through an occasional trace of scent, but nothing to elevate Keta's interest. Thickening clouds bury the heights of Kluksa Mountain, foggy streamers drift along the lower slopes, and dusk broods in every cleft. Because I haven't set up camp, there's no choice but to hurry back, hoping we might happen onto a careless deer along the way. Dark forest impinges on either side of the narrow muskeg where we started hunting an hour ago. I've often attracted deer to a call in this place, but the light is fading quickly now.

From my hurried, noisy strides, Keta knows our hunting is finished, so she grabs a stick, dashes madly through the grass, crouches ahead of me, and gives me that border collie stare, asking to play. Each time I approach she races off in a wide circle, joyous as a kid erupting from a school bus.

Then, unaccountably, she drops the stick, walks up into the wind testing a scent, and makes one . . . two . . . three suspicious whoofs, hesitates, then whoofs again. I've never heard this breathy, huffing sound from Keta, but I know it well. Koyukon people often describe such barks as a bear warning, and once, in a northern Alaska fishing camp, a sled dog tethered outside my tent made exactly this sound as a black bear approached under cover of twilight. Luckily, the bear ran off after we shouted a few times.

There are no black bears on this island, only the weighty, formidable, and cantankerous brown bear. If Keta were an experienced northern husky, I'd know without question what's going on, but she has yet to encounter one of the big animals at close range. And would a border collie raised in suburban Wisconsin react like a wolfish sled dog to fresh bear scent? Maybe she's just caught a peculiar smell or heard something unusual.

Keta stares across the muskeg toward the place where we met the deer earlier. I see nothing in that direction except an oddly shaped stump; perhaps she's mistaken it for a person or animal. After a few minutes' watching I decide to ease over that way—bullet chambered and rifle ready—to make sure we're not being shadowed. Keta balks at my side, tentative and anxious, not at all the way she'd react to a deer, and when we reach the misshapen stump she ignores it, peering farther into the muskeg. It's getting late, I can't distinguish anything except brush and meadow, and it seems best to turn back. Keta hesitates until I whistle for her, then reluctantly tags along.

Fifty yards ahead of us the muskeg narrows to a cul-de-sac where we'll pick up the trail to our anchorage. As an experiment I toss a stick for Keta. Incredibly, she pays no attention to it, but stays out in front glancing nervously from side to side. Even if she's detected an animal, I think it must be long gone after all the disturbance we've caused, so I let myself relax and watch Keta instead of our surroundings.

Then it happens.

PSHEEEEEEAAAAWWWWWWW! An explosive, wheezy snort shatters the silence, unleashing an electrified jolt that shocks every nerve in my body. Stopping short, acting without thought, I jerk the rifle to my shoulder. And at the same instant, a dark, hulking shape rises thirty yards ahead.

Brown bear!

The animal towers up on thick, bent legs, showing the mass and girth of his body, immense forelegs opened at either side, platter-sized paws hanging down. Staring at us through the impending dusk, his head looms like a stony butte, his chest heaves ponderously, his body sways from side to side.

In a single motion, the bear turns and pitches down on all fours, gathers himself like a landslide, and hurtles off, smashing violently through underbrush at the forest's edge.

Stunned beyond movement, I trace the bear's pounding retreat into the woods—just where I'd beg for him to go—until the bedlam abruptly stops. After a tremendous quiet lasting a few seconds, the animal charges off again, either coming toward us or skirting the muskeg just behind the trees. During these moments I remember Koyukon hunters describing the brown bear's preternatural strength, incredible speed, and vehement temper. And I wonder if this beast will turn away in fear or come bursting out in anger.

At this point I have the presence of mind to speak—or perhaps yell—so the animal knows without question that the thing it saw or heard or smelled is in fact a human. The words are something akin to what Koyukon elders taught me to say:

"Bear.

"I am a man. I don't want trouble!

"If you'll go your way, I'll go mine!

"Bear. I am a human! I didn't come here to bother you!"

The words overflow from a part of my brain that leaves no memory afterward, as someone might forget what he thought in the last instant before colliding with a dump truck.

Again and again I call out, trying to be heard over the cacophony of splintering branches and thundering feet. At one point I realize my voice is so loud and low it could be mistaken for a growl, so I force myself to talk more easily, which helps settle the storm inside my brain. It also allows me to hear the bear, who sounds as if he's bowling over everything in his path except full-sized trees.

There's such fury in all this, I can't help imagining the bear has circled back to teach me a lesson for some nameless offense I've committed against his kind. With this thought, I lift my anchoring feet and scuttle backward, gawking around for a climbable tree. There are none, but of course it wouldn't matter, because I'd be lucky to get off the ground at all—much less the required fifteen feet—in the time it would take a bear to get here. The rifle seems equally useless. How could I take lethal aim at an animal rumbling toward me at full speed, head bobbing and shoulders rolling, only half visible in the swarthy light?

Meanwhile, Keta's reaction, as far as I can tell, is totally opposite from mine. She's dancing toward the woods, ears up, ready for a chase. "Get back here!" I shout, and she cringes to my side. "You stay now," I order again and again, not just to get my point across but to make sure the bear hears my voice over his own racket.

At the same time, I've angled toward the exit trail, rifle still at ready, looking ahead so I won't stumble but keeping an eye behind for trouble.

Then everything falls silent. I have no idea if the bear has fled, stopped to reconsider, or slowed to a predatory stalk. I also can't tell if Keta, scampering ahead as we enter the forest trail, has picked up my fear or feels playful after so much excitement. As all this unfolded, I now realize, my hands never got shaky and my heart didn't race; there was only that hard twang of fright, followed by a state of intense concentration and an absolute resolve to do whatever became necessary. By some quirk of instinct, the jitters haven't begun until now.

When we're well inside the woods, I stop to catch my breath and settle my brain, figuring the bear is gone. And then, looking down at the muddy trail, I discover the impression of a bear's front paw. More prints reveal that the animal had followed our own freshly scented tracks through this forest and into the muskeg.

Keta snuffles every footstep until we reach the shore, where one of us, at least, is incredibly glad to get out of those murky woods. Here—etched on clean, smooth sand exposed by the falling tide—is a record of how our encounter began. The bear came ambling southward along the shore, got within thirty feet of where Keta and I first landed, then turned abruptly into the woods, laying its tracks atop our own.

These, incidentally, are about the largest bear prints I've ever seen on the island. The hind feet, measured from heel to toe and excluding the claw marks, are a bit longer than my size eleven boots and about twice as wide. Almost certainly it's a male, who followed us more out of curiosity than deadly intent. Possibly he's learned, as bears have on Kodiak Island, to track hunters in hopes of finding leftovers from their kills. Whatever the case, I realize there's a fair chance of meeting this bear again, since we both favor the same territory.

Above all, I marvel that I could have been so lucky. Had we

started back fifteen minutes earlier I would have blown the deer call, possibly bringing the bear at a full charge expecting a helpless fawn. Or we might have startled the bear at close quarters in the woods. Or if I were carrying a fresh-killed deer, the bear might have come to take it away.

As the bear's chuffing and snorting reverberate in my mind, I understand as never before that I am nothing more than an ordinary member of this island community. I cannot know if this animal was hunting us, or if we've been stalked at other times without realizing it—an ignorance I frankly welcome. And I will say this: Without denying the terror those last moments would bring, I'd rather die as a bear's prey than keel over on my desktop or meet my fate in rush-hour traffic. What an afterlife, to march around as part of a bear's muscles, bones, and brain!

Despite these romantic thoughts, I don't feel like sleeping here in a flimsy tent, being startled by every click and shuffle in the nearby woods, so I pull anchor and head farther up the shore toward an old, mossy-roofed shack in Bear Cove. As we idle away, it seems both prudent and appropriate to thank the bear for going easy on us.

Awake in my sleeping bag, I stare into the black fissure of night, listening to raindrops flail against the cabin roof, gusts hiss in the treetops, waves pound on the nearby rocks. I reassure myself that the skiff is securely anchored and tethered by a safety line to a tree on shore. At last, in the dim light before dawn, I can see the boat still nested in our sheltered cove. Haida Strait, on the other hand, is a pandemonium of whitecaps, with thick-bellied swells pouring across submerged reefs and detonating against bare islets.

Half a mile offshore, there's a flock of several hundred gulls, circling and undulating like mist in a cataract. What inspires these birds to seek out the storm instead of heading for a protected bay? Do the frothing waves stir up food? Or do gulls simply love riding the wind, as I would if I had wings? Never mind such questions, I tell myself: the searing, storm-sung enchantment of the world is reason enough.

Obviously, Keta and I won't be going home this afternoon as planned. Through a spatter of raindrops on the window, I peer into the gloom, watching black water tremble in the cove. I could fire up the woodstove and hunker inside, since most of the deer will bed in thickets until the wind and rain diminish, but I can't resist the temptation to head outside, drawn by an urge to stalk through the woods and muskegs, and to feel the storm's onrushing power. A full suit of rain gear might seem perfect on a day like this, but wearing nylon or some other noisy outfit makes it almost impossible to approach wildlife. Instead, I'll wear my usual outfit—wool jacket and polypropylene pants—soft, quiet clothes that keep you fairly warm even when they're soaked.

Keta and I trudge up the long, wooded slope behind Bear Cove, and by the time we reach open muskeg there's sweat on my brow. From then on we set a slower pace, staying near the muskeg's fringe, where forest creates a sheltered lee and deer might abandon cover to feed. Although it's quieter here, the wind and rain make enough noise to help mask our sloshy footsteps.

Everything around us is alive with raindrops—dappling tea-colored ponds, shimmering on gray trunks, clinging to needles and boughs, hanging from cottongrass fluff and withered shooting stars, splashing on mushroom crowns and bog cranberries, running down salmonberry leaves and blades of grass, soaking into sedges, saturating the soil, trickling down rivulets and streams.

Half a mile into the muskeg, Keta starts lifting her snout and peering ahead. I'm sure she's caught a rich blacktail scent . . . but has the deer already detected our approach? In hunting or watching wild animals, it's crucial to remember we carry around us a shifting halo of scent that drifts on the breeze, stretches into threads and plumes, gathers in pools and eddies, and flows off into the distance—totally beyond our own senses but unmistakable to deer. At the same time, we produce a halo of sound in the pattern of our footsteps, breaths, and scrapes against vegetation; and we create a visual halo that betrays us at ranges varying with cover, light, and terrain.

I try to imagine how far and in what direction our halos disperse, while I stay alert for the muted halos of sound and sight also given off by deer; and at the same time I watch Keta to borrow acuteness from her senses. Both the deer and I strive to conceal ourselves, as we also try to break through the other's concealment. For countless millennia, hunters and prey have carried out this complex interweaving of mind and senses; it lies at the core of our existence; it braids our separate lives together.

Keta's eagerness heightens as we track slowly upwind, immersed in a dense streamer of scent. Finally she hesitates, stiffens, and stares intently. Kneeling beside her, following her gaze, I eventually pick out a doe—smaller than I would hunt—almost perfectly camouflaged amid a backdrop of tawny beige grass, dusky tree trunks, and whirling rain. A prolonged standoff ensues, the deer absolutely motionless while I struggle to keep almost as still. For fifteen minutes she never stirs, never unfastens her eyes, never so much as twitches an ear, until I can't help feeling perplexed and wonder if she'll ever turn us loose. It's as if time moves differently in our two minds, as if this extended wait is nothing but a moment—or nothing in the world at all—for the deer.

When I glance away and then look back, the doe seems to have dissolved; but then, meticulously searching the spot, I discover she's still there, half lost in the mysterious perceptual veil that always seems to surround deer, the marvelously perfected cryptogram shaped by a million years of evolution. Deer are not *supposed* to be seen by predators, after all.

At last the doe breaks our impasse, reaches down to nibble a wet petal, flicks the raindrops from her tail, and struts away in an exaggerated gait reminiscent of a prancing show horse, forelegs raised high and bent elegantly above her hooves, as if to render me harmless at the sight of her unalloyed beauty. Then she bursts into a four-footed trampoline stott, hesitates once to glance back at us, and flounces off like tumbling water. I watch her vanish into the forest, rain flowing like a river in my eyes.

In the hours that follow, Keta and I drift along the muskeg's border without coming across another blacktail. Keta's soaked, clinging coat makes her look skinny and a bit wretched, although she's as lively and wagtailed as ever. My clothes are totally waterlogged, but I'm still fairly warm, thanks to steady trekking and southerly gales bringing temperatures well up into the forties. Despite the pleasure and excitement of rambling around in a storm, I also feel a growing urgency about the hunt. We're short of camp food, so we must head back tomorrow if the wind subsides. At home, last year's venison is about gone, and this is the ideal season for replenishing our supply—a time when bucks, especially, have reached maximum size and prime condition just before the rut.

Around midafternoon I abandon the muskeg and work along a narrow peninsula of forest with a deeply incised creek rushing through the middle. Here, during a long session with the call, a small, spike-antlered buck emerges from the underbrush, eases in our direction, head high and ears wide, but then flashes away—as if the wind has made him frazzled and hypersensitive.

A bit farther on, we come across a thick cedar tree with long pieces of bark peeled off, as you might tear vertical bands of tape from a wall. Some lie coiled like wet pythons beneath the tree, but others are still attached fifteen feet above the ground, hanging loosely over the smooth, shiny wood. Undamaged bark covers about half the trunk and the tree looks healthy, although it's too soon to know if it will survive. A wildlife biologist told me that brown bears sometimes pull off cedar bark this way in springtime, then lick the heavy-flowing sap either for a tasty treat or a nutritional boost.

Closer inspection of this tree reveals faint tooth marks, some well above my head, and the surrounding earth is worn raw, indicating the bear stayed here for a while, scraping and rolling and scuffling. Although there's nothing subtle or inconspicuous about these workings, and although I must have passed many trees like this over the years, I never noticed them until I'd talked with the biologist. It's often like this, I think: we're blind to much of the world until someone tells us how to see it.

The storm shows no sign of relenting as afternoon gives way to evening. From a ridgetop, I look out over Haida Strait—still a torrent of whitecaps, the offshore islets half lost in rain squalls, thick stratus surging overhead. I turn my face toward the sky, let the raindrops prickle my skin, and feel grateful to be alive in this saturated kingdom of clouds. After months of tranquil weather, the whole world seems caught up in a boisterous celebration, as if the season isn't just turning, it's doing handsprings. I'm exalted by the wildness of it all, ready for the cold and fire and passion of winter.

At times the gale blows so hard that the rhythm of my tired footsteps seems almost inconsequential, but I still try to keep quiet, staying on the highest, least spongy ground as we trek along the muskeg's edge. Little time remains before nightfall, so there's not much chance we'll come across any more deer. And yet, judging by the abundance of tracks, droppings, and clipped vegetation, more than one blacktail would hear the sound if I clapped my hands.

All around us is lovely parklike heath scattered with bonsai-sized pines, veiled in mist and rain. It's as if everything had been set perfectly in place, according to some meticulous yet whimsical design, and even I—a man freshly rooted here—feel myself a part of it, a single voice in a deafeningly beautiful chorus. I am an *animal*, moving among other animals, surrounded by plants, wrapped in a cloak of rain, breathing wind, feet sunken into the moss, the great earth plunging away below.

With the approach of dusk, I have no choice but to head back toward the cove. We haven't come across fresh bear signs today, but I'm still jittery from last evening's experience and don't care to grope through the woods in darkness. Retracing our earlier route, Keta and I approach the spot where we saw the first doe this morning. It's fairly calm and quiet under the leaning brow of trees, so I move along slowly and pause every few steps to look around . . . but just ahead is a broad, open meadow—not the sort of place where I'd expect to see deer, especially during a storm.

Keta grabs a stick and begs me to play, but I motion her to settle down; if nothing else, stepping along carefully and silently will keep my senses alert, heightening my awareness of the wind, the rain, and the softly dwindling light. I pick my way through a patch of deer cabbage, then look up to scan the area ahead.

In that fraction of a second, everything is changed, and I catch myself in midstep as the truth of it bolts through me. At the same instant, Keta sags into a half crouch, her neck leaning forward, her ears honed and eyes riveted, her legs quivering, one forepaw lifted off the ground.

There, standing atop a low rise about twenty yards ahead, silhouetted above the crowns of two stunted pines, hard edged against the faded, hoary overcast, are the chest and neck and head of a deer, faced directly toward us, eyes shining, ears in a wide V, and a beamy crescent of antlers bending above.

Without hesitating and without conscious thought, I sink onto my knees, raise the rifle to my shoulder, and brace it against a slender tree. During these seconds, I'm taken by a powerful sense of déjà vu. At this same season a few years ago, a buck stood against the evening sky less than a hundred yards from this spot, and I did exactly what I'm doing now.

Perhaps this is why the outcome seems just as certain. There is no tingling apprehension, no pounding heart, no shaking hand. The rifle sights come to rest, unwavering. I breathe deeply, and deeply again, eyes opened wide. It's as if everything were preordained and the animal had come—as Koyukon elders teach—to give itself.

I feel absolutely, jarringly predatory, like a cat splayed against the grass, simmering in ambush. And utterly alive, in a way that defies language, that scarcely renders itself in conscious thought. I am a living creature questing for its food. Whatever ambiguity I feel about the hunt, it now lies far beyond reach. And I say this: No tiller of soil, no herder of flocks, no gatherer of plants, no browser of grocery shelves will ever cross this same emotional terrain. As for me, I would rather be a rock on a hillside than exist without knowing in this way the animal who lives inside me and gives me life.

The buck pumps his head up and down, telegraphing his uncertainty. Then he stands utterly still, his shape incised above the curving cloud of branches, as if the full truth of him had leapt down into the fluid of my eye.

Lightning flashes brightly in the blackness, and thunder pours away over the land's edge, tumbling and tumbling beneath the storm.

There is a burst and a shock and a jarred half vision of the deer's fall, as if he were completely released, like a puppet whose strings have all been snipped at once. I stand, breathing heavily, and rush toward the empty place between the pines with Keta bounding alongside. She reaches the spot before me, circles, and snuffles the soft edges of the buck. He lies on a mat of crowberry and bog laurel—soft and quiet and midnight-still—as if the gale had instantly grown calm.

At first I hear only silence. Then I hear my heart pounding and the ringing in my ears, and finally Keta panting at my side, the swashing of wind in high boughs, the distant drum of surf.

I kneel beside the deer and touch his warm, silky eye to affirm the certainty of death. Then I run my hand along his flank, whispering words of thanks that seem inadequate and frail against what I've been given here—a life that will enter and sustain my own. Beaded raindrops roll down over the dry, brittle fur.

I am not a guiltless hunter, but neither do I hunt without joy. What fills me now is an incongruous mix of grief and satisfaction, excitement and calm, humility and pride. And the recognition that death is the rain that fills the river of life inside us all.

Keta prances back and forth excitedly, looking in all directions for another deer, as if animals fascinate her only when they're running or might do so. I hold her by my side, rub her fur, and nuzzle her wet face. The deer is a prime, heavy, thick-coated buck, bearing modest but lovely antlers, their slender beams stained dark maroon at the base, fading to polished gray on each of the six elegantly tapered points. I will leave them here, although it's not hard to understand why someone might hang them on a living-room wall.

After dragging the buck to a nearby tree, I fasten a rope around both forelegs, loop it over a branch, then hoist the animal off the ground. With a small pocket knife, I sever the neck and spinal cord, then make a shallow incision, slightly longer than my hand, down the middle of the deer's belly, being careful not to puncture its stomach, which would foul the inside with spilled contents. Next I reach up into the hot, moist cavity to pull out the stomach, intestines, and fatty mesenteries, leaving the heart, liver, and kidneys in place. Keta nudges close, trying to lick the blood that drips down, but I shoo her away out of respect for the animal. Later on, when we butcher the deer, Keta will have her share of scraps.

I take some fat from inside the body, plus a few slivers of meat, and leave them with the viscera for the other animals. It's important, Koyukon people say, that wild creatures feed on remnants left in the woods by hunters, but other than small tidbits, nothing should be abandoned except parts we can't use ourselves. The eagles and ravens will come at first light tomorrow and within an hour they'll clean up everything but the skull bones and stomach contents.

To make sure no dirt gets inside the carcass, I cut small holes through the skin around the belly and neck openings, then lace them shut with cord. Next, I half sever the forelegs at their "knee" joints and toggle each front leg through a sliced opening in the hock of the corresponding rear leg. This makes it possible to carry a modest-sized deer as if it were a pack, putting your arms through the fastened legs and hoisting it up so the animal's belly lies against your back. With darkness looming above mountains to the east, I start the final trudge. Keta dances alongside, perhaps anticipating tonight's dinner. I'll cut a few pieces of fresh venison to fry in a skillet atop the wood-burning stove—the most delicious and elemental feast I can imagine, making the deer a part of me.

In the last stretch of muskeg, just before we'll enter the woods behind Bear Cove, I angle over to a small, rain-dappled lake, put my load on the ground, and rest beside the water. Keta slumps against me, finally getting tired. But she perks up a few minutes later, when a large doe ghosts out from the trees directly across the lake from us and steps to the water's edge, nervously switching her tail. She reaches down and touches her nose to the water . . . and it's as if I have drifted into a deer's dream.

I slowly bend over, dip my hand beneath the ripples, and fill it with the same chill water. And there, embraced by the island and the sky, we drink each other down.

Nature writer and cultural anthropologist RICHARD NELSON has lived in Southeast Alaska for twenty-five years. His books include Make Prayers to the Raven *(University of Chicago, 1983),* Shadow of the Hunter *(University of Chicago, 1980),* Hunters of the Northern Ice *(University of Chicago, 1969), and* The Island Within *(Vintage, 1991), which re-ceived the John Burroughs Medal for outstanding natural history writing. His latest book,* Heart and Blood *(Knopf, 1997), explores the complex and increasingly problematic relationships between people and deer in modern America. Apart from writing, Nelson's life centers around watching wildlife, hiking, surfing, kayaking, subsistence hunting and fishing, and camping with his partner, Nita Couchman, in the wildlands and waterways of the Tongass National Forest.*

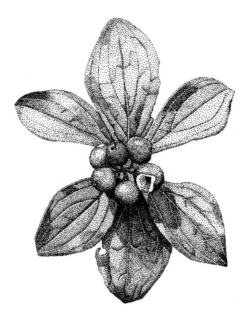

bunchberry, *Richard Carstensen*

The Weave of Place and Time

CAROLYN SERVID

In the summer of 1995, my Sitka neighbors' customary summer fishing trip led to a remarkable discovery. Natasha Calvin and Bob Ellis, longtime Southeast Alaskans, had taken their boat out for several days and headed south along the fragmented outer coast of Baranof Island, a shoreline buffeted by the whims and weathers of the North Pacific Ocean. Ready for a break from that wide-open water, they had anchored in a small bay, a place new to them but known for its good salmon runs. True to their usual practice, they had gone ashore to walk along the beach and, in this particular bay, along the stream that flowed from an upland lake into the estuary. Sockeye and pink salmon were already running in substantial numbers. Coho would soon follow. That day the stream was swollen with the water of heavy summer rains and was cutting away its banks. Fishing bears that had been tromping through helped the erosion, as did high tides, winds, and waves that carried stream debris out into the bay. At low tide, a walk along the streambed put the grassy top of the steep bank at shoulder and eye level. When the tide came in, it flooded the bed so that the water was lapping in the grass.

Natasha and Bob are both trained scientists, retired from full careers in marine and fisheries biology. Careful observation comes naturally to them, and they were looking closely at things as they went along. Natasha had also just taken an archaeology course, and they both have a keen interest in local history. So when they saw some newly exposed wooden stakes embedded in the freshly eroded mud of the stream bank, they stopped to investigate. Ancient fishing weirs are occasionally found in salmon streams in Southeast Alaska. They had seen such weirs in other places, and this seemed to be another one. But Natasha's attention was captured by what looked like a layer of woven branches embedded in the mud between the stakes, the very weaving that would have served to catch the fish. This was something they knew was uncommon, so they made a careful note of where it was and what it looked like. When they got home a couple of weeks later, they shared the news with a Sitka archaeologist.

Eager to take a firsthand look, the archaeologist arranged a floatplane flight to the bay, and Natasha and Bob found themselves headed back to walk the streambed with a team of Forest Service staff. The stakes were easy to find again and not a surprise to the Forest Service. They had been documented in 1991. But a careful, lengthy search turned up no sign of the layer of woven branches. The rapid erosion of the stream bank had quite likely sent the bit of woody net out into the bay. Everyone was disappointed. As they were getting ready to leave, lead archaeologist Karen Iwamoto went back to the bank for one last look down over the edge. She turned to the others, her eyes wide with astonishment, and then stared again into the stream below. There, under about a foot of water, in clear view, lay a four- to five-inch piece of a finely woven basket. The whole group crowded at the bank's edge, their several pairs of eyes corroborating what Karen could hardly believe. Twelve inches of water magnified the view of the basket fragment and offered further reassurance. And it looked as though another piece was still buried in the bank's mud. A rush of excitement ran through each of them, grounded only by the truth of their find. The chances of running across such an artifact in the moisture-rich, decay-enhancing climate of Southeast Alaska were extremely rare, but there it was. And it quickly became clear that if they wanted to save it, they couldn't delay. The natural forces that had for millennia unraveled the human story in the region were doing their steady work—organic matter decaying, rains accumulating in lakes and streams, water changing its flow and course, washing away soil and debris and evidence.

Their scheming began on the return flight to Sitka—how to get back to the streambed as quickly as possible with proper equipment to extract the basket and all the required Forest Service and archaeological protocols in line. This was not a simple process. Forest Service personnel arranged for another flight down, but since there was limited room in the plane, Natasha and Bob returned in their own boat. The slower route by water turned out to be the more reliable, however, and after two days of a blanketing fog that prevented any planes from landing in the bay, the archaeologists arrived by boat as well. The sense of urgency was palpable. Natasha and Bob had already discovered that part of the basket had been washed away. It was late afternoon. Afraid that the rest would disappear during the night with the next high tide, the archaeologists wrapped the remaining fragment as best they could with fabric they stapled into the mud. Their protection worked. Early the next morning they began their meticulous extraction. It took hours. The basket was only a couple of feet below the high tide mark, and to get at it they had to stand in the stream. The rains continued, and the little enclave of the bay was alive with the peak of summer. Sockeye and pink salmon splashed around the archaeologists' legs. Gulls wheeled and cried overhead, eagles waited in the trees. Later on, two brown bear sows with cubs and a fifth lone grizzly came out of the woods to feed in the fish-rich waters. The scene was not unlike what it might have been when the weaver of the basket or the carvers of the weir stakes were there. It was not hard to imagine the weir extending into the stream, men and women collecting salmon, baskets for fish and other gatherables left along the shore, including the one that just now was emerging from the mud.

When the archaeologists' detailed and careful work was done, they took back to Sitka with them a two-foot-square block of fine anaerobic sediment that had served as the basket's muddy safe-keeping. The woven fragment was left embedded inside. They also took a sample from the jumble of wood and debris that made up a stratigraphic layer just above the basket. And they took pieces from the stakes of the weir that had been strung across the stream. Fragments from each were sent off to a lab for radio carbon dating tests, and when the results came back, most everyone was aston-ished. Each of the weir stakes went back two thousand years. The woody debris found above the basket was a little less than five thou-sand years old, the basket itself a full five thousand years. The evi-dence unfolded ancient stories of people coming to that Baranof Island stream for salmon, one story interrupted, perhaps, by a natu-ral catastrophe that buried the basket under the rubbly layer of wood and anaerobic sediment that preserved it for five millennia.

When I try to grasp the significance of these dates and time spans, I have trouble. Perhaps that's because I don't have much to consider by way of comparison. I don't know of stories in the his-tory of my own Western heritage that go back that far. By contrast, the Tlingit people of Sitka had little difficulty taking in this infor-mation. Of course, they said. Our stories tell us that our people have been here from time immemorial. When a group of local weavers had a chance to examine the basket, they recognized ex-actly what they saw—two-strand twining, virtually the same as their own, creating a solid section that seemed to be the side wall of the basket, and a technique that used a cross warp to create an open weave in the curved section that was probably the bottom. What did surprise them was that the weaver used hemlock branches for the warp and hemlock root for the weft, rather than the spruce root that was considered customary. But there was undoubtedly a reason. She seemed to have made a disposable utilitarian basket, they noted. She had not made much effort to keep the weaving lines straight. Baskets like this were commonly used to store stink eggs, fermented salmon roe that was buried as a means of preservation. Further, they said, hemlock lasts longer in the ground. Could this basket have been full of the harvest, waiting for a time of feasting? Or had it already been emptied and simply left behind, then buried by an episode of geologic history?

The answers to these and other questions will never be known, of course. Archaeologists and anthropologists can't say that these artifacts are unquestionably linked to Tlingit history and culture. The Tlingit themselves have no doubts. The bay where the basket was found is an area claimed by the Kiksadi, one of the first Tlingit clans known to have settled in the Sitka area. And while the precise date of that settlement is unknown and the debate between Western archaeological science and Tlingit oral traditional and knowledge will go on, the ancient and millennia-long history of human inhabitation in this region is indisputable. What is striking is that throughout most of that history, these indigenous people left so few marks on the landscape. There were no gross alterations of the forest or shore. Ninety percent of the cultural artifacts that were left behind—dwellings, clothing, tools, household items—decayed right back into the woods and soils and waters from which they came. To find evidence of that early human presence, your eye must be trained to see detail and subtlety: an arrangement of rocks on a beach that might have aided in the haul-out of a canoe, a tall vertical stripe of missing bark on a particular cedar tree in the middle of a forest, a design etched with a dull tool into the surface of an inconspicuous stone. With luck, the stakes of a fishing weir; with good fortune, a piece of a basket.

I like to hold that woven hemlock artifact in mind for a variety of reasons. For one, it is a classic example of human ingenuity, of people's ability to figure out how to make use of materials at hand to craft something that complements and eases the tasks of daily living. It also is the source of contemporary knowledge. Twentieth-century Tlingit weavers have refined their techniques, but their basic skills aren't much different from those developed by the creative hands of five thousand years ago. I like to remind myself, too, that our ancient weaver's basket-making skills rested on a foundation of local knowledge. She knew that hemlock branches and roots were suitable, where to find them, how to gather them, how to prepare them for weaving, why they might have been better than other kinds of roots or branches. And, finally, that local knowledge enhanced the foundation of what seems to me most important—the sensibilities of a culture to accommodate itself to the parameters of a given landscape, to the particularities of place.

I admit that I envy the Tlingits their heritage. Their traditions and stories and art forms are all cultural aspects I respect and admire, though I recognize they can never be mine, nor should they be. But it is not the cultural artifacts that are the source of my covetousness. I long for that sense, so deeply rooted in the antiquity of their history, of belonging to a landscape, to a place. It is both a personal yearning and a sensibility I believe is critical for the long-term well-being of our species. There are plenty of people from my own Western tradition who would tell me I've got it backward, that land and places belong to people rather than the other way around. My government, after all, claims most of the land in this region as the Tongass National Forest. But from the back of my mind, I pull out a story told by Mary Kancewick in her essay "Of Two Minds" that opens the anthology *From the Island's Edge: A Sitka Reader.* The story is about the testimony of the late Tlingit leader Austin Hammond at a public hearing in 1984 about Native land claims in Alaska:

> The Tlingit elder travels to the meeting to present his people's deed, as recorded on a ceremonial blanket of

his Sockeye Salmon Clan. The blanket has been passed from generation to generation in an unbroken line, this history of the land and its people woven into mountain goat wool, from a time before the Puritans' first Thanksgiving. His granddaughter holds the blanket for him, translating his Tlingit words. Her grandfather tells how the Tlingit land was formed, how Raven made the waters, how the trees and plants came to be, how the people realized their kinship with the sockeye salmon, how the rules governing the use of land and waters came of the need to protect that kinship. Her grandfather shows how the Tlingit people and their land and its resources continued as one for thousands of years, continues to this day. Her grandfather says, "You say this is your land. Where are your stories?"

Austin Hammond's question recognizes a fundamental connection between place and culture. And it is that relationship that is at the root of both my envy and my concern for our species. The paradox that turns inside the concept of *belonging*—the possibility of taking possession or being possessed—is a distinction that shapes, in an essential way, the cultural attitudes of a people toward the place where they live. It is the turning point on which a culture either grounds itself in a place or separates itself from it. Our choice of one sensibility or the other determines what kind of inhabitants we are, how we behave toward the land and the larger natural community.

There is another cluster of concepts that is useful in sorting out these connections between place and culture. The English words *habitat, habit, ability, rehabilitate, inhabit,* and *prohibit* all come from a common Latin root, *habere*. According to Eric Partridge's etymological dictionary, they all spin off of a fundamental concept of relationship: "to hold, hence to occupy or possess, hence to have." From that nucleus, the English language radiates out to the family of words that, in an interesting sort of reciprocity, holds *us*. They ground us by describing where we live, how we live, what we are able to do, how we heal ourselves, what our connections are to the landscape around us, what the boundaries are for our behavior.

The integrated concepts embedded in these words seem so basic, so essential, as to be a prescription for survival. It is no wonder they cluster together around a common root. I imagine words like these developing within a language as the accompanying culture developed, as people came to understand and lay out ground rules for the way they should live in a particular place if, like the Sockeye Clan, they aimed to protect the kinship to the land that had been established. And I imagine that the necessary connections between these words remain clear as long as the culture is inherently linked to place. When a culture's ties to place weaken, when the kinship is no longer acknowledged as a priority, these prescriptions for living lose their relationship to each other. Such is the case for many people living at the end of the twentieth century—Southeast Alaskans included—when, thanks to industry and technology, the world is virtually at our fingertips. Where we live is no longer necessarily connected to how we live or how we heal ourselves or limit our behavior. We no longer link these aspects of our lives as ground rules to live by. Instead, we remember these associations when we happen upon them—when we research words in a dictionary, for example. They are not necessary relationships, but, rather, connections we can choose to make if we are so inclined.

When Austin Hammond made the connection between stories and the land, I think he must have understood that stories contain the metaphorical ground rules of a culture. They reflect our sensibilities about the places we live and our understanding of our own character—our capabilities, our habits, the bounds of appropriate action, our prescriptions for healing. The stories Austin Hammond knew from the Tlingit oral tradition tell of human lives inextricably intertwined with the land. They are about people and salmon, people and brown bear, people and killer whale, people and glaciers and tides and mountains and trees, people who go under the blanket of the sea to visit distant relatives. Like the stories of any literature, they profile human character through accounts of pride, greed, envy, alienation, allegiance, honor, and love. But they also describe primary relationships of obligation and appropriate behavior—of reciprocity—between people and the web of living things on which they depend.

It's hard to know how far back the Tlingit oral tradition extends. "Time immemorial" seems to encompass trickster Raven's creation of the Tlingit world as well as the migration of people into it and their occupation of it. Perhaps the weaver of that hemlock basket knew the stories; perhaps the fishers who carved those weir stakes told them to their children. However far back the stories go, their effectiveness in laying out the ground rules for inhabitation is manifest in the landscape European explorers found when they sailed along this coast two hundred and fifty years ago—forests and rivers and bays and uplands rich with a diversity of wildlife, unmarred by human hands. There may have been other contributing factors—a small human population spread over a large, species-abundant territory—but the stories and the land together offer compelling testimony of a culture that developed around a sense of kinship with the larger natural world, of a people that belonged to a place.

The stories Austin Hammond knew are juxtaposed against another set of stories about Southeast Alaska. They are stories rooted in that other sense of belonging—the sense that prefers domination and control to indebtedness and reciprocity. They rise out of notions of independence and opportunity. They are stories of uprootedness, of immigration and transience, of exploitation, often of confusion, and are the primary stories pulled together to relate the comparatively brief history from that time of European exploration to the present. They are stories of adventurers charting "new" territory, naming and claiming places for themselves or their homeland; of missionaries claiming souls for their God; of company-connected and entrepreneurial fur traders, miners, loggers, and fishers seeking to capitalize on what the earth provides; of people escaping into lives they hoped would be free from the fetters of civilization and government; of families left behind. They are stories easy to criticize for their insensitivity, their colonial outlook, their arrogance.

But beneath the surface—and not all that far down—it becomes apparent that many of these stories are about the very disconnection they reflect. They are about people in search of a place to which they might, in fact, belong. Often they are stories of people taken by the forest-clad, icy-summited mountains stretching skyward, northward, eastward, southward, by the dark spangled waters tracing those steep shores, by the allure and mystery, by sheer beauty. They are stories of people who unwittingly became possessed by the land.

My own story and my decision to move to Sitka were rooted in a subconscious desire for just such a sense of belonging and a similar unanticipated response to the land. I have no family or cultural ties to this northern temperate rain forest, but neither can I claim those ties to any other particular place on earth. As the daughter of medical missionaries, I spent my formative childhood years in a coastal village in India, a place I loved but to which I didn't really belong. Our return to the United States was considered a return *home,* yet it brought little comfort or surety, and I wrestled all through adolescence and college with the uncertainties of where I did belong. In a move characteristic of young adulthood, I took time out from a checkered working life to accompany a new friend on a summer adventure to Alaska, out of an interest not so much in seeing the country as in taking a chance on his heart. While the romance faltered, I ran headlong into a much greater presence that I could not face down: the horizon-wide landscape of mountains and glaciers and forests and waters—powerful, indifferent, complex, staggering, sublime. Its vast wildness breathed a fundamental question: What is the appropriate relationship between human beings and the land? The notion had never struck me so starkly or been so compelling. For the first time, my imagination stumbled over the possibility that the boundaries of my life might be defined and supported by the earth itself as much as by other people, and I found myself dreaming of being steadied by those tangible realities embodied in the land.

Theologian and historian Walter Brueggemann describes the desire to belong in a place as a decision to enter history. Place, he says, "is a declaration that our humanness cannot be found in escape, detachment, absence of commitment and undefined freedom." In other words, our humanness cannot be found without context. It strikes me, looking back, that the choice I made to live in Southeast Alaska grew out of a yearning for my own specific habitat, parameters that would give definition to my life—particularities of landscape, a point in a specific timeline, connections to a community, both natural and human. I longed for the set of ground rules that connected *where* I lived with *how* I lived, that defined the bounds of appropriate behavior and relationship to a place, that offered a source of inner healing.

My story has its own particular nuances, but it is not exceptional. The communities of the Tongass are full of people who have become possessed by the place they live. We may not belong to the place in the same way the Tlingits do. Our cultural stories are not inextricably rooted here. But we have been taken by the landscape. We have fallen under the undeniable spell of the earth. We are captive. Ask people why they came to these isolated forest communities, why they stay, what it is that has a hold on them, and the answers start to repeat themselves. The wildness. The natural setting. The remoteness. The beauty. The rugged mountains. The forest. The opportunities to be outdoors—to hunt and fish, to hike and get out on the water. Jobs, family, good schools, and safe communities are also common answers, but a recurrent refrain in story after story specifies a human affinity with the land.

And yet, when we try to answer Austin Hammond's question, we still come up short. Our cultural stories seldom encourage our kinship with the larger natural world. They tend, instead, to delineate our separateness from it. And so while we revel in the magnificence of this place that has captured us, we struggle with the paradox contained in the concept of belonging. The strong pull of our society is away from an attitude of beholdenness and toward the presumption of possession, the desire for control. We are encouraged to stand by our right to develop, manage, and use the land and its resources to our most immediate advantage. Our democratic ideals confirm these rights for us, and our communities and economies are built on these assumptions. The accompanying values are deeply ingrained in us, and though we sense their flaws, we can't simply abandon them. To do so might mean that we lose ourselves, our identity. Individually, we might easily acknowledge our strong sense of connection to this landscape, but we're not quite willing to submit our own sense of power to the greater authority of the natural world. We're not quite comfortable giving full acknowledgment to the source of our being, to our dependence on the earth. We can't quite admit what it means when we say we love this place where we live.

Since coming to Sitka in 1980, I have been lucky enough to live most of those years on nine acres of wooded land overlooking the inner reaches of Sitka Sound. Outside my windows are the waters of Thimbleberry Bay and Eastern Channel rimmed by the forested mountains of Baranof Island, a wedge of a landmass a hundred miles long and thirty miles across at its widest point, one of the largest islands in Southeast Alaska's archipelago. Behind the house, a stand of second-growth hemlock, yellow cedar, and spruce graces a slope that climbs three thousand feet steadily and steeply from the water's edge to a triangular rock summit known by present-day locals as Mt. Arrowhead. Today the boughs of cedars next to the house flutter in an unusually icy wind. Raven, the trickster of Tlingit legend and the creator of this world, calls from a high perch on one of the trees that shelter this house. He has plenty of company. Juncos and chickadees flit back and forth to bird feeders, fortifying themselves against the cold. A red squirrel scampers up and down tree trunks, scouting out things to eat. Across the water, the tall, wind-billowed spouts of humpback whales glisten in bright sunlight. The smaller spitting puffs of sea lions accompany them. In the closer reaches of the bay, I watch a seal stretch its nose out of the water, and I marvel at the strands of light delineated by its whiskers. Three mergansers swim nearby, poking their heads into the water in search of food.

There is no doubt in my mind that I have fallen in love with this place. These trees, these animals, these waters are faithful companions. They have steadied me in ways I have yet to understand. I like to think I am a fellow inhabitant of this island, but still must acknowledge one thing that differentiates me from everything else that is here. I have made a conscious decision to make this place my home. While all the other components of this ecosystem are *necessarily* intertwined, I am here by choice. Their habits and patterns of living are driven by biological and ecological factors, by the natural cycles of this particular landscape. Mine are driven by the realm of human possibility. Whether or not I belong in this rain forest ecosystem—in the sense that Raven and humpback whales and seals and chickadees and juncos belong—is a question of how I choose to behave, a matter of heart and mind. The choice begins with my love of this place. My obligations follow.

If, as Walter Brueggemann suggests, my yearning for place and my move to Sitka constitute a decision to enter history, then it is the history not only of the human community of Sitka, but of the natural community as well. In being mindful of my own life here, I must be mindful of how it affects my fellow inhabitants in the ecosystem. Dan Kemmis, author, teacher, and former Montana politician, put it another way. On a visit to Sitka in 1991 to help local citizens think about issues of community conflict, he said he often found it useful to think not just about things that were happening at the present time, but to try to put these events in historical perspective. He suggested that we try to imagine how it is that we will be remembered. What kind of civilization will we be known for? As he noted, "We don't often think of ourselves as part of history in that way. History or civilization is something that happens some other time or some other place. It's not us. But if not us, then who? And if not now, then when?"

Dan Kemmis's questions push Austin Hammond's into the future, and they are appropriate questions for all of us who live here. What stories will we leave behind? Not only the stories our ancestors will tell about us, but the stories the landscape will tell about us? What kind of inhabitants will we be known to have been?

The questions Dan Kemmis posed point out the fact that our day-to-day lives are telling the story of late-twentieth-century civilization. Those of us living in the Tongass at the end of the current millennium have been living out the ongoing story that was imposed on this place some two hundred years ago, a story that overpowered the existing ancient one that had endured for thousands of years. In the span of his lifetime, Austin Hammond watched the shift manifest itself among his own people as the steady pressures of education and legislation imposed new values that countered the traditions of their ancestral history. The dominant Western culture has shaped communities, politics, family, and individual lives according to a set of ground rules that strive to keep people in control of this place where we live. Using resources for our own economic advantage, we—Native and non-Native alike—have radically altered parts of the landscape. The half a million acres of clear-cut Native lands are even more devastated than the equal number of cuts on national forests. The resulting Native corporate and shareholder bank accounts rival and outdo our own. The resulting landscapes, Native and federal, relate a story that is difficult to bear.

There are telling signs that our late-twentieth-century Tongass story is failing us. Our very trust in the future is at stake. The steady timber economy of forty years has faltered. Communities that became polarized over issues of clear-cut logging and pollution from the associated mills are now divided over issues of growth and economic development. Native groups are divided as well: tribal members intent on reviving and sustaining traditional ways of life are challenging those who have clear-cut aboriginal homelands. We are at odds with ourselves over the conflict between our love of this place and our right to use it. There is a slowly growing recognition that we have taken too much and taken too much for granted. The story we've been living has been narrowly centered on self-interests. It has not offered much in return for all we've taken and been given.

The wonderful thing about stories, though, is that they call on the human imagination, what poet Wallace Stevens referred to as "the necessary angel." It provides us, he says, a means to press back against the pressures of reality. We can, in fact, create new stories. We can imagine them into being. Certainly we can fabricate things that simply are not true, but we quickly find that those stories are not particularly useful and get us into trouble. We can, however, also imagine the possible. We can pool the best of our knowledge and create a story grounded in both our experience and our hope for the future.

What has been taken for granted in Southeast Alaska for the past two centuries is the abundance of life in this northern temperate rain forest. That very abundance was at the core of the ancient story that Austin Hammond could trace back through time immemorial. I believe it is buried, as well, in the affinity with the landscape that so many Southeast Alaska newcomers acknowledge. Perhaps it might also be at the heart of a new story to be imagined into being by the people and communities of the Tongass. In the preface to his second book, *The Good City and the Good Life,* Dan Kemmis makes a simple and rather startling assertion about politics. Looking for an improvement to what he characterizes as our currently dehumanizing political structure, he suggests that "we might do worse than to repair to the biblical measure, 'that they might have life and have it more abundantly.' *It is the deep and varied bounty of life that we dimly but fervently seek to nurture and secure through politics, and it is by this measure that we might judge any framework within which we conduct our human affairs."* (Italics mine.)

The story we are currently living in the Tongass subscribes to the political structure that Dan Kemmis suggests needs to be changed. Interestingly, our hope may lie in the fact that the story is failing, that it's likely to be relatively short-lived. Because it is also true that the Tongass is one of the last places in North America where every plant and animal species that existed at the time of European contact still exists. There is no doubt that, in places, the earth's largest remaining temperate rain forest has been significantly altered by our human hand, but that deep and varied bounty of life, the abundance of the Tongass, still surrounds us.

What if we took Dan Kemmis's charge seriously? What if we conducted our human affairs in the Tongass in such a way that the abundance of life was our focus? And what if we repaired, as well, to the impulse that drew us to this landscape, that affinity we can hardly acknowledge without full hearts? If we embraced the strength inherent in our fundamental kinship with the larger natural world? If we gave our imaginations over to ways we might nurture and secure that abundance, if we grounded ourselves in our love of this place and took up the obligation that follows? What if we took on the task of reimagining how we inhabit this place? It might allow us to picture a future for ourselves that could heal the rifts we have created in our communities, one that might restore indigenous traditions, one that might unite us as people who belong to this place. It is true that there are plenty of instances in which this possibility has passed us by. We have violated the landscape and are left with a wounded world. We are faced with the ache of poet Robert Frost's question of what to make of a diminished thing. But elsewhere, the landscape is still whole. It *gives* us life. Within its abundance, there is room to imagine a new story of inhabitation, one that reflects what we know in our hearts, one that might balance our dominance and indebtedness, our ignorance and grace. There is room to imagine a new cultural sensibility rooted in and bound by the parameters and particularities of this place we call the Tongass.

CAROLYN SERVID has lived since 1980 in Sitka, Alaska, where she cofounded The Island Institute, a nonprofit organization whose aim is to encourage people to think creatively about how they can best live together in communities and best inhabit the places they live. She and her husband, Dorik Mechau, are codirectors of the organization. She is the editor of From the Island's Edge: A Sitka Reader *(Graywolf Press, 1995), an award-winning anthology of poetry and prose by participants in the Institute's Sitka Symposium on Human Values and the Written Word. Her essays have appeared in several magazines and collections, among them* Nimrod, Alaska Quarterly Review, Great River Review, *and* The Great Land: Reflections on Alaska *(University of Arizona Press, 1994).*

Artist Credits

More Books on The World As Home from Milkweed Editions

To order books or for more information,
contact Milkweed at (800) 520-6455,
or visit our website (www.milkweed.org).

Brown Dog of the Yaak:
Essays on Art and Activism
Rick Bass

Boundary Waters:
The Grace of the Wild
Paul Gruchow

Grass Roots:
The Universe of Home
Paul Gruchow

The Necessity of Empty Places
Paul Gruchow

A Sense of the Morning:
Field Notes of a Born Observer
David Brendan Hopes

Taking Care:
Thoughts on Storytelling and Belief
William Kittredge

Ecology of a Cracker Childhood
Janisse Ray

The Dream of the Marsh Wren:
Writing As Reciprocal Creation
Pattiann Rogers

The Country of Language
Scott Russell Sanders

Homestead
Annick Smith

Testimony:
Writers of the West Speak On Behalf of Utah Wilderness
Compiled by Stephen Trimble and Terry Tempest Williams

Other books of interest to The World As Home reader:

ESSAYS

The Heart Can Be Filled Anywhere on Earth:
Minneota, Minnesota
Bill Holm

Shedding Life:
Disease, Politics, and Other Human Conditions
Miroslav Holub

CHILDREN'S NOVELS

No Place
Kay Haugaard

The Monkey Thief
Aileen Kilgore Henderson

Treasure of Panther Peak
Aileen Kilgore Henderson

The Dog with Golden Eyes
Frances Wilbur

ANTHOLOGIES

Sacred Ground:
Writings about Home
Edited by Barbara Bonner

Verse and Universe:
Poems about Science and Mathematics
Edited by Kurt Brown

POETRY

Boxelder Bug Variations
Bill Holm

Butterfly Effect
Harry Humes

Eating Bread and Honey
Pattiann Rogers

Firekeeper:
New and Selected Poems
Pattiann Rogers

Literature for a Land Ethic is an anthology series that addresses the need to preserve our last wild places. These books offer prismatic portraits of endangered landscapes across our continent through the various perspectives of some of the best of each region's writers.

The World As Home, the nonfiction publishing program of Milkweed Editions, is dedicated to exploring our relationship to the natural world. Not espousing any particular environmentalist or political agenda, these books are a forum for distinctive literary writing that not only alerts the reader to vital issues but offers personal testimonies to living harmoniously with other species in urban, rural, and wilderness communities.

Milkweed Editions publishes with the intention of making a humane impact on society, in the belief that literature is a transformative art uniquely able to convey the essential experiences of the human heart and spirit. To that end, Milkweed publishes distinctive voices of literary merit in handsomely designed, visually dynamic books, exploring the ethical, cultural, and esthetic issues that free societies need continually to address. Milkweed Editions is a not-for-profit press.

Interior design by Wendy Holdman
Typeset in Legacy Serif and Sans Serif
by Stanton Publication Services
Printed on acid-free 55# Glatfelter Natural paper
by Edwards Brothers